THE
AWAKENED
HOMEOWNER

ORCHESTRATE YOUR DREAM HOME
A Guide to Design and Construction Success

THE AWAKENED HOMEOWNER

ORCHESTRATE YOUR DREAM HOME

*A Guide to Design
and
Construction Success*

W.W. REID

This publication is designed to provide accurate and authoritative information in regard to the subject matter covered. While the publisher and author have used their best efforts in preparing this book, they make no representations or warranties with respect to the accuracy or completeness of the contents of this book and specifically disclaim any implied warranties of merchantability or fitness for a particular purpose. No warranty may be created or extended by sales representatives or written sales materials. The advice and strategies contained herein may not be suitable for your situation. You should consult with a professional when appropriate. Neither the publisher nor the author shall be liable for any loss of profit or any other commercial damages, including but not limited to special, incidental, consequential, personal, or other damages.

ISBN

979-8-9903921-0-6 (Paperback)

979-8-9903921-1-3 (eBook)

979-8-9903921-2-0 (Hardback)

979-8-9903921-3-7 (Audio Book)

Library of Congress Control Number
2024939379

First Edition 2025

Published by:

BuildQuest
MEDIA LLC

Northern California

contact@BuildQuestMedia.com

DEDICATION

This book is dedicated to those who entrusted me with the privilege of creating their homes. Your dreams, visions, and stories have been the foundation of my work, and it is an honor to have been a part of your journeys. Thank you for your trust and for allowing me to create spaces where your lives unfold.

To my family—your unwavering support inspires me to leave a legacy. To my grandchildren, who remind me daily what true love is, my children, whose lives continue to motivate me, and my wife Sue, who has stood by my side for over forty years through thick and thin—your love and outlook on life continue to inspire me every day. This book is as much yours as it is mine.

MISSION

"To laugh often and much; to win the respect of intelligent people and the affection of children; to earn the appreciation of honest critics and endure the betrayal of false friends; to appreciate beauty, to find the best in others; to leave the world a bit better, whether by a healthy child, a garden, or a redeemed social condition;

to know even one life has breathed easier because you have lived. This is to have succeeded."

— *RALPH WALDO EMERSON*

DISCOVERY 1.

THE WORLD OF DESIGN 2.

THE WORLD OF CONSTRUCTION 3.

BUILDING YOUR TEAM 4.

CONTENTS

"Bill and his team
are an awesome
group of people
really dedicated to
helping their clients
fulfill their dreams
of remodeling
their homes."

- David P.

PROJECT BY BILL REID
OF REMODELWEST

PREFACE

My name is William Reid. In 1992, I founded a design and construction company, RemodelWest, located in Saratoga, California. For over thirty years and counting, I've helped thousands of homeowners design, build, and remodel homes of their dreams. I wish I could create your new home, too! *The Awakened Homeowner* is my next best way to help.

Throughout my journey as a general contractor operating a design-build business model, I've developed many internal processes, systems, and philosophies to achieve our company's core value: providing a quality experience for our clients. It doesn't come easy and it has proved to be a lifelong journey! To this day, I continue to learn from the economic turbulence and evolution the industry has experienced for the past 30 years and—most notably—how valuable my clients have been. I've seen positive results in the worst of times and negative results in the best of times. Being conscious of this has established my unwavering single value of caring for our clients by providing them with a quality experience.

In a way, I want to remodel or build *all* homes nationwide! Of course, it didn't take me long to realize that's not possible. I must admit that I thought about it in my younger, more ambitious years. Fortunately, there *is* a way to help everyone, and that's by sharing my knowledge with others. I genuinely enjoy creating new homes for people. I also see how daunting such tasks can be for homeowners and how scary it is for those who've never taken on a building or remodeling project before. If that's you, my mission is to help you overcome your fears through arming you with the knowledge and tools you need to take action.

"After 30 years of guiding homeowners to their dream homes, I feel a deep calling to share my experiences through this guide. My goal is to empower you to navigate the challenges ahead with confidence, turning the journey to your new home into an enjoyable and fulfilling experience."

–W.W. Reid

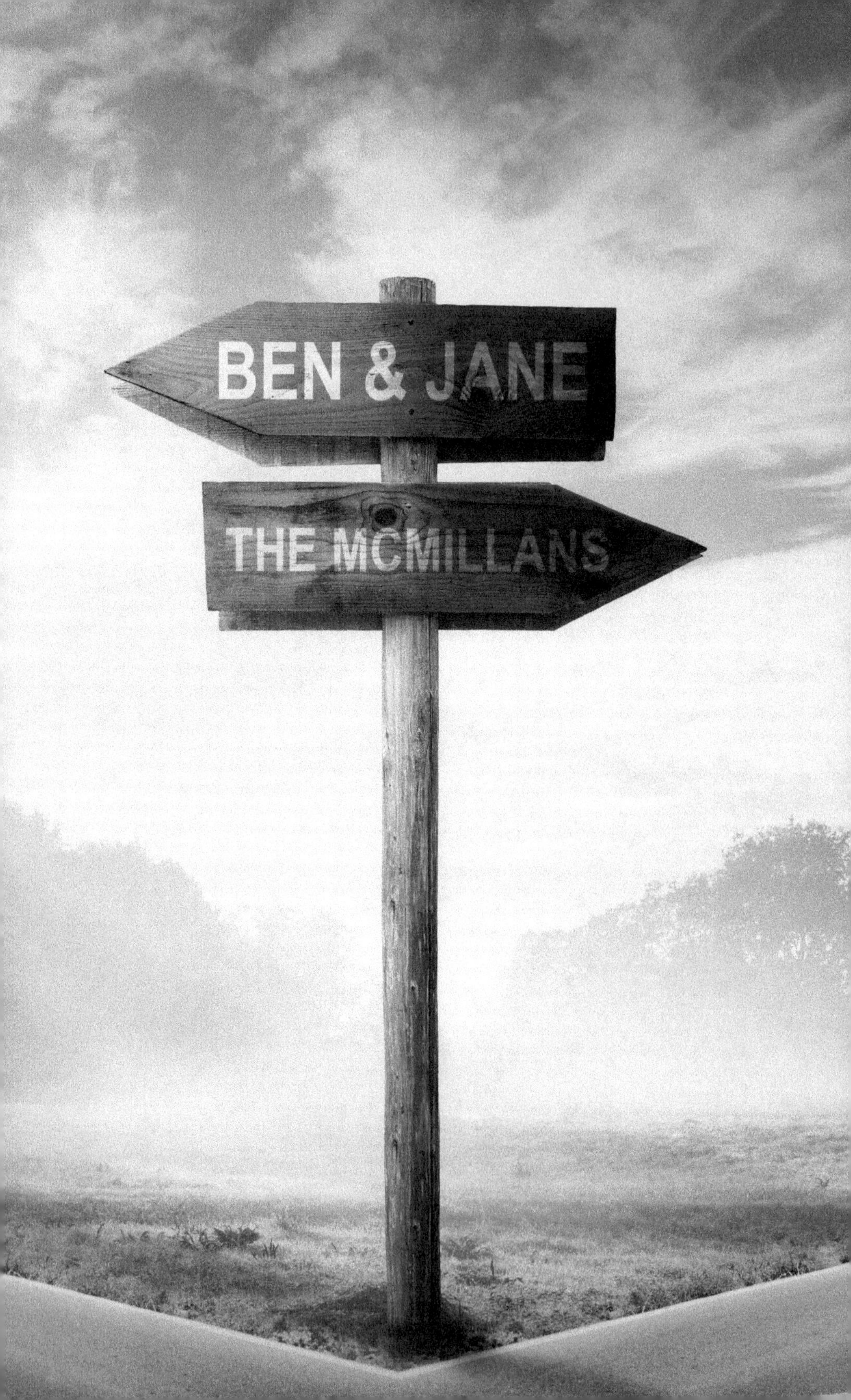
BEN & JANE
THE MCMILLANS

PROLOGUE

A TALE OF TWO HOMEOWNERS WHO TOOK VASTLY DIFFERENT PATHS TO THEIR NEW HOMES

As the sun set in the west, Ben and Jane knew they had found it. "It" was the perfect lot high atop a ridge in a new mountain development; it was secluded and reached via a long driveway bordered by oak and pine trees. The view immediately tapped into their emotions. With their kids Nathan and Betsy playing with butterflies in the tall summer grass, everything just seemed right. Ben and Jane would do it! They'd purchase the lot and build their dream home.

Across the ravine, two other people were walking along another lot. It was slightly lower in elevation and the view could have been better. Determined to make sure they could secure the lot they loved, Ben and Jane hopped into their car and sped down the curving road to the developer's office. The road led them past the couple walking along their lot, and when they spotted them, they thought it would be courteous to hop out and introduce themselves to their new neighbors. Sure enough, the McMillans were equally excited about their prospective lot. Ben and Jane thought the four of them might wind up building an enduring friendship, but back to business—it was time to put that deposit down on the lot. Ben and Jane congratulated the McMillans as they hurried back to their car.

Before they left, Ben noticed something strange: two other people were walking to the far end of the McMillan's lot while driving in stakes and taking pictures. Ben briefly wondered who they were but then quickly returned to the excitement of the moment.

The two people turned out to be the McMillans' architect and construction agent. They were previewing the lot to decide if it was a good site for the McMillans' new home. It wasn't. They ended up purchasing a lot nearby that had better access to utilities, was more level, and was just large enough to achieve their goals. Ben wouldn't know that until much later. This is where the paths split for the two couples. One was Awakened; the other was not. You get the drift.

Fast-forward 18 months. The rain was relentless as Ben and Jane drove to their new home site for what seemed the hundredth time. They looked sternly at one another as Jane mumbled, "There had better be something done!" The beautiful view on the ridge had cost them a fortune just for the hillside foundation work and the storybook driveway. No one had told them that running underground utilities a mile would cost as much as their first house. Consequently, the kids had been relegated to going to a junior college. "They had better get a damn scholarship!" Jane exclaimed, more loudly this time. Stress and anguish had set in for her and Ben just as they have for so many homeowners.

Regardless, it was exciting to see the progress...or at least they thought it would be. As they pulled off the road onto their storybook driveway, the car abruptly stopped. It was stuck in the mud. Unbeknownst to the couple, their contractor had not included any roadwork in the plans. Crap! Fortunately, they'd come prepared with some rubber boots and umbrellas.

They sloshed their way forward. As they rounded the last bend, their home came into sight. It was reminiscent of a horror film: dark and abandoned, there was nary a construction worker in sight. It was just a rain-soaked windowless gray house discolored by exposure to rain. Frustrated, they reached for their cell phone to hunt down their contractor and architect, but just then, it hit them that the workmen couldn't put the windows in because they didn't have them. It took much longer to get the windows than everyone had expected. Similarly, the roof wasn't on because Ben and Jane hadn't picked it out in time.

As Ben and Jane dodged the raindrops, they remembered that their architect wanted extra money to help with more details on the plans and assistance with managing construction. Ben and Jane had decided to take it all on their own and even complete the interior design themselves, so they cut him loose. Even worse, they prayed that their contractor could figure everything else out on the fly. An absolute recipe for disaster that they could now taste with every raindrop! Thank goodness they had gotten three bids from contractors. Sure enough, they liked the least-expensive guy, and the price was right. It had seemed like a match made in heaven…until it quickly dissipated. Turned out he was a one-man show who didn't know how to work a computer and had trouble with his cell phone.

Ben and Jane worked their way over to the terrifying structure and climbed up a teetering plank to reach the cavernous hole that would be their front door…someday. "Has the door been ordered?" Ben wondered aloud. "Shoot, did we pick it out?" Jane responded. Did *anyone* know the door's status??

The plywood subfloor was drenched. It felt like an eternity since anyone had been here, although Ben and Jane had no idea what the holdup was. They meandered around their dream that had turned into a nightmare, visualizing where their new spaces would be. It was still a little exciting, but definitely…"dampened," if you will. But the view! Nothing could take their view away.

Perched above the mountainside, they peered towards the west and noticed a glow going down the mountainside along the curving street. They both wondered what it was and then looked back at their view. "It will all be OK," they said simultaneously. Then they laughed and then they cried. The rain had subsided and the sun had begun to reappear as they navigated along the small lake back to their car. Down the curving road they went for the hundredth time. Things were wearing on them at this point—they had no one to turn to. But then they spotted that glow again. It was growing larger. It was a home! A *completed* home! They slowed to a crawl and extended their necks out the car windows like nosy ostriches. There they were: the McMillans, framed by their new windows, clinking two wine glasses together as they celebrated their housewarming. What! Both couples had purchased their lots at the same time! How was it possible that the McMillans had already moved in??

"We may need an exorcism performed before we can get into our house this decade!" Ben nearly shouted. "It's not fair!" Jane half-yelled. And the stress exploded…

…to be continued…

While this is a composite story and not a biographical one, people are surely screaming their lungs out right now. Or maybe you are or hopefully you want to avoid the infamous terror by learning before you leap. There's so much more to this story! (Perhaps I feel a novel coming on.) But for now, let's dive in and learn how to be Awakened homeowners like the McMillans. This is our mission together.

"I find that the harder I work,
the more luck I seem to have."
– Thomas Jefferson

INTRODUCTION

I hear many homeowners screaming the same thing: "I don't know what I don't know!!" Would you agree it would be beneficial to learn about those unknowns and then apply your knowledge to achieve your dream home? Let's tackle those unknowns together!

Your first step is *not* picking up the phone or searching the internet for five-star-rated contractors. It's *not* about running out and buying granite slabs you fell in love with or ripping your kitchen out before it's designed, and it's certainly *not* about following in Ben and Jane's footsteps by purchasing that "perfect lot."

The truth is, you may feel overwhelmed and scared because you don't know where to start. Just the thought of tearing your home apart or staring at a blank lot without a clue about how to proceed is paralyzing. You have no idea where to start and your neighbor can't stop complaining about their contractor. It's so overwhelming that you do nothing. Worse yet, you call your neighbor's contractor to see what happens.

If you read my opening story, you know that Ben and Jane had a miserable experience for many reasons. Well, those all began with them. Right from the beginning, their emotions got the best of them, and they compromised their experience by purchasing a lot without the due diligence they needed to protect their investment. This emotionally driven choice set the tone and momentum for subsequent poor decisions and ultimately a horrible experience. On the contrary, the McMillans had their lot inspected by a contractor and an architect. (That contractor may have been me and I might have helped them find the architect...) The McMillans chose the right path by becoming educated and making informed decisions. They were, in other words, Awakened homeowners.

Contrary to what many people believe (and may have experienced!), remodeling or building a home *can* be an enjoyable experience. I aim to help you overcome the fear of taking on a remodel or home building project by using my experience to build a bridge between my knowledge and you! Think of me as your guide, concierge, and guardian angel who is going to empower you with the knowledge and expertise you need to take on a remodel or home building project.

The keystone to success is committing to learning and then planning before a single scoop of dirt is dug! Becoming an aware and educated homeowner enables you to make informed decisions every step of the way. This ensures your enjoyment throughout the journey of designing and building your new home. After all, it's probably the most significant investment you'll make in terms of affecting your quality of life every day, so it's best to take control of the situation and enjoy the journey—when it's all over, you'll be the last one standing.

This guide and its accompanying resources for The Awakened Homeowner (TAH) community is designed for homeowners who are ready to invest a fraction of their time in learning and planning, and—with some hard-earned luck—become empowered to successfully take on a significant remodel or new home project. This is what *The Awakened Homeowner* achieves.

This book is perfect for anyone who's planning to design and build a home, hire a contractor, or plan a home remodel. If you're a DIYer looking to build a home, you can likewise use TAH resources to learn how to hire an architect and design your home and then get to work.

Even if you're an aspiring architect, designer, or general contractor, *The Awakened Homeowner* can provide you with a wealth of knowledge about how to build your career and your business and form strong alliances with your clients.

THE GUIDING PRINCIPLES

While I was writing this guide, I knew I wanted to make homeowners feel in control of their project. (And their life, for that matter.) As I wrote, the constant theme of values kept surfacing; finally, I pinned them down. We'll begin the Awakened homeowner mission by talking about what I call the Guiding Principles. I hope these will empower you as you're embarking upon possibly one of the most significant experiences of your life!

THE THREE GUIDING PRINCIPLES ARE:

✓ To **enlighten** you with knowledge and experience so that you take the prescribed steps and ask the right questions at the right times,

✓ To **empower** you by allowing you to leverage your new knowledge to make informed choices and plan intelligently, and

✓ To **protect** you and your family by arming you with the knowledge and tools you need to enjoy the design and building experience and be satisfied with your home.

And there's one more element that's always at the forefront of my mind and should be at yours as well. This one can be elusive and cause you to become delusional if it goes sideways, but if you braid it into the three principles, it can smooth out the trail: **expectations.**

Expectations is a core value of this guide encapsulating the Guiding Principles. I use this word every day in my design and construction business with clients, designers, employees, subcontractors, and

The
Guiding
Principles

suppliers—the entire team I pull together on a project. I liken this word to being accountability in disguise. Expectations are defined as a strong belief that something will happen or will be the case in the future: "Reality has not lived up to expectations," Jane may have thought at some point.

Synonyms for expectations are many: suppositions, assumptions, presumptions, conjectures, surmises, calculations, predictions, hope, anticipation, expectancy, eagerness, excitement, and suspense. These synonyms—or perhaps it's better to call them *symptoms*—are a few examples of the traps that expectation set for us. Setting them seems so easy: "I want my job done in six months," you might say, or "I expect high quality." But what did you do to ensure that this will happen? Who's out there helping you?

Achieving expectations takes work. *By you!* But how can you do the work if you don't know what you don't know? That's the purpose of this guide: to do some personal discovery, soul searching, and number crunching in order to pull back the veil of the world of design and construction enough for you to see its inner workings well enough to know what to ask. Only *then* will you be empowered to set and achieve realistic expectations.

HOW TO BECOME AN AWAKENED HOMEOWNER

If you've ever played in a sports event or if you're a sports fan, orchestrating the design and construction of a significant home project is much the same. Think of design as assembling your coaching staff, building your playbook, strategizing, recruiting your players, and training them. Essentially, you're preparing for the big game. Think of construction as the game itself: you'll be positioning the players, studying the playbook (your plans), and strategizing the plays (project management). Keep in mind the most important critical factor, which is that *you* are the owner, general manager, and head coach, all wrapped up into one super homeowner. *You* are ultimately account-able for all aspects of your team and the game's outcome. It seems daunting, but with the proper knowledge and an action plan, deter-mined homeowners can orchestrate a stellar team performance. *The Awakened Homeowner* will place you in the coach's chair by teaching you what you need to know so that you can then apply your knowl-edge, set realistic expectations, and hold everyone accountable. In-cluding yourself!

HOW TO USE THIS GUIDE

Our mission together is to build a solid planning foundation by in-vesting in some discovery time and doing some exercises to em-power everyone involved in your home project. We'll also build your knowledge of the world of design and construction and investigate the minds of professionals to learn what *they* need to know to be able to meet your expectations.

I've structured this book in four parts that will take you from the first days of dreaming about your new home to the breaking-ground or demolition party on your site. Each part serves a purpose, and each builds upon the previous one. All have the master goal of em-powering you to intelligently orchestrate the planning and building of your project.

PART ONE: DISCOVERY

PART TWO: THE WORLD OF DESIGN

PART THREE: THE WORLD OF CONSTRUCTION

PART FOUR: BUILDING YOUR TEAM

STEPS TO USING THIS GUIDE

1. Begin by absorbing the Guiding Principles.

2. Sit back and spend some time reading Part One: Discovery in its entirety. This will form the foundation of pursuing your project. Be prepared to revisit this section when you are ready to begin planning!

3. Part Two: The World of Design is where we build your knowledge of all aspects of design. This will be your first foray into bridging the gap between your dreams and reality. Soak it all up, knowing that when the time arrives to hire your design team, this knowledge will be at your side.

4. The knowledge mission continues by enlightening you with Part Three: The World of Construction. I recommend you absorb as much as possible during your first go-around and highlight the areas that apply to your project and are most important to you. When you shift gears into the planning phases, you can hop back into this section to be sure you're protected.

5. Part Four: Build Your Team wraps up Parts Two and Three and shapes them into strategies and options that you can utilize to build your team of design and construction pros. Review this section carefully and see which path feels right for you.

Here is a closer look at each Part and what the objectives are of each.

PART ONE: DISCOVERY

This is the time to look inside and focus, sometimes even *before* you purchase that lot you love or a home you think you can transform into your own. It's about introspection: you'll begin by allocating time and using a system to look within, discover, and set some early parameters. Discovery presents a methodology you can use to meet your expectations—by collecting vital information before you venture out on your project, you'll lay a foundation to build your new knowledge upon.

The goal of the discovery phase is to overcome common fears, delusions, and mental paralysis by providing clear and concise design desires and financial information to professionals. This will yield the most effective and efficient design experience.

THE DISCOVERY STEPS ARE:

✓ Collect the dreams and visions of your new home.

✓ Share a story of your family and your home or property.

✓ Dodge the prevalent delusions that too often can undermine expectations.

✓ Take a deep dive into your finances and set an investment goal.

✓ Package it all up and begin your search for design and construction pros.

PARTS TWO AND THREE:
BUILDING YOUR KNOWLEDGE

The Discovery section information and clarity is our foundation to build upon and is paramount to ensuring your success. Next we will begin to build *your* house, so to speak, by enlightening and empowering you with knowledge.

The number one contributor to a painful remodeling or home building experience is poor planning. What's interesting and scary with this pervasive problem is many homeowners don't even realize that they are headed for disaster until it's too late. Why? Because you don't know what you don't know! My job is to wake you up and then build your knowledge as we head towards planning your project intelligently.

In preparing for your new home journey, we'll assume that you have ventured out on weekend projects but that this is your first time tackling a large-scale remodel or new home project. Or perhaps in the past, you attempted a project with little success. No matter how you slice it, you'll need a team comprised of a designer to capture your goals within plans and specifications, a contractor to put it all together, and the knowledge to make it all happen. The amount of new knowledge I could immerse you in is immense, so I've intentionally brought in only key components and essential elements. Then you'll be a step ahead when the time comes to leap!

THE GOAL OF KNOWLEDGE _____

Utilize your knowledge and tools to meticulously plan your project.

Build Your Team: *Select a design and construction team best suited to meet your expectations.*

Design Your Project: *Coordinate the vital resources you'll need to prepare comprehensive plans and specifications.*

Ready to Build: *Pull together the final cost, select your builder, execute contracts, and obtain approvals.*

_____

Now that you have some visibility into your desires and budget, next up is understanding all the aspects of design, who to hire, the design process, how to navigate the design steps, and what to know when it comes time to deal with your city. We'll dig in further to expose you to the world of builders, contractors, costs, and contracts and how insurance is vital to your protection. While there's more than one way to pull your team together, all depend on your experience, time, and comfort levels, so I'll introduce various options when it comes to hiring designers and contractors.

We'll divide our knowledge base into the **World of Design within Part Two** and **The World of Construction in Part Three**.

HERE'S WHAT WE'LL COVER! _____

The World of Design – *Learn about design professionals, each of their roles, early obstacles and limitations, the methodical steps of design and their deliverables, plans and documents that will make you ready to build, and how to obtain approvals from your city.*

The World of Construction – *Learn about contractors, what they bring to the table, contracts and the different types, managing your risk, and how to estimate the cost of your project.*

_____

Within each area of design and construction, I'll present the human aspects, methodologies, processes, and challenges you could face. You'll gain insight into designers and contractors, who they are, how they work, the procedures to follow, and their deliverables. Next up, you'll learn how to use the information generated on your behalf to obtain costs, hire your contractors, and get approvals from your county or city. All with our Guiding Principles in mind so that your expectations will be met!

PART TWO: THE WORLD OF DESIGN

To build a project, you need plans and specifications, and the more accurate and thorough those are, the better your construction experience will be. Transforming your discovery exercises into reality involves your first planning step: selecting professionals to develop design concepts, plans, and specifications that meet your expectations.

You'll learn about the world of design by understanding design professionals and their agreements, the regimented design process, vital information about limitations that may already exist, what constitutes a set of plans and specifications, and how those documents are created. The design process will also include obtaining approvals and permits from your city, so we'll also delve into the inner workings of Planning and Building departments.

The goal of understanding the world of design is to gain the knowledge you need to hire a design team, hand off your discovery package, and then experience the design and approval process. You'll build a set of plans and specifications you can use to interview contractors, obtain estimates, and hire your pros.

THE WORLD OF DESIGN STEPS ARE:

- ✓ Learn about design professionals and their characteristics.
- ✓ Based on your project type, determine the type of designer you need.
- ✓ Learn how design pros structure their agreements.
- ✓ Learn about the methodical design process and how your discovery exercises play a significant role.
- ✓ Become aware of the many limitations that can derail your goals early on in the design process.
- ✓ Take a deep dive into understanding design and plans.
- ✓ Become aware of the approval processes within your city and county.

PART THREE: THE WORLD OF CONSTRUCTION

Handing off all of the work accomplished during the design process to the person who will actually build your project is one of the most significant milestones in your process! Therefore, it's vitally important who your team of construction pros are. In Part Three, we'll build a solid foundation for you to make intelligent decisions about these professionals.

You'll learn about the world of construction by understanding contractors and what value they provide, how your project costs are determined via an estimating process, and the different methods a contractor may use to manage the finances of a construction project. Eventually, you'll sign a contract with your contractor, so I'll highlight some of the more important components of a contract that will be crucial to you. And because protecting yourself during the construction process is also vital, I'll introduce the main elements of managing risk.

The goal of understanding the world of construction is to gain the knowledge you need to select your contractor by matching your project type, personalities, and contracting methods with the right person.

THE WORLD OF CONSTRUCTION STEPS ARE:

- ✓ Educate yourself about the types and characteristics of contractors.
- ✓ Gain an understanding of the attributes of a quality contractor.
- ✓ Learn how contractors make their money and the different financial management methods they use.
- ✓ Educate yourself on the basics of a construction contract.

✓ Learn how to protect yourself during the construction phase.

PART FOUR: BUILDING YOUR TEAM

Parts Two and Three allow you to see into the world of design and construction by peeling back some deeper layers and exposing you to a deeper level of knowledge. Part Four is our first foray into what to actually *do* with your new knowledge. In this last section, you'll assemble your orchestra of design and construction pros. How you build your team depends on how you answer the following questions:

✓ How much experience do I have?

✓ How much time do I have to devote to learning and navigating through all of the processes I just became aware of?

✓ Do I like to be in the middle of the battle and do I enjoy controlling every detail?

✓ Am I the planner type who'll spend a lot of time up front but then sit back and let the pros do their thing?

The goal of building your team is to learn how to search for design and construction pros. That includes understanding the two well-traveled paths you have in front of you to begin your project based on your characteristics and abilities and the type of project you're pursuing. You'll also gain some insights into two specialized options for those who have a lot of experience and those who don't.

THE STEPS TO BUILDING YOUR TEAM ARE:

✓ Learn about search strategies beyond default Google searches.

✓ Tap into industry resources to filter out candidates.

✓ Study the two paths to a successful project. I call them the "self-guided" and "guided" options.

✓ Become aware of what an "owner-builder" is and how that may be a fit for very experienced homeowners who are willing to hop into the trenches.

✓ Understand that there are options to extend yourself with an "owner's agent" status that frees you from the trenches.

TAKING ACTION

This guide is packed with a plethora of knowledge that will become your best friend! But gaining knowledge is just the starting point— you can't stop there. What you'll *really* need is guidance on how to put your new knowledge to work, a system that breaks everything down into a plan. That's where'll we expand past the covers of this book. These pages are just the beginning!

As I developed this guide, it quickly became clear to me that it needed to go beyond a typical how-to book. Therefore, I am taking it further by developing an action plan that reaches past just telling you what to do—it also supplements the steps with tools, systems, consulting, and coaching. This action plan is comprised of the TAH Planning and Building Workbooks under development, which assembles all of the knowledge and methods detailed in this book into chronological phases and steps. The steps of each phase are outlined with goals and instructions on how to apply the information found in each part of the guide.

When the time arrives to begin your planning mission, visit and join the TAH community to learn about our services and systems that will wrangle everything you're about to learn into a surmountable task.

www.TheAwakenedHomeowner.com

Let's
Start
The
Journey

1.

DISCOVERY

*"Without leaps of imagination
or dreaming,
we lose the excitement
of possibilities.
Dreaming, after all,
is a form of planning."*

Gloria Steinem

DISCOVERY 1.

1.0 INTRODUCTION

There's a reason you discovered *The Awakened Homeowner*: the time has arrived to pull up those stakes and get more serious. It's irresistible *not* to consume all the media out there of finished projects! Without a doubt, those images are inspirational. Let's face it—this is the fun part, because who's talking about *how* they got there? Not many. Well, we're about to!

Part One of this book is designed to complement those late-night swipes that save picture after picture of your dream home. My goal is to empower you with information so that you can get as close as possible to your expectations.

- ✓ We're going to talk about **your dreams and realities.** It's important to take the time to look within so that you can share your goals and ideas with the people you'll need to help you with your project.

- ✓ We'll delve into **how to build your budget.** You'll gain insights into how to think about your project from different financial perspectives and how to establish an investment goal and then balance it with your dreams.

- ✓ We can then zero in on your project parameters for your own focus and for the design pros who will be designing and building your project.

- ✓ You'll learn how to guide all involved parties to adhere to your goals, achieve the design, and prioritize your finances.

Let's first begin with time for personal discovery and financial reality checks before you pick up the phone in search of a contractor. You've spent quite a while obsessing over ideas, drooling over your friend's new home, and/or driving miles and miles to search for that perfect lot. Now we're going to establish the personal goals that will guide you down the path of planning your project.

Doing a little introspection to get into the right mindset can begin to alleviate the overwhelming feeling of tackling a project. It's about soul-searching, gaining clarity, setting expectations, and building a solid project foundation by thinking about your lifestyle, property, wishes, and ideas. We'll cover how you can think about what your desired project may cost and we'll discuss how your property value may affect your dreams. All of this will tie into a budget-building method that we'll call an investment goal.

1.000 DREAMS, REALITIES, AND FOCUS

It's crucial to do some soul-searching and document the goals and vision of your new home *before* you start planning the project or hiring a team. This exercise will help you set clear expectations and find the right people to participate in achieving your dream home. To begin, capture your thoughts and ideas in a format that can be easily shared with the design team you intend to hire. Remember, the success of your project largely depends on setting expectations, and *that* begins with defining and conveying your vision and goals.

HERE'S WHAT WE'LL COVER _____

- ✓ You and your property: Sharing about your family and property today.
- ✓ Your dreams and visions: Sharing your goals, inspirations, and ideas.
- ✓ Delusions! Resetting your thinking before beginning.

Building or remodeling your new home is one of the most personal and exciting adventures you can embark upon! It's not just about creating a beautiful space, it's also about fostering a lifestyle that complements your unique needs, preferences, and goals. To help you achieve this, your first point of contact will most likely be an experienced architect or designer who can guide you through the process.

To ensure that your design team fully understands your vision, you must provide them with as much information as possible. You can accomplish this by sending them a package introducing you and your family and outlining your property details, lifestyle, and investment goal. By providing your design team with this comprehensive information, you can bring clarity to your vision and empower them to succeed—they can use the detailed information you give them to create a design that meets your expectations and enhances your lifestyle.

1.001 YOU AND YOUR PROPERTY

The better your design team understands you and your family, the more empowered they'll be to respond with thoughtful design. It's simple: just share your family dynamics through a short narrative. Talk about your family, lifestyle, future, career, hobbies, and experiences. Upload photos if you like; the more a design professional personally connects with you, the better.

1.002 PERSONAL PROFILE

*SAMPLE: THE SMITH FAMILY*_____

We are a busy family of four—we're Ben and Jane and our two kids Nathan (age 10) and Betsy (age 8). We don't have plans for more kids, but we all enjoy our dog Rufus. We both work in the high-tech sector and often work at home, yet we have limited time to tackle our projects. We enjoy spending time with the kids and their sports. Nathan is starting a band and Betsy is passionate about gymnastics and music. We both enjoy mountain biking. Our parents live close by and enjoy spending time with the family. We hope to craft a home for the long haul, at least long enough for the kids to get through college. We've remodeled before, but not to the extent we desire to do this time.

1.003 PROPERTY PROFILE

Provide details about the property you intend to build on or remodel. It would be helpful if you started with the property's address, age, number of bedrooms, bathrooms, and other rooms. Although most of this information can be found online, it would be valuable if you could share additional details about the property that cannot be obtained through a web search.

SAMPLE: RENOVATION PROJECT_____

222 Mary Drive, Sunnyvale, CA 23444

Our home is situated on a normal city lot in the Cherry Chase neighborhood. It's 2,000 square feet and we think the lot is 10,000 square feet. We back up against a schoolyard, which is a noise issue. We purchased the home in 2000 but have not remodeled it since. We think the home was added onto in the '90s and the kitchen was remodeled as well.

12888 Forest View Lane, Lake Tahoe, CA 34567

Our lot is 2 acres and has a slight slope to it. We purchased it because we like the view and the privacy.

In each of these cases, a narrative combined with the standard available data will build a profile and give the design team insight before they even visit the property. I'm willing to bet the McMillans took those steps and that's why they purchased a different lot!

1.010 DREAMS AND VISIONS

Once you have your family background and existing property information in hand, your next step is to drill down further and share visions of your new home and spaces. You can convey this valuable information to your design team by writing narratives and sharing idea books, websites, images, and sketches. We'll delve into that now! First we'll create a design statement and explore your inspirations; after that, we'll get into your specific ideas. The more granular your input is, the better your architect's output will be and the more likely your expectations are to be met.

1.011 DESIGN STATEMENT

Your first deep dive is sharing overall goals for your new home. We call this a "design statement"—it's the term used in the world of design for a narrative about your new home or remodeling dreams. Think of it as a short story of your life as you envision living in your new home. This kind of vision won't offer specific solutions—it's more about your home's overall look, feel, and global requirements. You will have an opportunity to dive deeper into the next steps. If you create a thorough and thoughtful design statement, it will immediately set the tone, direction, mindset, and especially productivity for your design team candidates.

SAMPLE DESIGN STATEMENT

We envision our home to be a single-story, modern style with warm materials, four bedrooms, three baths, and a comfortable place for our parents to visit for extended periods. A private office or workspace would be ideal for Jane as she works from home and has international calls at odd hours of the day.

HINT!

Avoid prematurely coming up with specific solutions when thinking about your new home. I commonly refer to this as being "stuck in the mud." For some time now, you've likely been spinning your wheels with ideas and no way to evaluate them. This unproductive whirlwind leads to a lack of focus and can hinder your design team when you introduce them to the project and then—in the same breath!—blurt out the eight options you've been pondering for ten years. Instead, focus on what a designer cannot see by sharing your dreams and visions of your family living in your new home or kitchen. Offer insights into your lifestyle, existing home, potential site, and attributes. Let a creative person listen and respond with aligned solutions.

1.012 INSPIRATIONS

As you collect pictures of homes and spaces that catch your eye, they can be used as inspirations to support your design statement. You may not even know why you like a particular picture of a space or a home, but sharing it with professionals opens up the opportunity for quality discussions.

Inspirations can take the form of detailed lists, images, and web links that offer more insights to your design team. It's essential to prioritize your list and revisit it during the estimating stage. However, don't try to come up with solutions during this exercise! Instead, use these visuals to guide your design team towards achieving your design statement and your overall big picture. Once you've laid the groundwork, you can start enjoying the fun part of design.

HINT!

Visit a few home-design-specific sites like Pinterest and Houzz. Create a profile and idea books or boards and then begin saving your inspirations. Categorizing your idea books by "exterior," "interior," "kitchen," "bath," etc. is best. Eventually, share these with your designer candidates. Gathering these resources takes some time, but it also makes your design team more likely to hit the bull's-eye.

1.013 IDEAS

Precisely because no one knows your lifestyle, home, and family better than you do, you actually *won't* be able to help yourself by imagining ideas and solutions. I realize this sounds counterintuitive, but discovering ideas can be one of the most enjoyable stages of the design process, whether it's your own ideas or your architect's ideas.

Although it's irresistible to come up with and discuss ideas with anyone who wants to listen, beware! Doing so can influence your designer and even handcuff them if you're adamant about your long-established ideas.

The last thing you want is a designer who simply regurgitates your ideas! I've been involved with numerous projects where our design team developed concepts and the client said something like *"I had never thought of that!"* or *"How did you come up with that idea? It's fantastic!"* Professional designers will listen and respond with solutions you may not have considered. The better your input is and the more closely they listen, the better the design results will be.

HINT!

Use the same methodology as you did with your inspirations, but dig even deeper by sharing your specific ideas and scaling your list by priorities like "must-haves" and "nice-to-haves."

To review, the goal for the first discovery stage was to capture as much as possible about you, your property, your inspirations, and your goals. Collecting this information and passing it along as a shareable document is powerful and your architect will love you for it!

1.020 DELUSIONS AND REALITIES

The excitement and emotions surrounding thinking about a new home are powerful, so much so that they can cloud your decision-making. Early-onset delusions can undermine dreams and expectations, potentially sidelining a project. The solution to protecting yourself is establishing a solid mindset. That begins with awareness! I aim to bring these delusions to the forefront so that you can overcome these potential pitfalls by gaining focus for yourself and the team of people who'll help you get to the finish line.

1.021 DELUSIONS

Almost everyone asks the two quintessential questions until they hear what they want to hear: how much will my project cost and how long will it take? You were likely doomed when your friend puffed out his chest and boasted that he spent 20K on his kitchen remodel and it only took a week. There are no silver-bullet answer to these questions. The more architects, designers, builders, and friends you ask, the broader range of answers you'll get. This confusion and the ensuing contradictions stem from the diverse experiences people have had with design and construction businesses that operate in numerous ways.

Every day, I'm amazed by folks who have burned unrealistic ideas of costs into their mind, so I've thought about this a lot. So much information is coming at you from so many resources that you'll inevitably find what you want to hear and you'll believe it. But remember, I'm positioning you to have realistic expectations that lead to intelligent decisions. We can set you free if you're able to start with a clean slate by thinking for yourself!

Before we begin building a "bridge of reality," as I like to call it, let's closely examine some common delusions you could succumb to. Knowing what may work against you can help you set your mind right before you even contemplate a budget. (And the budget is the last piece of the discovery puzzle that could trigger you to adjust your aspirations.)

1.022 MEDIA

Home improvement channels, DIY networks, social media, and the like are the first culprits that distort the actual time it takes to build a project, not to mention the actual costs. Let's remember that these productions and influencers are based on entertaining, grabbing attention, and earning a buck. Basing your planning and expectations on this misinformation can immediately send you down the wrong path. It's worth examining why.

Missing pieces: *The cost of a construction project is not limited to the construction itself—various other expenses come into play before the actual construction begins. For instance, there are costs associated with design and planning, such as fees for architects, designers, and consultants like engineers. Other expenses include Planning and Building department fees, permits, site preparations, etc. These costs can account for 20% to 30% of a project's total cost depending on the project's size, complexity, and quality.*

Materials: *Drilling down into these projects, you'll certainly find "arrangements" that have been made by product manufacturers to provide materials to projects for little to no cost in exchange for visibility during programming. Furthermore, when costs of materials are referenced, said costs are frequently wholesale costs. This is unrealistic for the end user.*

Labor: *This is also a significant expense in any construction project. However, actual costs can be distorted when the media attempts to convey them. Service providers may donate or discount their labor to a project for visibility or charitable reasons, for example.*

The process of creating a TV show project is quite understandably time-consuming. It involves producing and then editing the show, all of which can take multiple weeks or even months before being filtered into an episode that's a mere 30 to 60 minutes long. This process can lead to false expectations and unrealistic beliefs that a project can be completed quickly. Moreover, the considerable number of labor resources applied to a project can also create confusion about how a project can be accomplished so fast. A popular TV show called *America's Home Makeover* used hundreds of people to build their projects. This served the show's production well. However, if the cost of all those resources were to be included in the project value, the amount would be staggering! To avoid fixating on unrealistic expectations and costs, you must get what you've seen on social media and TV shows out of your mind before you engage with your teams.

1.023 FAMILY, FRIENDS, AND COLLEAGUES

I have formed a strong opinion after having designed and built hundreds of projects: your friends and colleagues tend not to fully share what they spent on their project. They even treat how little they supposedly spent as a badge of honor, to the point where they're delusional. During prying conversations, I've uncovered diverse ways of thinking about cost, from "I don't count the design or the appliances in my budget" to leaving out that they performed some or all of the labor themselves.

Talking about costs with friends and then relating those supposed costs to your own project will certainly cloud your thinking as you tackle the big "How much will this cost?" question. Because this is such a custom business, from the scope of work to the material choices, asking "How much will this cost?" only helps to understand costs on a very high level. In other words, does a kitchen remodel cost 20k or 200K? Believe me, you'll hear numbers throughout this range. To get more usefully specific, you need more information.

1.024 CONSTRUCTION AND DESIGN PEOPLE

Naturally, going to the source—the professionals—is the way to better understand what kinds of resources, efforts, and costs go into a project. Knowing what to ask is the first hurdle and understanding the roles of different disciplines is the next one. Being able to articulate your project details is an even higher hurdle. But the wall you'll *really* ultimately hit will be obtaining consistently objective input.

When it comes to creating custom homes and remodels, each homeowner has their own financial priorities. One person's return on their investment may weigh heavily on their financial decisions; others may value achieving their dreams more and resale takes a back seat. Therefore, it's difficult for a design or construction pro to pin down costs when a homeowner asks the elusive budget question until more information is available.

With that said, when homeowners do ask the budget question, it's common for contractors to blurt out a wide range of numbers, further exacerbating the difficulties of creating a budget. Inevitably, homeowners lock onto to the lowest number they hear. That's when delusions set in. This common pitfall is not helpful and potentially leads to a poor experience. But where do you turn? You must start *somewhere* to see if your dreams are even close to reality. Well, nobody knows the cost of construction better than a contractor. Thus a typical next step is to find a contractor and ask how much he charges. Let's look at some real-life scenarios.

Perhaps you want to add a primary suite. You ask Ace the Builder how much it will cost. The reply is "Sure, no problem! My guys can build your addition for $300 bucks per foot!" You crunch the numbers: 500 square feet multiplied by $300 equals $150,000. "I can pull that off!" you say excitedly. You immediately start spending money on plans. This stopping-there mistake is a chronic problem in the home building and remodeling process! More questions should be asked before any planning begins.

Experienced building professionals will have a plethora of information to offer when the time comes to build your project. As you peel back the layers of this experience, you may find that other areas of the business take a back seat. When you asked Ace the Builder how much your primary suite addition would cost and he said "$300 bucks a foot," what exactly did that mean? Did he ask *you* any questions? Is that his cost and then you must pay his profit and overhead? Does that amount include the plans? The permits? The tile material? What about the plumbing fixtures for the primary bath? Do you want skylights? Oh, or a fireplace? Hardwood floors? The list goes on and on.

As you navigate through the process for your supposedly $150K primary suite, there's an excellent chance you'll hear "Oh, the plans are extra" and "Our clients usually provide all the finish materials" and "Do you want hardwood floors? Our base is carpet."

Design professionals come with all sorts of experience levels, credentials, and licenses (or not). While many people think these folks would have a better grip on costs given that it's their job to design solutions that meet your budget, unfortunately, such is often *not* the case. The reality is that design professionals are not in touch with construction costs as much as construction professionals are. By "construction professionals," I mean general contractors and subcontractors.

Having an elusive and unrealistic budget is where the process begins to fall apart. Designing towards a budget—especially if you need clarifications and don't convey your actual budget—is a challenge, and it puts your designer in a tough place. I often see a few scenarios in particular:

- You go to Fred the Architect with your ideas and you have Ace the Builder's $300-cost-per-square-foot budget locked into your brain. Since you are "comfortable" with Ace's price, you begin the design process without bothering Fred with your understanding of what the project might cost. Fred listens well, responds with useful design solutions, and even offers a few new ideas that may cost a bit more. You're okay with that because there's some "wiggle room" in your budget.

- You go to Fred the Architect with your ideas and share your budget goal. Fred stares blankly and doesn't believe you; he thinks you're sandbagging him because that always happens—homeowners always exceed their budget. So Fred nods and takes your money to design the project. The plans are completed and ready for the permit. You go back to Ace to get a final cost and are floored by the budget, which is now double what you had in mind. The plans are worthless.

- You go to Fred the Architect and share your budget, and Fred says the budget is unrealistic based on his experience. It's hard to convey how much more it could cost until the design has been completed. You now must make a call, but if you're like most homeowners, you have zero experience in these matters. "Okay," you think, "how much more could it be compared to Ace's quote? Twenty percent? Thirty percent?" You decide that you can handle that and you'll take the plunge. "If Ace's cost winds up being too high, I'll find someone else," you mutter to yourself.

The end result is that you're a loser in all of these scenarios because your expectations were unrealistic. And it's mostly your fault, with some help from Ace and Fred.

This delusion is our first introduction to accountability disguised as expectations. Who ultimately is accountable for your budget? Fred? Ace? When it boils down to it, *you* are accountable for your budget. "That's not fair!" you say. "I've never done this before! How can I possibly accomplish this project?"

By becoming informed so that your expectations are achievable. You need Ace and Fred, yes, but *you* will take control and lead the pack during the upcoming planning processes because you will be an Awakened Homeowner.

1.025 SELF-DELUSION

Project costs can often be elusive, possessive, and blinding, leading to poor decision-making when starting a new project. To better understand this scenario, imagine that you're about to embark on a multiday hike. You've done your research and you bought the necessary gear. Now you're standing at the trailhead ready to begin. The trail is clearly marked, but there are a few alternate routes. As you take your first steps, your mind starts racing. You start thinking that there must be a better, quicker, easier, and cheaper way to reach your destination. Maybe there's a secret path that nobody else knows about. You decide to branch off the main trail and start blazing your own path. You convince yourself that you can overcome all of the advice you've received and achieve a faster and cheaper result. Spoiler: most people who do this end up regretting it.

You start picking and choosing what you want to hear based on your "research." You have no quantifiable data to base your conclusions on, but Ace the Builder's low cost sounds good. You may think that you can lower the cost even more by selecting cheaper materials. In fact, you believe that you can do it for cheaper than your brother-in-law did. He had no idea what he's doing, and now *you* do! You haven't even started really going down the trail yet, but you're already following the wrong path. It instantly takes you on a steep uphill slant. Your heart begins pounding.

Instead of going down the wrong path, it's better to follow well-traveled paths, empowered with the knowledge and resources you need to help you understand the actual cost of your project. As you progress through this book, I'll present you with methods that will allow you to tackle the monumental questions.

DREAMS, REALITIES, AND FOCUS REVIEW

The goal is empower your design team to achieve your goals.

Step One: Share your personal story.

Step Two: Share your property details and dynamics.

Step Three: Share your vision of your new home.

Step Four: Share your inspirations and idea details.

1.030 HOW TO BUILD YOUR BUDGET

What better way to gain focus than to break free of delusions and balance your dreams with an investment goal? Misunderstanding costs is the number-one destroyer of projects and relationships, and it often happens before a project even gets started. Worse yet, it happens *after* the project has already begun. It's the chicken-or-the-egg dilemma, a question that's virtually impossible to answer until a project is completely designed. The natural and negative instinct is avoidance, with everyone glossing over the cost until it's too late. There's no secret answer. Becoming aware by going through some exercises provides metrics to make informed decisions, protect the experience, and maybe even put the kids through college.

HERE'S WHAT WE COVER _____

- ✓ Break Free of Delusions
- ✓ Reasons to Build a Budget
- ✓ What Is a Budget?
- ✓ Two Steps to Building a Budget
- ✓ The Components of a Budget

1.031 BREAK FREE OF DELUSIONS

By now, I wouldn't be surprised that your ideas have been a constant stream to your Pinterest account, Houzz idea books, web links, and untold hours spent watching HGTV and DIY networks. You may have ideas on what you want to accomplish—perhaps you downloaded a free design software application and played with your ideas. This is an exciting and inspiring part of planning a renovation or new home project! You might have been pondering hundreds of ideas for years, and now you know what you want to achieve. But some concerns are lurking in the background. How much is the project going to cost? How much should you spend? How do you know that what you're looking at is *it*? And on and on. It's never too early to think about cost; each homeowner has their particular ideas and comfort levels. You'll have to prioritize the cost on your own, but addressing the budget as early as possible is crucial. Otherwise, you may undermine the entire project!

Establishing a budget for your project *before* you engage in the design process is one way to wrap your head around costs and tamp down the delusions that could otherwise creep in. The financial aspects of a project revolve around personal life situations and goals. As the homeowner, these multifaceted dynamics mean that *you* are ultimately responsible for communicating and controlling the elephant in the room: cost. But how can you possibly do this if you don't know what you don't know?

With a sound methodology for approaching the budget question, that's how. The first step has been becoming aware of the delusions that can derail you from the start. Unlinking the emotions caused by the new kitchen you're drooling over—you love that granite slab!—or the fairytale-perfect modern farmhouse plastered all over the internet is the next step to detaching from your delusions. Doing so is vital to keeping your thinking process clear.

The less focus you have, the less decisive you become, and that leads to your design and construction team having to spin more wheels at your expense. Setting yourself free, on the other hand, empowers you to think about your investment realistically, enabling your design team and contractor to be at their most effective and productive when providing solutions. Throughout this guide, remember that I'm streaming all of these ideas, suggestions, and supporting tools your way to empower you, hold those you hire accountable, and prevent your kids from requiring a college scholarship because you had to have that red granite from Mars.

1.032 WHY A BUDGET?

It may seem silly to think about cost so early, but in most cases, cost is what drives the design decisions. Skipping the budget process could undermine all of the time and money you ultimately spend on design, whereas getting an early start can only help as important decisions arrive. This vital step happens *before* you hire designers and certainly before your contractor digs out a single scoop of dirt! It's up to you how far you reach to get your arms around cost, but I bet Ben and Jane wished they had taken it more seriously. Establishing and communicating an investment limit to their architect would have allowed them to avoid many of their ensuing disasters because it would have placed a spotlight on the cost at key stages of design or even before they purchased the lot.

Effectively prioritizing and communicating a budget to those helping your dreams come true shares accountability so that your dream doesn't become a nightmare. A budget can immensely help the subsequent design and cost-estimating processes! For example, a budget will place values on options you may be considering and can phase out a remodel project over time. Perhaps you're building a home and are curious how much it would cost for a basement or how much the master bath would cost for your remodel project. Again, identifying these components with your designer and contractors early on enables them to be at their most productive while designing and costing out construction. Most importantly, having a budget empowers you to make educated decisions, meaning you can design and build a project you feel financially comfortable with.

WHY YOU NEED A BUDGET _____

- ✓ To establish a financial benchmark to work towards.
- ✓ To share accountability across design and construction pros and you.
- ✓ To foster an effective and efficient design process.
- ✓ To identify phases, options, and alternatives early on.
- ✓ To empower decision-making.

1.033 WHAT IS A BUDGET?

The term "budget" is frequently used in the context of construction, but maybe you're wondering what exactly it signifies. In the realm of home renovation and construction, a budget refers to the amount of money you're comfortable investing in the property to help you achieve your vision. That's it! A budget does *not* attempt to predict final construction costs, although we'll tackle that issue soon. A licensed contractor will determine the actual cost of your project once the design, plans, and specifications have been prepared by your design team.

Establishing a budget begins with deciding how much you prefer to spend regardless of your dreams. I like the to use the term "investment goal" to describe this end point. Deciding on your investment goal involves setting a dollar value based on metrics outside of the world of construction costs, such as property values before and after a project is completed. Then as you progress through the design process, you'll have a benchmark—it's the missing piece of the puzzle that empowers you to make informed decisions tailored to your personal financial goals.

There's a deeper level of budgeting that cracks open the door to predicting construction costs. In our discovery stage, we take this further by analyzing how your hypothetical project aligns with your investment goals before you even speak with an architect or contractor. This deeper dive helps you get a clearer picture of the costs involved in building your dream home and enables you to make informed decisions about the path you want to take. Our system exposes you to potential expenses early, empowering you to seize control of your project and ensure that you stay within a reasonable budget. To quickly recap:

WHAT A BUDGET IS
- ✓ An investment goal.
- ✓ A dollar amount you feel comfortable investing in the property.
- ✓ A dollar amount you can afford.
- ✓ A method to compare your investment goals to your dreams.

WHAT A BUDGET ISN'T
- ✓ A construction estimate.

1.040 TWO STEPS TO A BUDGET

The time has come to couple your dreams with a first look at the financial aspects of your property and project! These two steps determine how much money your project may take vs. the value of your property and the surrounding properties. Understanding the value of your property today and in the future when your project is complete empowers you to balance your dreams with costs from an investment perspective. Your budget may consume all of your equity in the property or surpass other homes in the neighborhood, or you could ratchet back your dreams because you plan to sell the property in the not-so-distant future. Ultimately, the decision is yours. My goal here is to provide you with the guidance, information, and tools you need to make informed decisions, refine your goals, and direct your design team as clearly as possible.

The first step is to understand your property value today along with the equity you may have, the value of neighboring properties, and how your dreams can affect your property values. This step allows you to look ahead and reality-check your ideas. With this valuable information, you can capture a rough dollar value for your dreams. You can then compare your future value to your property value today and ultimately declare a budget that will guide you and that you'll share with others. It's not an exact science, but it's much better than being encircled by false information.

1.041 STEP ONE: DETERMINING YOUR PROPERTY VALUE TODAY AND IN THE FUTURE

"How much should I spend?" you ask. "Well, that depends," your guardian angel responds. That's because remodeling or building a new home is a highly personal and individual endeavor. Instead of using the word "should," consider replacing it with "could," "can," or "will." Or respond to your own question with "I don't know until I see ideas." A good starting point is to understand your property's current value and its potential value after your dream home is built, viewed purely from an investment perspective. This analysis will help you prioritize costs and create a budget and will potentially influence your project ideas.

When it comes to custom home building and remodeling, homeowners may not always prioritize resale value. Nevertheless, it's still a valuable exercise to go through to evaluate your project from the investment angle. This exercise can provide a sanity check and empower your decision-making by understanding your property's current value and equity, your borrowing power, and your property value after completing your project.

With so much information available online, you can evaluate your property's current value in an hour or two. The following steps and tools examine the following key elements to explore:

STEP ONE

✓ Research your existing real estate market to understand the estimated value of your property today.

✓ Identify comparable properties in your area that are currently on the market and then compare them with properties that recently sold.

> **HINT!** Create an account at Realtor.com and save searches by neighborhoods. You can get updates and notifications frequently to stay in touch.

> **HINT!** Create an account at Zillow.com. For active urban and suburban markets, you can click on properties and drill down deeper to see the sale data. The same thing can be done with Realtor.com.

✓ Consult with a local real estate agent who's familiar with your area.

> **HINT!** Rockstar real estate agents usually target specific neighborhoods with a sharp focus on daily

transactions. They call this their "farm." Connecting with this agent will provide you with the most valuable information.

✓ Collect the information into a small spreadsheet to quickly analyze values by square footage and the features of each property.

> **HINT!** Determine an average value by square foot. You'll use this cost-per-square-foot method and value throughout the budgeting process.

✓ Determine your borrowing power by including your mortgage vs. the estimated value.

> **HINT!** Visit a mortgage broker or construction lender early on to understand how much of your equity you can leverage and how much of your own money you'll need to pitch into a financing package to fund your project.

With your estimated values and available funds in hand, you now have the information you need to identify how much you'd prefer to invest in your property. This analysis should happen before your dreams are finalized, any designs begin, or you determine a project budget. As we delve into the next step of building your budget, this analysis is your reality check.

1.042 STEP TWO: BUILDING YOUR BUDGET

"How much will my job cost before there's a design and some specifications to price out?" Practically everyone has this elusive question, but again, there's no dependable way to find an answer. What we *can* tackle using some tools to drill down and narrow in is to gain an understanding of where your project could go financially. Keep in mind that building a budget at this early stage is just a few steps removed from flat-out guesses or delusions. Still, it's a way to balance your dreams over the value of your property, empowering you to make intelligent decisions regarding design and finances. This process may feel like going down a rabbit hole, but it's worth going through it once and then revisiting said rabbit hole as you begin planning your project.

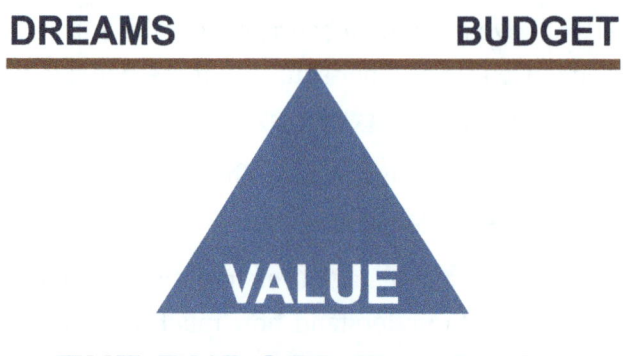

THE BUDGET BALANCE

The diagram above represents three components for evaluating a project from a financial perspective. It all boils down to balancing your dreams with your budget. Knowing the value of your home today and possibly in the future gives you one checkpoint. Ultimately, you'll prioritize your dreams vs. the budget, and knowing this crucial checkpoint early enough is the objective of building a budget.

Earlier in Section 1.010, I introduced the concept of exploring your dreams and visions. While these are essential to convey to prospective designers, this exercise can help in even more ways: these statements can be used as a baseline to analyze an early look at your project budget, how your dreams impact your existing home, and ultimately what the cost will be. Below is an example of a design statement with more details:

We would like to expand our home to include an additional bedroom and bathroom that would act as our primary bedroom suite.

We anticipate approximately 500 square feet at the rear of the home. Also, we would like to remodel the kitchen and would consider redesigning the space to achieve a more efficient workspace. New hardwood flooring throughout the main living area, kitchen, and the new primary suite are desired. The home has not been updated since the original construction in 1965; therefore, new windows, doors, and a roof are also included in the project.

This design statement is a quick example of adding more detail to the scope, which helps break down the budget. But before you do so, understand that your ideas will likely impact the existing home in a remodel project because it's nearly impossible to expand your home without affecting the current structure in one way or another. A 500-square-foot addition can frequently become a 700-, 800-, or 900-square-foot project, impacting your cost study. Your architect and contractor are the professionals who will determine the impacts, but sharing what you desire in your own words points them in the right direction. The budgeting exercise will also expose potential impacts, thus creating a solid set of expectations.

HOW TO CREATE YOUR BUDGET

❏ Enter the square footage data of your existing home.

❏ Enter the square footage data of your new home or expansion.

❏ Enter the square footage of the areas impacted by your existing home.

❏ Budget other special items.

❏ Select square footage values.

❏ Estimate the cost of design, permits, and other ancillary costs.

❏ Determine a budget range.

Once you're ready to begin your planning, exploring the TAH Planning and Building Workbooks is your next step. In "How to Build Your Budget" at the TAH home, you'll find a sneak peek into our application with detailed instructions, resources, and tools you can use to carry out your planning.

1.050 BUDGETING METHODS

Analyzing the cost of construction per square foot is an age-old method for estimating the cost of building a home—and, let us not forget, placing a valuation on properties. Using the value-per-square-foot method for budgeting at this stage is just about your only option until you have actual data like designs and specifications.

In many respects, building a new home from a blank canvas is more straightforward to construct and analyze on a cost-per-square-foot basis than a custom home or remodel project. If you were to talk to a larger-production home builder about how much they charge per square foot in your market, they would likely know a dependable range. This precision is especially true if the company builds multiple homes with similar floor plans. This history of costs factors into many elements, such as repetitive designs, efficiencies in construction, and exceptional cost concessions they receive due to volume. However, if you were to go to the other end of town where a contractor is building larger custom homes for individual clients, you might hear a much higher cost range per square foot.

Remodeling is even more challenging to pin down the cost per square foot due to the inherent custom nature of designs and how an existing structure poses challenges, which drives costs in many directions. This is why when they're taking the plunge to remodel their home, many folks have no clue what it will cost and are often disappointed initially. So, with all of that said, what we're trying to do here is develop a cost that's a couple of notches up from flat-out guessing and submitting to delusional forces. But make no mistake: a budget is *not* a construction cost estimate. Although using cost-per-square-foot estimates can be useful for budgeting purposes, remember that those are *not* a definitive measure of construction costs and can vary significantly depending on the specific circumstances of the project.

1.051 BREAKING DOWN A BUDGET

Before embarking on a budget-building exercise, you need to understand some terms and methods that are collected within three budget components. You can do so by asking yourself these questions:

- ❏ How much new square footage do my dreams include?
- ❏ How much square footage of my existing home would I like to remodel?
- ❏ What is my scope of work? (This needs to clearly identify *all* of the work you'd like to have done.)

THE BUDGETING BIG THREE

The three components that need to be analyzed for budgeting are:

- ❏ New square footage
- ❏ Existing square footage
- ❏ Scope of work

NSF = New Square Footage
ESF = Existing Square Footage Impacted
SOW = Scope-of-Work Across Project

THE BUDGETING BIG THREE

1.052 UNDERSTANDING SQUARE FOOTAGE

To begin with, let's have a clear understanding of what we mean by the term "square footage." It is not as straightforward as it may seem. When we talk about square footage, we're referring to the livable space within a home, *not* including areas such as garages or unfinished basements. One way to determine the square footage is to check the listing from when the house was on sale. If you're unsure about that, visit your county assessor's website, use the property look-up tool, and input your address. This data should give you accurate square footage. However, it's essential to note that if the house has been expanded without building permits, the record may not be correct. For example, enclosed covered patios and converted garages may not be included in the square footage that the county has on record. If you prefer to measure the square footage on your own, just remember that measuring from the outside of the exterior walls is the correct reference. This DIY approach commonly involves breaking your home up into individual shapes and then totaling up the areas.

We're going to divide the square footage into two categories: new square footage and existing square footage. This division will help us analyze the budget more accurately, as costs can vary significantly depending on whether new square footage is added or existing portions of the home are modified.

1.053 NEW SQUARE FOOTAGE (NSF)

NSF will be relatively easy to capture as this is purely the new portion of the house that will be added or the total living area square footage in the case of a new home. The next two components get a bit foggier because a remodel project involving an addition will trigger work that needs to be completed on the existing structure, and you may not have thought about this added-on work.

1.054 EXISTING SQUARE FOOTAGE (ESF)

ESF includes the square feet of the existing home as impacted by two drivers: the NSF and the remodel areas. For example, adding on the primary suite may require redesigning the home to gain access to the new space—a bedroom may need to become smaller, a bathroom may need to be moved, etc. Secondly, in terms of the existing areas of your home that you want to remodel, although it's possible that remodeling existing square footage will be less expensive than creating new square footage, don't let that fool you! A kitchen remodel has many components crammed into a small space, inflating the cost per square foot. The ESF method will allow you to assign a price per square foot to capture a more accurate budget.

1.055 SCOPE OF WORK (SOW)

The term "scope of work" or SOW will be used throughout this guide and will progressively get more detailed as we reach deeper into planning. For budgeting purposes, this is your opportunity to elaborate on the ideas you may have that cross over between the new and existing square footage (such as the detailed design statement that we discussed earlier). Think of a SOW as a more descriptive and directional narrative that allows others to fully understand what's to be accomplished. For example, our design statement declared that we need a new roof as part of the project. This work would span beyond the new and existing areas, effectively distorting the cost-per-square-foot calculations. Instead, we'll place this third SOW component within the analysis to capture this cost.

Focusing on the three main components of a budget within the living areas gets us pretty close, but we're still not all the way there—depending on the project scope, there will be other costs beyond your living area. These potential impacted areas include:

✓ Attached and detached garages, shops, and studios

✓ Unfinished and finished basements

✓ Utility work: power, water, and sewer service

✓ Landscaping and pools

✓ Design costs, architects, interior designers, and consultants

✓ Planning and Building department fees

To learn more about budget building methods, costs per square foot, establishing an investment goal, and how to factor all these potential costs into your project visit www.theawakenedhomeowner. com/category/project-budgeting/

RECAP OF YOUR NEXT STEPS

✓ Take some time to think through your goals and write them down.

✓ Be aware of the outside forces that can steer you off track.

✓ Understand the value of your property today and tomorrow.

✓ Make an informed decision on how much you prefer to invest.

✓ Build a budget that goes beyond delusions and guesses.

✓ Balance your budget with your dreams.

✓ Share your goals with your design team.

✓ Set the expectations for everybody, including yourself!

Once we get deeper into the upcoming section on the world of design, our mission will be to link design with specifications and expectations that are balanced with your budget. We'll perform budget checkpoints, fine-tune your dreams, and pin down your construction cost by using an estimating process.

PART ONE CONCLUSION

Laying the groundwork for your project began with some introspection as you contemplated your new home and your financial goals. These methods and eventual actions fall directly under the umbrella of our Guiding Principles because they set expectations for you and the many people you'll engage to complete your project. You began by looking within and sharing your personal and property profile with your design team, and you also created a design statement that captured your visions for your new home. This vision can be supported by different tiers of inspirations and ideas.

Now you know how badly delusions can derail a project from the beginning and the significant role that reality plays in your dreams. You've gained a better understanding of how difficult it is initially to answer the inevitable question of "How much could my project cost?" and you've learned that you should instead be asking "Should or could I spend that much?" Tackling this huge question by doing budget exercises wraps up the first part of our guide.

"Bill Reid and his team are extremely professional, finished the project exactly on time as per the project plan that was updated weekly, and responded to all our questions/concerns within hours."

- Dagmar S.

PROJECT BY BILL REID
OF REMODELWEST

THE WORLD OF DESIGN

2.

*"Design is creative solutions
woven with aspirations
and beauty while balancing
practicality, aesthetics,
and value."*

W.W. Reid

THE WORLD OF DESIGN 2.

2.0 INTRODUCTION

The result of your project will only be as good as your design, which is articulated in drawings, details, and specifications aggregated into construction documents by your design team. If you rush through the design process and then select the cheapest designer and handcuff her, don't expect her to meet your expectations. Those who don't prioritize and value design should be prepared for a teetering and crumbling experience, also known as missed expectations. Ben and Jane come to mind.

Researching design ideas on the web can be exciting and inspirational for your new home. You may have discovered the websites Pinterest and Houzz, where you can create idea books. It's a great way to capture and share your ideas and expectations for your home! Conceptualizing ideas is the easiest part of designing. However, planning to achieve concepts is *not.*

This is where a design pro comes in. A common attempt to remedy inferior design and planning is to shift responsibility to your contractor, expecting them to solve incomplete design challenges during the heat of the battle. They don't enjoy this burden (to put it mildly), and it will materialize in increased costs, delays, substandard quality, and even dissention. Your expectations are under *your* control! Once you have the knowledge and awareness that design is valuable, you're well on your way to matching your expectations to reality.

Proper design is your first step to protecting your experience and investment. Part Two will enlighten you about many aspects of the design world, positioning you to take the right actions and hire the right people to meet your expectations. Remember, *you* are the conductor. You may not know how to play the violin, but you sure know when it sounds funny. Let's pull back the curtain! To kick everything off, here's a snapshot of what we'll be talking about:

THE DESIGN TEAM: METHODS AND AGREEMENTS

✓ Learn about architects, designers, and consultants that make up the design team.

✓ Dig into the design process to understand the methodology that your design team will deploy to shape your discoveries into reality by composing your design, plans, and specifications.

✓ Monitor your budget during the design process.

✓ Learn how design agreements are structured and other important considerations when hiring an architect or designer.

KNOW THE DETAILS

✓ Understand how design limitations already in place can affect your ideas even before you begin design.

✓ Learn about your designer's work product—what are architectural plans? You'll find out how they're organized and what information should be included.

✓ Get to know the intricacies of permit processing and approval by your local city or county Building departments.

✓ Manage your project during the design process, starting with permits, plans, and specs and going through to the ready-to-build stage.

2.000 UNDERSTANDING DESIGN PROFESSIONALS

Design is the most undervalued and overlooked aspect of a project. Design quality is the keystone of a successful project—it's a funnel point and a bridge to your new home, and it begins with your first call to a qualified designer. The type of designer you may hire depends on your project scope and experience, coming in the form of architects, residential designers, or interior designers who have varying credentials, professionalism, and levels of experience.

A designer's job is to provide solutions by first understanding and respecting their clients and their objectives. They achieve this by listening to the client's wants, needs, likes, and dislikes—basically, all of the areas we covered in the opening discovery stage in Part One. Once the design criteria are understood, a professional designer taps into their knowledge, experience, and tools to present design solutions and shepherd homeowners through the lengthy design process until the day of groundbreaking.

Because it's so crucial to find the right designer for your project, this section will enlighten you on how to achieve a quality design by matching the right designer to your experience, project type, and goals so that your expectations can be met. As you work your way through this and the next part on your way to Part Four: Building Your Team, you might want to refer to the Project Design Pro Matrix (see page 344) to help decide who you need to hire. First, though, we'll cover:

- ✓ Architects: Who they are, their distinctive styles, and what you need for your particular project.
- ✓ Residential designers: Who they are compared to architects.
- ✓ Interior designers: Who they are and why they're so important.

✓ Designer obstacles: How to maneuver around potential roadblocks.

✓ Consultants: Who they are and why you may need them.

Within the world of residential design, two essential people become key players for the team: architects and interior designers. Intelligently investing time and money into the first planning stage with these professionals is paramount to enjoying the ultimate outcome, so let's delve into their roles and responsibilities, how they differ, and how a collaborative effort can foster a wonderful experience and a beautiful home. As we dig deeper into the design process, many opportunities will arise that will allow you to further qualify your designer. But first, let's talk about architects, who are the most common type of designer for residential projects.

2.010 ARCHITECTS

Architects are creative and technical individuals who have studied design and engineering, obtained the appropriate credentials, and passed the state board exams. They possess a license issued by the states they practice in and actively practice in your community. When considering larger projects such as a new home or significant remodeling and expansions, hiring a licensed architect will likely be your first point of contact. That said, this is not necessarily the only path you can take to design a project. (See Options for Hiring Design and Construction Professionals on page 346.)

The term "architect" is only intended to be used by individuals who have accomplished the above-mentioned credentials. Note that the residential design field is filled with very competent individuals who may have obtained a degree in architecture from an accredited institution but elected not to pursue their licensure for various reasons. Many of these people are employed by architecture firms or practice on their own, but in either case, they should not use the term "architect" within their title description. Instead, they commonly use the term "designer" or "residential designer." In rare occurrences, a person or company who does not hold the appropriate credentials could be using the terms "architecture" or "architect" in a way that misleads the public. Taking a close look at this qualification will be your first task when hiring an architect—you must research whether or not the person or company you're talking to has the proper licensing.

When you interview architects, you'll be searching for someone who demonstrates a genuine passion for their profession. You'll want them to have superior creative talent and take progressive actions to address rapidly changing building systems. You'll want an architect who's enthusiastic about pragmatic solutions that balance project design with cost and the production of quality design, drawings, and details. Like any other profession or trade, there are varying levels of architects. My mission here is to give you enough knowledge to be able to confidently filter your options. Some characteristics of an architect are influenced by personal and industry forces that may or may not benefit you. Let's look at a few profiles of architects I've worked with over the years and see if one resonates with you.

THE GATEKEEPER

Perhaps you know what you're doing and don't need a guide or you aren't interested in paying for one. However, it would help if you had a map! This kind of designer is a guide who hunkers down at the trailhead. You state your destination and they hand you a trail map. Then you ask for minimal directions and you set out. Your survival is not a priority for the gatekeeper—that's on you. Many designers are gatekeepers. They prefer to do the bare minimum and are sometimes unconcerned about the dangers on the trail or the end result.

Part of what you need to know to understand the full landscape of home building and remodeling is the unofficial phrase "the permit push." We'll talk more about this later, but the short story is that the designers and architects who are engaging in the permit push are trying to put as little information as possible on their plans when applying for their permits. Scary! Believe it or not, this option can work, but you better *reeeeally* know what you're doing and have plenty of experience designing and remodeling homes. But sure, a homeowner who wants to drive the design and have someone get it on the plans can "benefit" from the permit push approach by paying the least amount for the plans and obtaining permits in record speed. I say this in jest, because the odds of this approach being successful are extremely rare even if you think you're ready. The bottom line is that if you don't know you're interviewing a gatekeeper, you're doomed. This kind of designer will provide minimum information on the plans, leaving you to fight it out with contractors, suppliers, and the Building department.

Ask yourself the following questions—and be honest!

❏ Am I in a hurry?

❏ Do I know what I'm doing?

❏ Am I willing to go into my project blind?

❏ Is cheaper better?

THE ADVENTURER

Equipped with the most current design tools and technology, a creative mind, and the necessary skills to push you forward to a superb project, an aura of excitement and passion exudes from the adventurer architect. Their portfolio is superb—the photos of their projects resonate with you—and some of their projects have received awards and been published in architectural magazines and on websites. The larger and more innovative a project is, the better it is to have someone alongside you throughout the entire process who's genuinely interested in seeing their work applied in real life. From design through construction, this person has your back and is your advocate. This style of architect is a perfect match for a homeowner who recognizes the value of design; the adventurer architect can be fun to work with and will achieve stellar results. That said, however, you still need to peel back some layers to keep your priorities intact.

Brilliant design comes at a cost in terms of both design fees and construction costs. Creative design is an exciting experience, but unintended consequences can manifest if the budget is subconsciously deprioritized by your designers. And another danger lurks—people may not follow through on the details that are necessary to achieve the ideas you've fallen in love with. That's because highly creative architects can sometimes lack the stamina to follow through with all of the details required in the plans. This deficiency can lead to you expecting your contractor to read the mind of the architect, resulting in mistakes, escalated costs, delays, and missed expectations. Ultimately, you'll have to depend on your contractor to interpret the plans during the estimating phase and then follow up with the architect. Keeping an eye on the budget is already difficult within the world of design, and when you hire an adventurer architect, it may become even more difficult. As "perfect ideas" crop up in your plans, it will be up to you to prioritize the budget, call a time-out, and rein in the team.

Ask yourself the following questions—and be honest!

- ❏ Do I want as fabulous an outcome as possible? Is the cost of design *not* a huge priority?
- ❏ Can my ideas take a back seat so that my designer is uncuffed?
- ❏ Am I prepared to invest in design?
- ❏ Am I prepared to adjust my budget if I love the design ideas?

THE OUTFITTER

This seasoned guide has traveled to your destination numerous times, has pack mules loaded with gear and food, understands your objective and physical capacities, and leads you to the summit. This designer style is often the most seasoned and experienced and may be ideal for an experienced homeowner who has definite ideas but who also appreciates the value of design.

An outfitter architect is keenly interested in your discovery input, doesn't ignore the investment goal you've declared, and is genuinely interested in seeing the project through to the end. An outfitter may or may not be the most creative designer, but frankly, you may not need that. If you have definite ideas and are willing to listen and leverage experience, an outfitter can comfortably get you there. Deciding if an outfitter is a good fit boils down to the specific project and your experience.

Ask yourself the following questions—and be honest!

❏ Do I know if I need creative help?

❏ Who will be my advocate during the project—me, my designer, or my contractor?

❏ Is this the type of designer I can direct or are they stuck in their ways?

❏ Would I like my architect to be at my side through the construction stage?

KEY ASPECTS OF AN ARCHITECT

✓ Architects are the most qualified and most professional designers.

✓ Qualifying your candidates is paramount! You must check their credentials.

✓ Architects come in a variety of styles.

✓ Reconcile the scope of your project, experience, personality, and available time with your candidates.

Once we've covered design professionals and the design process, I'll present design agreements. In Part Four, we'll explore the various options you have when it comes to hiring your design team.

2.011 RESIDENTIAL DESIGNERS

Residential Designers are generally individuals who may or may not have formal training but possess the knowledge required to design and prepare a plan set for your project. It's also possible someone has a college degree in architecture but has yet to pass the state board exams and is therefore considered to be a designer rather than a full-fledged architect. Unlicensed designers practice under the mentorship of architects, and some may be current or past contractors or remodelers with a reasonable sense of design and structure knowledge. Interior designers armed with technical competence and some experience in structural aspects is another profile that falls under our "residential designer" classification. In Part Four, you'll learn how hiring a design team comprised of a contractor, residential designer, and structural engineer (known as a design-build business) can be a good path to take for the right project.

Typically, someone who occupies this niche in the design community possesses a moderate level of engineering knowledge, design knowledge (with limitations), and professionalism when it comes to drawings and details. Within this niche, you'll likely see companies called, for example, "ABC Design." Note that they don't utilize the words "architect" or "architecture" in their business name (or in the titles of their employees). Becoming a licensed architect entails a considerable commitment and is a significant accomplishment; you may discover more designers than architects as you search for your design team. Inevitably, you'll realize there's a price difference between the two, and rightfully so.

In many states, a designer needs no credentials to draw plans for a single-family home and assumes practically no liability. My experience is that there are very talented designers—it's not an option that should automatically be discarded. As a homeowner, understand the person's reputation and review their design work, 3D renderings, and plans. And never forget the adage "You get what you pay for."

Ask yourself the following questions—and be honest!

❏ Does my project involve major structural changes or is it more cosmetic?

❏ Is the designer I love backed up with structural design support such as an outside engineer or in-house construction personnel?

❏ Have I looked closely at past projects and plans my designer has done?

KEY ASPECTS OF A RESIDENTIAL DESIGNER

✓ Residential designers are *not* architects.

✓ It's prudent to compare architect vs. residential designer candidates.

✓ Residential designers can have a wide variety of backgrounds.

✓ Residential designers can be a good fit for the right project and homeowner.

2.012 INTERIOR DESIGNERS

In dealing with thousands of homeowners over the past thirty years, I've discovered certain prevalent misperceptions, namely that interior design is optional and/or reserved for more elite, larger projects.

Many homeowners think that interior design is an expensive luxury they can accomplish themselves. But ultimately, *someone* must design the kitchen and baths in detail and then select and specify the myriad materials, document them into the specifications, scope of work, and drawings, and then procure them on time.

A common misunderstanding is that an architect or residential designer will handle all aspects of design, including materials, finishes, and the drawings and details needed. However, focusing on interior details and materials is not necessarily a priority for architects! Instead, architects tend to focus on the big-picture aspects of new homes: the plan, the overall look, the flow of the spaces, and the technical components of the structures. While architects occasionally become involved in interiors and provide superb drawings and details, this level of involvement is the exception rather than the rule. In some cases, architects suggest clients do it themselves or hire an independent interior designer. In other words, you're left to fend for yourself.

One of the biggest mistakes you can make is assuming this responsibility by inserting yourself into the design process. Although a homeowner can indeed take on a project's required interior design demands provided they have an understanding of what an interior designer contributes to a project, it isn't easy to do so unless that particular homeowner is an experienced homeowner. Be cautious about taking on this responsibility! Because this is where projects often fall right onto their faces.

In the design world, the term "interior designer" is used widely across all disciplines in the field. A qualified interior designer in residential remodeling or new construction projects is a technically competent person who likely has a four-year degree and is certified through various professional associations. Having a degree in interior design with an emphasis on architectural interiors *and* being certified by NCIDQ is one differentiator.

The terms "interior designer" and "interior decorator" sometimes need clarification. When we talk about what interior designers do, we are not talking about fluffing pillows and picking draperies. That's what a decorator does. An interior decorator is more associated with selecting furnishings and finishes and is not so apt to provide the architect or builders with details about integrating and installing materials. On top of creative aspects like color and material selections, the ability to conceptualize and study creative design concepts for feasibility and then articulate them into a detailed drawing is where the value of a qualified interior designer can be immense. Both skill sets are needed, but often an interior designer can provide both, whereas a decorator cannot.

The interior design process can impact a project just as much as the architectural design does, directly influencing the placement of rooms, the costs of materials, and the accuracy of the plans. Detailed kitchen and bathroom designs and drawings, material selections, coordination, and technical knowledge of appliances and fixtures only scratch the surface of the value an interior designer can provide. Homeowners who invest in interior design quickly come to appreciate an excellent designer's creative contributions and the emotional relief that ensues as they visualize their new home interiors. All of this expertise ultimately influences the look, cost, and satisfaction with the end product.

When and if you involve an interior designer will depend on your project type and what services your architect provides. If you plan to build a new home or do a substantial remodel, having an interior designer involved early in the design process is prudent. Suppose you're planning an interior renovation that revolves around kitchens and baths. In that case, hiring only an interior designer may be possible provided they have the right qualifications for drawings and details. Search out "kitchen and bath designers" to see what options you have. An interior designer trained in the appropriate technical competencies can perfectly fit this type of project.

Ask yourself the following questions—and be honest!

❏ Do I know where to start?

❏ Is it overwhelming to even think about all of my options?

❏ Who will specify all of the materials that will go into my home before construction?

❏ Can I visualize all of the materials for my project?

❏ Who will provide the design drawings, documents, and details needed to ensure the materials are in line with my expectations?

❏ Who will source the materials, place the orders, and have the multifaceted knowledge needed to ensure a smooth-running project?

WHAT AN INTERIOR DESIGNER DOES

✓ Is a part of the design team who collaborates with the architect.

✓ Interprets your design preferences and translates the spaces, materials, colors, and fixtures presented in physical or digital material storyboards into real life.

✓ Holistically conceptualizes the spaces throughout the home by using design software to visualize proposed solutions, including specific materials and colors.

✓ Creates detailed and technical drawings to convey installation and material specifications to you, the design teams, suppliers, and installers. Areas such as kitchen, baths, millwork, and cabinetry are primary areas of focus.

- ✓ Provides detailed material and equipment specifications within a document format.
- ✓ Assists with electrical and lighting design coordinated with interior design specifications and architectural plans.
- ✓ Supervises and assists with acquiring interior materials and monitoring construction progress.

2.013 DESIGNER OBSTACLES

As you begin to think about design professionals and you eventually take action to hire your designer, you can unfortunately sabotage yourself without even knowing it, and in a variety of ways. For example, difficulties could stem from how the agreement with your designer came about and the need for more focus on your end. Here are more few examples of obstacles you can avoid by knowing that they're lurking around the bend.

CONSTRAINING YOUR DESIGNER

Your financial arrangement with your design team can handcuff them. If you negotiate a "deal" with your architect at a low rate, you may just be cutting your own throat. Keep in mind that designers can tailor their design service offerings to meet your budget much more easily than a builder can build the project. Less budget spent on design means fewer plan details, more headaches, more missed expectations, and more compromises on quality. And the worst part is that you didn't even know you were undermining your project—perhaps your architect failed to mention that.

Countless times, I have built projects based on inadequate architectural plans. As I dug in to learn why plans are sometimes so mediocre, I realized that one contributing factor is the "The client did not want to pay for those details." But guess what? You *will* still pay later because the lack of details means it probably wasn't included in the cost, it didn't work, and/or you don't like the result. Be careful when pushing for the best deal for a design! You'll eventually pay with money and—worse yet—stress.

WHAT TO ASK YOUR DESIGNERS

- ❑ Can you tell me what the most critical aspects of design are?

- ❑ Would it be possible to show me designs you're particularly proud of and the details that went into the design to make it happen?

- ❑ What were some of your biggest challenges with this project?

- ❑ Based on your proposal, is this what I should expect? (You should only ask this if the architect can walk you through the plans and details and you're impressed.)

- ❑ Do you see any particularly tough challenges on our project?

- ❑ Would it be possible to speak with the contractor and client of the project you just showed me?

The idea is to see if your candidates provide comprehensive designs, meaning the appropriate quality and details that are required for a wonderful experience. You may not know precisely what you're looking at, but don't be surprised if you can follow along well enough to at least understand your candidates' principles and passion. You can compensate for inexperience by speaking with the client and contractor of a previous project—they can tell you how the design was applied in an actual project.

Engaging in this "power qualifying" exercise allows you to accomplish a few things:

1. Demonstrate to your design candidates that you're interested in a quality design experience.

2. Obtain a built-in client reference, one that may not have made the architect's client list.

3. Have a potential contractor candidate to fill in the gaps later when you begin your search.

THE PERMIT PUSH

A classic and infamous anomaly is having a minimum approach to developing a design and plans with just one goal: obtaining a building permit as fast as possible. Known as "the permit push," the consequences of inadequate information will put everyone at a disadvantage. This inferior method happens way too often and (inevitably) leads to disastrous results. Homeowners push to get their projects started, and because designers would love to get the project off their plate, they jump on the bandwagon, too. Or worse, they push to do the bare minimum. What your city or county needs to issue a permit is a C-; what *you* need to build your project is at least a B+. Ideally, you need an A.

It's very tempting to fall prey to prematurely submitting plans to the Building department for approval because it can take months to get your permit to break ground. If you're building an entire custom home or are engaged in a substantial remodel and addition, many decisions need to be made. In a perfect world, they would be decided and then you'd immediately submit for a permit. The reality is that this scenario rarely happens. When a designer and homeowner push to crank out a set of plans, deferred decisions and details pile up and must be eventually addressed to ensure a smooth-running construction project. The more these details build up, the better the chance is that they'll never make it to the plans and specifications.

Two categories of deferred information in particular don't necessarily delay obtaining a permit but can contribute to inaccurate estimates, schedule delays, and missed design expectations. Here are just a few examples:

ARCHITECTURAL DESIGN DEFERRALS

✓ Specifying the construction materials throughout the plans. (See Specifications in Design Process on page 155.)

✓ Complete information that instructs contractors how to build unique details. (See Architectural Pages in Understanding Plans on page 213.)

✓ Incomplete scope of work document. (See Scope of Work on page 162.)

INTERIOR DESIGN DEFERRALS

✓ Floor plan and elevation drawings depicting accurate material selections. (See Interior Design Pages on page 237.)

✓ Material and equipment selections and specifications. (See Specifications on page 155.)

✓ Incomplete scope of work document. (See Scope of Work on page 162.)

Fortunately, there are ways to mitigate the damage caused by minimal plans. That will take an advocate, which could be you, your architect, or your agent. Whoever it is must push for information, manage deferrals, and then pull the trigger for submittal.

WHAT TO ASK YOUR DESIGNERS

❏ Once the plans are ready to be submitted to my county, will decisions still need to be made? If so, can you explain some examples of those?

❏ Is there a system in place to capture all the deferred decisions so we can tackle them during the permit processing?

❏ Will the plans be complete enough when interviewing contractors and obtaining estimates later in the design process?

The idea is to realize that deferred decisions, design, and details are essential. Asking your architect these questions suggests that you have a keen interest in minimizing setbacks that fall under the control of you and your architect. Engaging in this "empowerment" exercise allows you to accomplish a few things:

✓ Inform your architect that you're aware of this anomaly during the design phase.

✓ Know that decisions and details will inevitably follow after submitting a permit.

✓ Realize that roadblocks can be minimized if a process is in place to manage any missing information.

✓ Best of all, know that you can have another pair of eyes— your contractor candidates—to determine if the plans and specifications are adequate to estimate and build the project.

I sincerely hope that by the time you digest all of the information in this book, you'll have the power to uncover these details that will cost you and only you! For now, bank the term "permit push" and do not succumb to it.

ALLOCATING AND PRIORITIZING ENOUGH TIME TO PARTICIPATE IN DESIGN

There's no question that life today can get busy, with people having limited time left over just for day-to-day life. Add on a remodel or new home project, and now you have a second job! Committing enough time to plan a project is a big hurdle for many homeowners. Overwhelming thoughts can stifle the design process, like, "I need to learn everything someone else has spent a thirty-year career learning and is still learning." Even if you gain some knowledge, then what?

In my experience, homeowners who hire a professional design team and are the most engaged are the happiest in the end. I attribute this time commitment to a productive design process, minimized surprises, and meeting expectations. If you believe it's inevitable that you won't have time to hyper-focus on the project, there are ways to compensate for that. Those ways begin with whom you hire.

Depending on the project, the design process can be lengthy and overwhelming. A large part of the initial discovery stage of this guide has been to focus on you and your design team as much as possible so that ideas are best aligned with your desires. Engaging in this kind of foresight means you'll optimize the time you spend on design and will also ease your decision-making as you're pummeled with ideas, questions, and approvals. But still, even with getting a jump start via the discovery exercise, you'll need to allocate a sizable chunk of time to keep your eye on the ball.

SUGGESTIONS FOR MAXIMIZING EFFICIENCY AND EFFECTIVENESS DURING THE DESIGN PROCESS

✓ Inform your design team about the best method of communication—voice, email, or text? Be consistent so as not to get lost between methods.

✓ Preschedule a dedicated day and time of the week to meet with your design team.

✓ Discuss your attributes with your design team. For example, are you the type who wants to understand every window product on the face of the earth before making a decision, or are you the type to say "Send me three options with pros and cons"? After all, your design team should be a filter.

✓ Ask for an agenda for each upcoming week's meeting. For example, your design team could say "This week is about windows, exterior doors, and siding" or "Based on your inspirations, here are some suggestions" (with links to materials).

✓ Dedicate days and times of the week to complete your homework.

✓ Review the Options for Hiring Designers and Construction Professionals section on page 346.

THE IMPORTANCE OF DECISIVENESS

The ability to focus on details while thinking holistically about a project is a skill that design professionals and contractors have developed. Expecting you as the homeowner to instantly develop this skill is unreasonable, which is why good companies develop a structured set of systems and processes to get their arms around a project and help homeowners tackle decision-making. Ask your design candidates how they can help you make decisions and where you as a homeowner can contribute to making their job productive and fun.

Once again, the discovery stage plays a role. Spend plenty of your time managing your inspirations! Assemble images of the homes you're attracted to, research some of the products you gravitate to, and deliver all of that information to your team. Then please wash your hands of things and let them go to work to earn your trust. Remember, it takes time to earn trust, so give them some rope and let them climb a bit. But of course, if they slip and fall, please hold that rope tight.

The single most significant roadblock to homeowners making decisions is them having difficulty in visualizing ideas and concepts presented by the design team. If you're presented with two-dimensional floor plans, make sure they're accompanied by a lengthy description of what exactly they mean. Most people need help to visualize a built environment no matter how much explanation occurs. Intelligent designers know that to get your head bobbing up and down and have you declaring "YES, I LOVE IT!" cuts through all indecisiveness, thus fostering productive meetings. In comes the three-dimensional presentations! Visualizing your new home and that new kitchen—all with the actual materials that you like—fast-forwards the design process, thereby achieving our Guiding Principles.

WHAT TO ASK YOUR DESIGNERS IN ORDER TO HAVE A PRODUCTIVE DESIGN EXPERIENCE

- ❏ Is the information I provided early on enough to point you in the right direction?
- ❏ How will you help me/us make decisions?
- ❏ Will you be using three-dimensional renderings in your presentations?
- ❏ Will the renderings include both exterior and interior views?
- ❏ Will 3D views include materials shown in my inspirations and ideas as well as any suggestions you may have?
- ❏ How will the interior design materials be presented to me?

The idea is to become aware that there's a way to visualize your project and thus empower you to make decisions. The world of 3D design is practically the norm now! If your designer hesitates about providing 3D presentations, I consider that a big red flag—they may not be a good fit for you. Perhaps now you know that they're a Gatekeeper and it's time to move on.

2.020 CONSULTANTS

A second tier of design professionals could be required depending on the size, complexity, and scope of your project. Consultants are design professionals who supplement your architect's work. If you're doing a basic kitchen remodel, then few of these will apply, but if you're building a new home, then likely most of them will.

Your architect's job is to bring in the required consultants as part of the design team when the time is right. One of the most considerable challenges an architect has is coordinating the consultant's design, plan pages, and specifications within the complete set of architectural plans used for obtaining approvals and constructing the project. Each consultant's deliverables usually arrive in the form of plan pages and specifications stemming from your architect's plans. When the architect begins interfacing with a consultant, the first step is to export the architectural design work into a format the consultant can import into their software. This design collaboration is the initial step to coordinating the design team and carving off many conflicts that could otherwise occur during construction, such as coordinating the location of plumbing, electrical, or HVAC equipment to be sure that the proposed connections will in fact adequately serve the home and not conflict with one another.

Numerous examples of this critical coordination exist, but here are a couple of significant ones:

- **Placement of structures relative to the surveyor and civil engineer data.** The earlier an architect has this information, the better. Knowing where structures will be placed will depend on how complex your property is based on the size and slopes and city or county regulations. In new home construction on a sloping lot, for example, there could be subtle to drastic revisions to maximize views and mitigate unnecessary construction costs. Moving a structure horizontally or vertically just a few feet can save thousands of dollars in excavation and foundation costs. In the case of a small suburban lot, you may desire to maximize the allowable square footage and push the boundaries of the setbacks to your property line. All of this starts with a survey.

- **Merging the structural engineer design with the aesthetic elements of the architectural design.** Coordinating with the structural engineer can feel like a reality check and frankly sometimes a gut punch. If there's been early collaboration between your architect and structural engineer during the design process, fewer surprises will pop up; likewise, the more skilled and experienced your designer is, the fewer knockout rounds will occur. The structural design is considered by the architect but then is validated by the structural engineer within separate plan pages and specifications that are integrated into the main plan set. It's not uncommon for an architect to revise the design to comply with the structural design.

As we move into the section covering the design process, I'll present more detailed design considerations to ponder as plans are being developed by your architect. The Understanding Plans section will allow you to be certain that your desires will make it into your plans and specifications to ensure that the work will be completed to your satisfaction. In the meantime, let's take a closer look at what each consultant would contribute to a project.

2.021 SURVEYORS

A licensed land surveyor can legally document your parcel within the plan pages. Key components of a survey are establishing property lines and corners, lot slope (known as a topographic map), heights of city streets, curbs and sidewalks, existing structures, existing hard-scaping, fencing, existing trees, recorded easements, and location of utilities. A survey can be very valuable to a property owner, especially for new homes, more extensive renovations, and projects where the new home will be close to setbacks.

Don't be surprised if your fences differ from the actual property lines—that's a common and crucial factor when placing your home or addition. As you progress through construction, some cities require a setback certification letter from a surveyor when a project pushes the limits. If required, during the construction of the foundation, your surveyor will mark locations before concrete is poured and will provide a letter to submit to the city. A survey can protect you by providing data for a more effective design and covering your liability for meeting city, county, and neighborhood regulations.

If you have a larger project, your survey will be the first thing your architect will require. Today's standard practice is for the land surveyor to provide a software file that can be imported into the design software your architect utilizes. This property data assists in areas such as floor area calculations, establishing setbacks, determining heights of adjacent grades and curbs, and—best of all!—placing the new home on your site within a three-dimensional model.

2.022 CIVIL ENGINEERS

A civil engineer becomes involved in designing any portion of the project that's outside of the structures by first understanding the subject property via the survey and topographic map. The civil engineer will evaluate adjacent sites, the regional climate, the architectural design, the proposed placement of structures, and the landscape design. Civil engineers then prepare plans and specifications for grading and drainage, retaining walls, sewer and septic systems, roads and driveways, and underground utilities. Your Building department may refer to these plan pages as the "civil plan" or "grading and drainage."

Water intrusion is the top destructive element for a home. Solutions to this begin with the roof design, runoff capture, and proper disbursement. Water *will* find its way into a structure, and a civil engineer's job is to accommodate these dynamics specific to your site and building within the design work. If you're building a modest home on a flat site, the drainage demand may be minimal. However, if your project is a larger home on a hillside with a basement, addressing the grading and developing a comprehensive drainage system is important. Disbursing water runoff from the site and structure is usually a main driving force to design and ultimately the scope of work for your contractor. Many cities and counties require water runoff to be dispersed on-site. Historically, you could discharge runoff into the storm drain system or street; today, jurisdictions prefer to keep runoff on-site to recharge the groundwater system. This often involves creating deep holes called dissipation pits.

There are many more aspects of what civil engineers provide for projects, but for now, the idea is to make you aware of this potential design requirement so that you know more about what you didn't know. Asking your architect or city if a grading and drainage plan is required is an excellent step.

2.023 GEOTECHNICAL ENGINEERS

The soil and conditions beneath the surface of your parcel support your new home and drive the design of the foundation and subsequent structure. Retaining a geotech engineer (also called a soil engineer) is done almost exclusively for larger new construction projects. However, don't immediately rule one out if you're expanding significantly or your existing home is on a sloping lot.

Not long ago, jurisdictions didn't require soil reports for single-family home projects—instead, past data and geological maps were used to make assumptions and the architect designed projects to a prescribed minimum established by the local Building department. However, relatively recently, soil reports are now a requirement in some states. Frankly, they should be! If you're building a new home or doing a significant remodel/expansion, be prepared to retain a geotechnical firm. Let's talk about how it works.

After you've completed the survey and done conceptual designs by placing the new home on the site *but* before any final decisions are made, a geotechnical firm will visit the site with your preliminary plans in hand. The engineering crew will obtain samples of the soil in various areas around the site near where your new home is proposed. These samples are obtained via drilling or digging test pits. As the crew digs, samples are retrieved at various depth intervals, recorded, and returned to the lab for testing. The tests determine the soil type, moisture content, and how much strength there is to support the structure. Because it's common for geology to change as you go deeper, the objective is to locate a soil layer that will provide adequate support.

The findings of a soil investigation will be captured within a soil report supplied by the engineering firm. A soils report will identify the soil types at depth intervals and a recommended depth for excavating for the foundation, the type and size of the foundation, specifications for concrete to be used, and various other considerations such as drainage. Your architect and structural engineer will use this data to design the home to meet the requirements. Geotech firms use many CYA clauses within the report to observe the soil as the foundation is constructed. This critical observation by your geotech engineer will be discussed later in our Building Workbook.

2.024 STRUCTURAL ENGINEERS

Think of the structure of your home as a skeleton supported by the earth you're walking on. The rest of your home's anatomy is comprised of the systems and materials that make it beautiful and sustainable.

Engineering the structure of your new home or remodel is typically completed by a licensed professional engineer. In single-family homes, a civil engineer seems to be more commonly used, but the term "structural engineer" is widely used, so we'll stick with that. On rare occasions, your architect can also function as your structural engineer, but this is fading away as building codes place more demands on structural design.

Your architect or residential designer will focus on your home's overall design and aesthetic—their structural design knowledge base will influence and direct the design. When the time dictates, the architect will engage with the structural engineer and hand off the plans for them to do their work. Ideally, the SE and architect will have worked together before and will work with the same or comparable software platform.

Your structural engineer becomes an essential part of your design team, interacting with the architect and geotechnical engineer. Think of a structural engineer as the person specifying the bones and writing the instruction manual to assemble the skeleton of your home.

The SE imports your architect's plans into their system, analyzes the design, begins the design of your skeleton, and outputs a complete set of plan pages and supplemental calculation documents. These skeleton plans will include the designs of the foundation, floor, wall, and roof systems and all of the components that go into each, down to the size of each stud and beam to the size of the nails. Although these plans are not as sexy as your architect's pretty pictures, they are *crucial* to those whom you hire to build the project. Your contractor will depend heavily on structural plans to provide accurate estimates, order materials, and construct the project.

In the upcoming Understanding Plans section, I'll introduce the contribution that a structural engineer makes to your plan set in the form of plan pages. At our TAH online home, I present a structural engineering primer and samples of actual plan pages.

2.025 MEP: MECHANICAL, ELECTRICAL, AND PLUMBING ENGINEERS

Think of MEP as the circulatory and respiratory system of your home. Mechanical, electrical, and plumbing engineering consultants are brought in for very sophisticated projects and are often referred to as MEP engineers. Their documentation is called the MEP plan.

- The M in **MEP** = mechanical, which = HVAC: heating, ventilation, and air-conditioning.

- The E in **MEP** = electrical: power and lighting systems.

- The P in **MEP** = plumbing: water, waste, and gas systems.

MEP subcontractors can be one of the most expensive and neglected subcontractors on the plan set, which leads to inaccurate and incomplete installations. Simply not taking the time to create a plan tailored to your needs can sabotage your project by forcing you to compromise on your expectations. Here are some of the instigators of that undesired scenario:

- The permit push leads the pack of Mistakes to Avoid when you may be anxious to start your project. Both designers and homeowners easily fall prey to this chronic problem in planning where the designer quickly creates a cursory plan that's sufficient for the building permit process but doesn't meet your needs. It's then expected that those areas will be addressed later...but they never are addressed to the point that will be needed.

- The lack of your designer's credentials and professionalism can result in incompetency or a lack of interest.

MEP engineers and designers can come from one firm or be individual consultants within each discipline. Coordinating all of the consultants is a big challenge, because the fewer individuals your architect must engage with, the better.

Some perceived benefits to hiring dedicated MEP engineers are that they'll be current with standards, codes, and equipment technologies specific to your project type. However, many MEP firms design large commercial and institutional projects and fill in with single-family residential projects as a secondary channel of business, so you'll need to interview each consultant by reviewing their past projects to be sure they're in tune with residential custom home construction and up to speed on the latest equipment technology.

Determining if your project warrants such consultants will be driven by the size and type of project coupled with your personal desires. Not surprisingly, this can quickly become complicated. Addressing whether or not you need consultants early on in the design process is highly recommended regardless of who you ultimately wind up going with.

MECHANICAL ASPECTS

HVAC work in a home has become increasingly complicated, driven by sophisticated equipment and building codes. The need to integrate HVAC equipment and ducting into the overall design process seems obvious but is often overlooked or at best a cursory approach is taken. Either one results in compromises and negative consequences. Being aware of basic HVAC components and how they're represented in your plans is all you need to empower yourself to set expectations for your designer, builder, and HVAC contractor.

There's a not-great alternative to hiring dedicated MEP engineers when designing an HVAC system: doing a "design-build." That means the HVAC contractor also designs the system, which could occur during the planning process but often gets deferred to the day they show up on the site to install your new system. Deferring the HVAC system design will undoubtedly lead to a host of problems.

In reviewing plans and talking with colleagues, I am constantly amazed by the challenges posed by inadequate HVAC design. If you were to poll a hundred contractors and list their top ten problems, I guarantee that HVAC design would be near the top. Having your architect coordinate with a very qualified HVAC contractor during the development of your plan would be the bare minimum you'd want to do to ensure success. If your project is large and complex and you have particular needs or interests in your home's indoor environment, it's prudent to also bring in a mechanical engineer consultant.

ELECTRICAL ASPECTS

Power and lighting represent the E in MEP. These may be shown on separate sheets depending on the size and complexity of the project. The electrical and lighting scope of work and material specifications are identified within dedicated floor plan pages and are tied to a legend that defines what each one represents.

Preparing thoughtful electrical and lighting plans is necessary for you, your local building department, and your electrician. To the extent that this occurs, it leads to our core objective of setting expectations, which in turn will result in accurate costs and installations. Often, a designer will prepare a "standard" plan and may not even ask for your participation. But seeing as no one else knows better than you how your home will be used, taking charge of this step is prudent so that when you reach for that outlet to plug in your phone, it's there.

One crucial analysis that must be attained is understanding the existing electrical service size for the property and what your new design demands. An electrical engineer can perform a load calculation based on the proposed equipment and other parameters to determine the size of electrical service you'll need. For example, in the case of a remodeling project, it's possible that you might only currently have a 100-amp main panel and the new design will require 200-amp service. The solution is not simply to replace the panel but quite possibly upgrade the power lines and transformer from your power company. This will lead to significant costs. The load calc analysis adds a missing piece of the puzzle when you're evaluating your desires vs. your electrical service—only then can you make informed decisions.

Having your architect coordinate with a qualified electrical contractor during the development of your plan would be doing the bare minimum. Adding a lighting designer to the mix could certainly maximize the quality of your spaces, and if your project is large and complex and you have particular needs or interests in the electrical system and indoor environment, then bringing in a consultant is a prudent step.

PLUMBING ASPECTS

While it's certainly not as inspirational as the comfort of your HVAC system or the ambient light throughout your home, your plumbing system still matters. The plumbing design will include the locations of the water supply lines to all of your fixtures, the waste systems that lead from your sinks, toilets, and other drains, and any natural or propane gas lines that go to your appliances.

Once the locations and fixture types are selected, a plumbing engineer or contractor will specify the diameter and materials. For most projects, it's more common for a plumbing contractor to perform the calculations and diagrams as part of their estimating process and for permitting. For larger and more complex projects, a plumbing engineer can become involved in specifying the proper equipment to serve the home. Examples of homes that may warrant an engineer are multistory homes or multiple buildings dispersed throughout a large site (i.e., over 4,000 square feet). Homes of this nature often include multiple water-heating systems beyond conventional tank units and hydronic heating, and all of these require detailed analyses and equipment specifications.

With the proposed architectural design in hand combined with the specifications for fixtures and equipment, a vital analysis must be performed to determine if the water supply line currently serving the property is adequate. A plumbing engineer or qualified plumbing contractor will consider the demands of all of the equipment that requires water and will then determine the necessary diameter of the water line. Considering that some projects require fire sprinklers to be installed, the existing water line may not be adequate. This is a common oversight.

Like HVAC design, the locations of waste lines within a structure can play an important role and also pose a significant challenge. The best way to avoid undesirable results is for the architect and structural engineer to coordinate to identify possible conflicts. Being able to hear the toilet flush and drain down the wall behind your bedroom suite, for example, wouldn't be great. Structural engineering is one of the main culprits behind pipes being routed to undesired locations. The structural design will specify beams, floor joists, and other members that your contractors cannot modify to accommodate pipes. The consequences can be built-out walls, dropped ceilings, and exposed pipes in the basement.

The goal is to know that potential conflicts, inferior equipment, and undesirable results can occur. The solution is for your architect to collaborate with a MEP firm by coordinating their design with the MEP firm's design. This collaboration occurs via exported and imported shared files that can be overlaid, thus exposing any conflicts. The process doesn't have to be complicated—in fact, it can be facilitated through separate engineers if someone who's qualified has their eyes on the bouncing balls.

The MEP world is filled with hundreds of possibilities, choices, and opportunities that you can utilize to create a superb home. In our Planning Workbook, I've developed a checklist to assist you in identifying possible conflicts and things to consider while you're designing your home.

2.026 LOW-VOLTAGE CONSULTANTS

The low-voltage (LV) trade is rapidly growing and encompasses many solutions, services, and products. Differentiating between an LV consultant and an LV contractor can be complex, as many who specialize in this industry cross over into the world of subcontractors who are interested in performing the actual service instead of only providing consultation during the design steps of a project. Deciding when to bring in an LV contractor will be determined by your interest levels in the solutions outlined below:

✓ Telecommunications

- Telephones
- Data network: wiring for computer networks such as Cat6 cabling and related equipment
- Cable and satellite

✓ AV systems

- Audiovisual systems

- Entertainment system design and equipment
- Distributed audio

✓ Security

- Alarm
- Video monitoring, cameras
- Gates
- Intercoms
- Window and door automation

✓ Home automation

- Lighting and power control: smart switches and receptacles
- Window blinds
- HVAC system control
- Smart appliances
- Voice control

✓ Monitoring and management systems

- Utilities: smart meters and equipment for power, water, and gas
- Solar
- Indoor air quality
- Irrigation: sensors, landscape, and agricultural

As you can see, many solutions fall under the low-voltage category.

The more boxes you check, the more likely you are to need to consult with a specialist during the design process.

To achieve having an overall comprehensive design by your architect and garnering accurate costs during the estimating process, bringing in an LV contractor as the design develops can ensure the best possible installations.

Because the low-voltage trade overlaps with the electrical trade, in some cases, your electrician could also be your LV contractor. But be careful! There's a vast difference between somebody who can pull network wiring around your house and somebody who's deeply entrenched in the rapidly evolving world of home automation. In my experience, it's rare to find an electrician who also specializes in the LV world, but I have, and when I have, it's been the best of both worlds.

2.027 FIRE PROTECTION CONTRACTORS

Having to install a fire sprinkler system can come as a shocking surprise to homeowners. This requirement for new construction is relatively new to the building code. It may also be required if your home expansion is on a larger scale. (Learn more about how projects are classified in the Project Classification section on page 203.)

Engaging with a fire protection contractor is the first step. Although some plumbing engineers are also certified to design fire sprinkler systems, the contractor usually provides the design and installation for these systems.

Once again, timing is crucial, because fire protection contractors will plan to poke many holes in your ceilings, potentially interfering with lighting, ceiling details, and beams. The time that the MEP plan is being developed is an ideal time to engage with a fire contractor. Once you have the MEP plan, electrical lighting, and reflected ceiling plan (coming up in the Floor Plans section on page 213), the next step is to provide the plan for the fire sprinkler design. This enables the contractor to place heads without conflicting with other elements.

Sprinkler design has its own set of restrictions for the spacing of heads; it also comes with other constraints that will affect your design. For example, if you have tall decorative beams in recessed ceiling details, large skylight wells over an island with pendant light fixtures, or other ceiling elements that could conflict with a design, now would be the time to get feedback and make adjustments with a click of a mouse. Otherwise, those changes will be made with a chainsaw during construction.

The sprinkler system's design and other water demands within the house will dictate the size of the main water line from your service provider. This frequent surprise requirement pops up when the sprinkler design isn't addressed early enough, leading to delays and unexpected costs. Significant remodel projects are the most vulnerable to this surprise since a water meter already exists. It's easy to overlook this requirement! If your plumber or plumbing engineer determines that the existing water meter is inadequate, then expect to pay to upsize your service from the water company and replace the water line from the meter to your home. For new construction, if you determined the size of your main water line *before* you broke ground, then you're in a much better position since the water line from the meter has not yet been installed. In the case of a subdivision of new lots, it's still possible that the water meter placed by the developer won't be adequate, so check on that early. Now you know what you may not have known!

One last element of a fire sprinkler system that affects your design is the equipment's location. All of the fire sprinkler piping distributed throughout the home ends up at what's called a "fire sprinkler riser." The riser is a combination of valves and monitoring devices and is often located at a point nearest to where the water service enters the home. This piping and equipment require space and clearances around other equipment and therefore should be studied and included within the MEP plans.

❏ Will my project require a fire sprinkler system?

❏ When should we engage with a fire sprinkler contractor?

❏ What is your process to coordinate all of the trades that will need to be involved?

❏ Where would the equipment be located?

❏ Do you think we'll have to upgrade our water line? And who determines that?

❏ How will the sprinkler heads look?

2.028 ENERGY EFFICIENCY EXPERTS

Building energy efficiency standards have been established by your state and the federal government and apply to both new construction and existing buildings. The policies are designed to reduce energy consumption and protect the health of the building and its occupants. Addressed within the design process by your architect, the first criterion that drives energy-efficient design is the climate zone in which your project is located (zones are defined by the US Department of Energy). The zone will influence how your architect designs your home and what compliance solutions your energy consultant will propose. Below, you can see eight main zones and subzones with their characteristics.

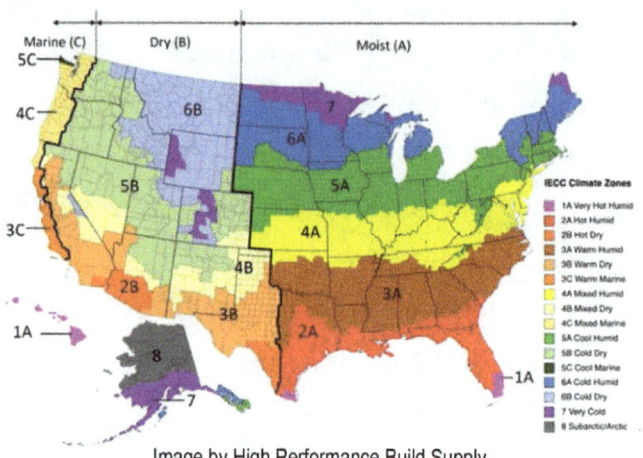

Image by High Performance Build Supply

Visit theawakenedhomeowner.com to see samples.

CONSTRUCTION COMPONENTS AFFECTED BY ENERGY EFFICIENCY STANDARDS

THE BUILDING ENVELOPE

Think of the building envelope as what separates the outdoor elements from the indoor elements. Within your envelope is your basement, floor, walls, and roof. Each construction element has many components that make up an assembly, a term you may hear as your architect explains the evolving design. For example, a wall assembly includes the following elements starting from the outside in:

1. Siding or cladding: This material could be wood, stucco, brick, composite, metal, stone, or a combination of those.

2. Exterior insulation: Yes, insulation on the outside! This offers a way to conform to requirements, especially in more extreme climates.

3. A WRB or weather-resistant barrier: A moisture protection layer that allows a wall to "breathe."

4. Exterior sheathing: The plywood or composite on the outside of the walls.

5. Studs: The vertical members making up the wall.

6. Cavity insulation: Insulation between the studs.

7. Vapor barrier: Needed in some climates.

8. Interior wall finish: Drywall.

As you can see, we have eight materials that make up a wall. If you want to dive deeper into this topic, search for wall assemblies within your climate zone and have fun! The point here is that energy efficiency begins with your structure being designed to achieve an acceptable level of insulation and moisture management.

Now let's look at key construction materials that affect compliance beyond building assemblies.

WINDOWS, EXTERIOR DOORS, AND SKYLIGHTS

- Anything with glass that transfers heat and cold affects energy efficiency. These products have performance ratings used by energy consultants in their calculations.

- Roofing material matters because its reflectivity mitigates heat transfer.

- When it comes to insulation, there's now a wide range of insulating materials and methods.

Your energy consultant will analyze these components and factor in their individual performance ratings. As an example, windows have different thermal ratings, and the more glass you have in your home, the more heat loss and gain you'll have. Roofing materials have different reflective ratings and insulation types, and installation methods vary on how they perform depending on the climate your home is in.

SYSTEMS

The systems of your home exist to provide comfort, safety, and a healthy environment. How your systems are designed takes many factors into account, such as your climate, size, home orientation, the design of the building envelope, and the occupant load.

- HVAC (or heating, ventilation, and air-conditioning) provides comfort and a healthy indoor environment. The energy code will mandate the performance specs of the system and will introduce a newer requirement of constant ventilation.

- Electrical and lighting play a role within the energy code and will affect the lighting design and type of fixtures for both the interior and exterior. In some states, a photovoltaic or solar power system is mandatory in new construction and natural gas is no longer allowed.

- Plumbing requirements apply to water heater performance and low-flow plumbing fixtures.

Before submitting your plans to the Building department for a permit, a certified individual must provide an energy report. This report mandates the specifications for the building components and systems.

The timing of when you engage with your energy professional is crucial and often overlooked until the design is far along. The degree to which this person needs to be involved is project-specific and also depends on the level of expertise your designer or architect has. Say you're building a second new home in a cold climate and you hire a local designer from your primary home location who's unfamiliar with the demands of a cold climate. In that scenario, design time and details could be wasted. High-performance insulation could require thicker walls and roof cavities, for example, and the amount of glass demanded by high-performance windows and HVAC systems comes with their own restrictions and performance requirements.

Architects commonly facilitate the energy report process, but understanding when this occurs and how it will affect the design and cost of your project is what you care about. So remember, if you're building a new home or expanding an existing home, an energy report *will* be required. Being involved with this stage of the process can reduce surprises.

2.029 SOLAR CONTRACTORS

A photovoltaic (PV) system will generate electricity from the sun, which couldn't be a better way to power your home. National and local energy codes may mandate installing a system if you're building a new home. Regardless of whether or not it's required, installing a PV system is a prudent consideration and may influence the design of the systems in your home. PV systems have multiple benefits, including reduced or eliminated power bills and backup battery systems that provide power during outages. PV systems can also be used during peak hours when electricity costs the most. If you own an electric vehicle, you could power your car with the sun by installing charging stations inside your garage.

What's interesting about solar power is that it can affect the architectural design of your home. In the early steps of design, the best-performing system will drive the design of the roof—the orientation of solar panels to maximize sun exposure is essential, and clearly, you'll benefit the most from a carefully thought-out design. In reality, installing effective PV systems boils down to compromising on aesthetics vs. performance. Unfortunately, however, solar designs often get deferred too far down the road and the solar contractor is handed a set of completed plans with little space to install adequate panels that face the right direction.

If your city or county requires a solar power system for your project, then expect to include one in your building permit application.

This submission will consist of a solar panel design and equipment specifications. Engaging with a solar contractor early on in the design process is beneficial, as they will be the person who provides the design that's suitable for the application process. In some cases, an electrical contractor will also perform the solar work. The latter is my preference seeing as the two disciplines are integrated and affect one another from a design and installation standpoint.

2.030 ARBORISTS

Trees can play a factor in your design and in some cases will dramatically influence what's possible on your lot. Hiring an arborist is almost always reserved for new construction and large renovation projects and is dictated by your city or county—if your project requires the removal of a tree, for example, hiring an arborist will likely be required by the city. The arborist's role will be documenting all of the on-site trees. To do this, arborists often use the site plan generated by the architect in conjunction with survey drawings. (There's another added value to obtaining a survey!)

The arborist will record the tree species, diameter, height, health, and if they are protected within the report and the plan pages that will be inserted into the architect's plan set. Recommendations will be made on protection, removal, and replacement based on the project's impact.

Many cities will require a tree protection plan. This identifies protected trees and specific methods for ensuring that damage does not occur to said trees. The tree protection plan could include fencing, trunk protection, signage, and water commitments. If your project involves removing significant trees, be prepared to plant additional trees to compensate for the ones that will be removed. If that's not possible, you may need to contribute to a fund as mandated by your city.

2.031 LANDSCAPE DESIGNERS

Involving a landscape designer in the project as early as possible can accomplish a cohesive design by merging the architectural design with the natural surroundings. Much like an architect, a landscape designer listens to the client, studies their inspirations and ideas, and then conceptualizes plans and presentations. Sometimes the ideas are so profound that they require the buildings to be moved within the site or set at specific heights; sometimes windows and doors must even be added, expanded, or eliminated.

Some jurisdictions require a landscape design before a permit is issued as part of the submittal to the Planning and Building departments *(see the Approvals and Permits section on page 242)*. The primary reasons for this requirement are to protect the quality of your neighborhood and to align with water conservation provisions. If your property is located within a homeowner's association, expect to provide a landscape plan during this approval process, which occurs before the building permit process.

Whether or not—and when—you'll want to engage with a landscape designer will depend on your project's size, priorities, local HOA and Building department regulations, and how many cooks you want in the kitchen during the design process.

UNDERSTANDING DESIGN PROFESSIONALS REVIEW _____

As you can see, numerous fields of design may apply to your project, from architecture to interior design. Now that you know about the characteristics of architects and designers, you'll be empowered to streamline the selection of your designer by marrying your project type to the right designer. Regardless of the designer you choose, they should be your first advocate in helping you navigate the design process as you obtain approvals, and they should keep an eye on the ball during construction.

2.100 THE DESIGN PROCESS

The process of designing your new home will be led by your designers and consultants and guided by the information you gathered during your discovery phase. This section dives deep into each methodical design step and introduces your design team's deliverables, plans, and specifications. Your plans will transform your ideas into a tangible and powerful communication tool that you can use to obtain dependable costs, apply for approvals and permits, perform the construction, and hold all those involved accountable.

Because plans deserve ample space of their own, I've dedicated a section to understanding plans later in the book. Once you have the concepts of the design process down and you understand how to execute agreements with your designers and what kinds of design limitations are out there, you can wade into the Understanding Plans section on page 208 as deeply as you want.

WHAT WE'LL COVER _____

- ✓ Design Planning
- ✓ Steppingstones of Design
- ✓ Pause points between steps.
- ✓ Monitoring the pulse of the budget
- ✓ The results of the process

2.101 DESIGN PLANNING

It's important to have a lead design professional such as an architect or a residential designer guide you through the design process and develop a plan. To make the process smoother, it's best to organize the upcoming steps into a structured schedule at the beginning of the process. That will help set expectations for you and your designers.

Creating a design schedule can be an intelligent way to understand what tasks need to be completed and when. However, it's crucial to determine who will create and manage the design schedule if there is one. When interviewing potential design candidates, be sure to ask them questions about how they manage their design projects! To help you wrap your head around design schedules, we're about to explore some snippets of two different schedules. The first one is a preliminary schedule that outlines an approval process for a new home in a planned development with an HOA, and the second one is a full design schedule outlining all of the upcoming design steps.

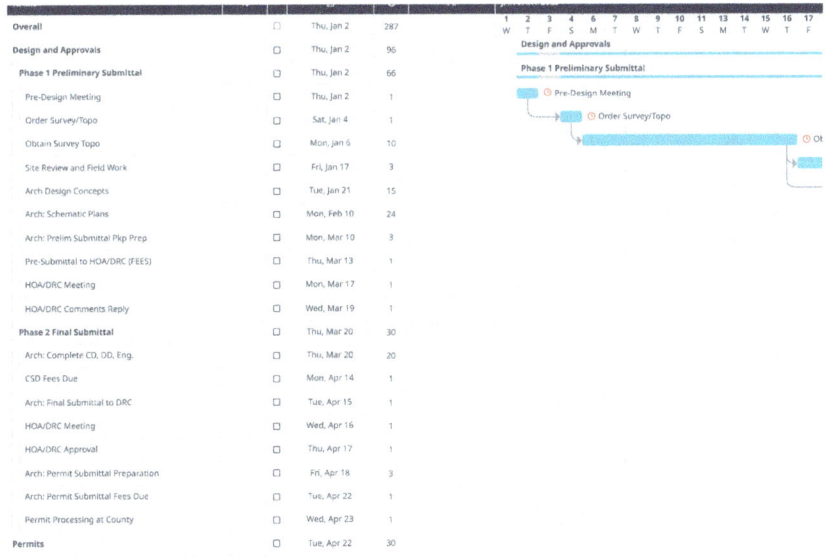

Visit theawakenedhomeowner.com to see samples.

Sample Job 2 Custom Home Schedule

NAME	%	✓	📅	🕐	👥	JUNE 2025
						2 3 4 5 6 7 9 10 11 12
						M T W T F S M T W T
Overall		☐	Mon, Jun 2	128		
Design Process - Custom Home		☐	Mon, Jun 2	1		Design Process - Custom Home
Design Agreement Approved		☐	Mon, Jun 2	1		Design Agreement Approved
Step One - Schematic Design		☐	Tue, Jun 3	30		Step One - Schematic Design
Discovery Package Received and Reviewed		☐	Tue, Jun 3	1		Discovery Package Received and Reviewed
QA#1: Design Parameters		☐	Wed, Jun 4	1		QA#1: Design Parameters
Site Visit and Measure (as applies)		☐	Thu, Jun 5	3		Site Visit and Measu
QA #2 Site Verifications		☐	Sat, Jun 7	1		QA #2 Site Verifications
QA#2: Site Measure Ck List		☐	Sat, Jun 7	1		QA#2: Site Measure
Generate As-Built Dwgs (as applies)		☐	Mon, Jun 9	3		Ge
Create SD Concepts		☐	Thu, Jun 12	7		
SD Meetings		☐	Fri, Jun 20	5		
Budget Check Point #1		☐	Thu, Jun 26	1		
SD Revisions		☐	Thu, Jun 26	5		
SD Finalization		☐	Wed, Jul 2	5		
Step Two - Design Development		☐	Tue, Jul 8	62		
Client Authorize DD		☐	Tue, Jul 8	1		
Prepare Planning Dept Approval (as needed)		☐	Wed, Jul 9	10		
Planning Approval - (as applies)		☐	Mon, Jul 21	10		
Site/Structure verifications, HazMat, etc.		☐	Wed, Jul 9	5		
Consultants		☐	Fri, Aug 1	30		
Structural Engineer and others		☐	Fri, Aug 1	30		
Architectural Design - Sheets		☐	Sat, Aug 2	30		
AD: Plan Pages/Coordination		☐	Sat, Aug 2	30		
Specifications: Scope of Work		☐	Sat, Aug 2	40		
Tier 1: Cabinetry, Floor, Slab, F/P, Sky, Wdws, Ext Drs		☐	Sat, Aug 2	10		
Tier 2: Tile, Int Doors/Mill, Elect, Plumb, LV, Mech		☐	Thu, Aug 14	10		
Tier 3: Side/Trim, Stucco/Msnry, Roof, Concrete		☐	Tue, Aug 26	10		
Tier 4: Glass, HDW, Paint, Drywall,, Insulation		☐	Sat, Sep 6	10		
Budget Check Point #2		☐	Thu, Aug 28	10		
Interior Design - Sheets		☐				
ID: Plan Pages, Specs, Boards		☐	Sat, Aug 2	40		
QA #3 Plan Review		☐	Thu, Sep 18	1		
QA #3 Review Check List		☐	Thu, Sep 18	1		
Publish Bid Set		☐	Sat, Sep 20	1		
Estimating and Contracts		☐	Mon, Sep 22	22		
Contractor Quest - Last Time		☐	Mon, Sep 22	5		
Request for Proposals		☐	Sat, Sep 27	1		
Site Evaluation (contractors)		☐	Mon, Sep 29	5		
Cost Evaluations		☐	Sat, Oct 4	5		
Design Revisions /Final Selections		☐	Fri, Oct 10	5		
Contract Approvals		☐	Thu, Oct 16	1		
Step Three - Construction Documents		☐	Fri, Oct 17	10		
AD: Complete Plans For Submittal		☐	Fri, Oct 17	10		

Visit theawakenedhomeowner.com to see samples.

2.102 THE STEPPING STONES OF DESIGN

Think of the design process as being stepping stones that lead towards your destination. Each stone is spaced precisely according to your stride and just far enough apart that if you try to skip one, you'll fall into the stream. Don't fall!

The design team takes three steps, each one more detailed and technical than the last, until a final work product called a plan set is delivered, coupled with specifications. Understanding the three steps and asking your design candidates to share their process will help you decide if they're a good fit for you.

While each step should have a goal and a value, the spaces between the stepping stones represent natural pause points and considerations that you should ponder before moving forward. Upon completing each step, you must feel comfortable with the outcomes before you move forward and build upon the design. Therefore, take your time, ask questions, and enjoy the design process.

But before we take our first design step, I want to emphasize one especially important aspect of design: visualizing your new home within the design work. This can be challenging for most homeowners. Luckily, nowadays, architectural software provides powerful tools to help homeowners understand the design by viewing three-dimensional color renderings of their project. (A caveat: it takes a significant commitment of time and money to perfect the use of 3D modeling features, so don't assume that your architect or designer will always present these to you.) When homeowners can visualize their homes earlier on in the process, that leads to more decisiveness, resulting in a more productive and satisfying experience for both the design team and the client. Ask your architect how they present their design work and view some samples of it. These questions are an excellent way to qualify potential design candidates and set expectations.

2.110 STEP ONE: CONCEPTUALIZING YOUR DESIGN

This is where your discovery activity goes to work by manifesting your discoveries through design. Your architect will absorb all of your input, analyze your property, and develop concepts and solutions that will achieve your dreams. This phase—commonly referred to as *schematic design*—is very flexible and allows for an abundance of creativity. Your design team will hopefully use software to present a variety of design ideas, from floor plans to 3D models, and you'll have the opportunity to review these, provide feedback, and make changes until you're satisfied with the concepts. This creative and flexible process is a fantastic opportunity to discover innovative ideas and explore possibilities that you may not have considered before!

Example of an exterior 3d rendering of a
new home our team developed.

Visit theawakenedhomeowner.com to see samples.

2.111 THE OBJECTIVES OF SCHEMATIC DESIGN

- See your visions and ideas come to life in design work.

- Explore design options and study construction and cost feasibility.

- Narrow down your design options into one direction.

- Build a solid design foundation to build upon in the next step.

2.112 WHAT TO EXPECT: REMODEL SCHEMATIC DESIGN PRESENTATION

Your first schematic design meeting can be compared to a big reveal party, where designers can be just as excited as homeowners are to share their ideas. Bear in mind that first presentations can vary widely—creating new homes and remodels is a very customized and personalized process. Let's look at two scenarios of first presentations. Let's say that within your discovery package, your criteria were to create a new kitchen and great room in your 1970s suburban track house on a quarter-acre lot. You're unsure if you want to expand your home, but you'd certainly like a more open floor plan and you'd like to understand your options and their costs. In order to explore these options, your designer will:

- Review your discovery package in detail, visiting your inspirations links and files, coordinating meetings, and asking many questions to gain focus.

- Discuss the budget criteria as they pertain to your ideas, then provide feedback and direction to determine which options to pursue, further gaining focus.

- Measure your existing home, document your home systems, and note any circumstances that could influence designs. This includes peeking into the attic and crawl space to understand the home's structure in order to be able to provide reasonably feasible solutions.

- Research your local Planning department and homeowner's association (if there is one) and their respective rules for your possible expansion option.

- Go away for a few weeks to prepare concepts for your first design presentation.

- Conduct the first schematic design meeting using 3D design software. This is when you sit back and let your designer dazzle you by showing you various documents:

  - An "as-built" floor plan, which is your home today before any modifications have taken place.

  - Various floor plans that articulate options for expansions within existing walls. Plans could be in the form of Plan A, Plan B, Plan C, etc.

  - Overlapping floor plans—i.e., the new ones over the existing one. This allows you to gain a better understanding of the impact of the ideas.

  - 3D renderings of each plan from exterior and interior perspectives that include the style and materials represented in your inspirations. This is super helpful when it comes to making decisions!

- Present a monologue explaining their concepts, their impacts, how they achieved your joint goals, and finally, ideas you've never thought of.

- Have a discussion with you about the pros and cons of each option, what you like and dislike, and possible directions to take with the design.

- Establish a budget touch point to keep your investment goal at the forefront.

A DESIGNER CHECKLIST

✓ Did my designer listen to me carefully and check off the boxes on my discovery criteria list?

✓ Did my designer research with my city and HOA and explain any limitations for the expansion concepts?

✓ Did my designer explain the floor plans and how they may impact my existing home?

✓ Did my designer provide 3D renderings to help me make decisions?

✓ Did my designer provide feedback on costs or a path to understand the preliminary costs of each design?

✓ Have I requested to engage with my design team's structural engineer or contractor to get a different perspective on how the structural concerns will impact my project?

✓ More about this in the Planning Workbook.

The first schematic design presentation for a remodeling project can result in various outcomes due to its highly customized and personalized nature. Ideas may surface that you'd never thought of before, or maybe you like certain features of each of the designs. A positive outcome from the first design meeting can provide you with plenty of information to give quality feedback to your design team! A good designer appreciates input; a great one puts their ego away and listens. In most cases, the first design round involves several iterations as various plans are merged into a more refined single plan.

When merging your budget with your remodeling ideas, discussions may arise about how to balance the two. Early thoughts about phasing portions of the project or identifying other options may help you understand the value of each option, thus enabling you to manage the budget. For instance, if you've been dreaming about having a big open kitchen, a great room floor plan, an additional bedroom, and an indoor laundry room for your growing family, an early budgeting exercise can help you find a way to make your dreams a reality. Still, though, a budget may not provide clear directions to your design team. In that case, breaking the project into two phases can help you understand the costs of each one. Identifying this possibility within a master plan can result in an efficient design and estimating process that will empower you to make informed decisions.

2.113 THE VALUE OF A MASTER PLAN

Over the many years of working with homeowners, I've heard similar stories of the untold hours they spent dreaming about their new homes, running in endless circles throughout the house with ideas, swiping the tablet late into the night...and ending up right back at square one with no results. A shortage of ideas isn't usually the problem. The problem is having too many spinning wheels, and the solution to *that* is being able to see and analyze ideas in order to calm said wheels.

It's not uncommon for homeowners to have big ideas with a budget that's not so big; often, homeowners need more information to be able to decide if the value of their ideas makes adjusting their budget worth it. By exploring a master plan with your architect, you can relieve this kind of stress! And then you'll have a tool to analyze the viability of all your ideas.

FEATURES AND BENEFITS OF A COHESIVE MASTER PLAN

- Having the ability to understand how various ideas relate to each other. In other words, can you add the primary suite without tearing out the other bathroom?

- Gaining an understanding of what project portions can be broken out into phases. For example, if you want a second-story addition, the impact on the first story may trigger additional work. Therefore, you must do the kitchen simultaneously.

- Identifying which whole-house systems will be impacted by phasing. For example, does the roof or HVAC system need to be replaced regardless of the phasing?

- Identifying a cutoff point for finished materials if you phase out the project.

- Figuring out if you can keep living in the house if you don't phase.

- Estimating the cost by phase to better understand the project's financial viability as a whole or in phases.

Iterating on the plan options, executing master planning, and referring to the original budget leads to a reasonable level of focus and direction for your design team. Successful schematic design is about you saying, "This is darn close to what we wanted." Changes can occur, of course, but the overall concept is hitting the mark. The result could sound like this: "Let's go ahead with the master plan but leave out the second story. Identify two phases so that I can have my contractor price it out separately from the beginning." Or maybe, "Let's go with Plan B but the primary bath design from Plan A."

The next step of design is design development. That means your design team takes your direction and digs deeper into the details. It's like when you're the coach and you arrive on game day and send your team onto the field: the game is *on*. Ideally, you don't change your mind on the game plan, but at this early stage of design, there are still opportunities to refine details. You can still improvise your play-calling and make final decisions (say, not doing one phase or moving fixtures around), but completely changing the discovery criteria—a.k.a. the game plan—will cause heartburn for all.

Before you move on to game day, you need to decide whether or not you cleared the first hurdle in design. If you're hesitating at all, I suggest not proceeding to the next step until you're satisfied. And if you can't get satisfied, cut your losses, pull up your stakes, and move camp.

2.114 WHAT TO EXPECT: NEW HOME SCHEMATIC DESIGN PRESENTATION

Although many of the same remodel project schematic design fundamentals apply to a new home project, you'll need to consider other components for a new home project. Let's go back to your discovery package and say that your criteria were to create a new home with a detached accessory dwelling unit for your parents and a man cave basement. Your lot is 1.5 acres with some slopes, rocky outcroppings, and potentially incredible views. In order to achieve your dreams, your designer will:

- Review your discovery package in detail, visiting your inspirations links and files, meeting with you, and asking many questions.

- Finalize the architectural style and programming (i.e., the rooms and spaces you desire).

- Discuss the budget criteria as they pertain to your ideas and then provide feedback and direction to determine which options to pursue.

- Hire a land surveyor to document the property lines, slopes, obstacles (i.e., rock outcroppings, protected trees, and easements), roads, and utilities.

- Import the survey into design software.

- Research your local Planning department and homeowner's association rules for new home construction.

- Go away for several weeks to prepare concepts for your review.
- Conduct the first schematic design meeting with 3D design software. This is when you sit back and let your designer dazzle you by showing you various documents:
  - A site plan depicting proposed structure footprints utilizing survey data (main home, garages, accessory dwelling unit or ADU, encroachments [access to property], and some hardscaping [driveways, walkways]).
  - Various floor plans articulating options in the form of Plan A, Plan B, Plan C, etc.
  - 3D renderings of each plan from exterior and interior perspectives that include the style and materials represented in your inspirations. This is super helpful when it comes to making decisions!
- Present a monologue explaining their concepts and the impacts of those concepts, how they achieved your joint goals, and finally, ideas you've never thought of.
- Have a discussion with you about the pros and cons of each option, what you like and dislike, and possible directions to take with the design.

When it comes to a new home project, before you get too far along, you need to consider important areas related to the upcoming section about understanding design limitations. Here are some examples of such considerations:

✓ Can my architect confidently confirm that the design meets all of the requirements of my local Planning department and homeowner's association?

- What research was done and what did they learn? Did any restrictions affect the design? How?

✓ How did the survey data affect the proposed layout of the buildings?

- Are any easements restricting the buildings?

- Are the utilities in a reasonable location?

- Are we maximizing the views?

- Can we still achieve the same footprint if we opt out of a basement?

Beyond those points, there's one last consideration to ground the project: budget checkpoints.

2.115 BUDGET CHECKPOINT #1

Prioritizing the budget will be your job as various concepts begin to surface. Architects often get scrutinized because unbeknownst to the client, architects overdesign and the homeowner ends up with a beautiful design that never gets built. But in all fairness to the designer, a homeowner is often unclear about their budget, and that uncertainty undermines the entire process. That said, I've seen designers dismiss a client's budget and design away, only to then plop the plans into the garbage. This dilemma occurs way too often and should be addressed during the design process.

Maybe it's been several months since you first thought about how much you may want to invest in the project. As the design takes on its own life, a budget checkpoint is your chance to ask yourself and everybody else, "Are we sure we're on the right track?" In response, is your design team nodding their head while looking at the ceiling? How confident are you that you can afford this project? It's up to *you*. And only *you* know how much you want to know the answer to that question.

At certain stages of the design process, a more refined budget can be established by revising your original budget to align with the data from your preferred design and then engaging with a contractor to validate your budgeting methods. Beyond these methods, the only way to determine a very accurate price is to initiate estimating (coming up in Estimating Your Project Cost on page 368) after the plans and specifications have been completed.

A refined budget validated by a construction professional protects and empowers you to make educated decisions. If for assorted reasons you and your design pro got carried away as the design progressed, it's good to know that as soon as possible, as in before you pay them thousands of dollars to complete the plans and obtain permits.

Take a few prudent steps before your design team initiates locking in your design:

❑ Revisit the budget exercise and review the information you've already input. Is the kitchen still in the same spot? Is the primary suite still 500 square feet? How many square feet is your new home, including *all* of the structures?

❑ Open a dialogue with your design team to discuss the impacts of the proposed design on your existing home. Use your instincts to determine if they have a solid understanding of said impacts.

❑ Reevaluate what other work will be required due to your selected design and its impacts.

❑ As needed, visit a contractor to get a second opinion. After all, the contractor is the person who will implement the design throughout the construction, and the odds are in their favor that they know more about costs and your structure than your design team does.

❏ Study Part Four: Building Your Team (see page 341) so that you can create a seamless experience for yourself, from design to construction.

2.116 STEP TWO: SELECTING DESIGNS AND OPTIONS

During the schematic design step, you may have explored different high-level options for your new home. Those could be a range of styles, configurations, or sizes presented in versions such as Plan A Single-Story or Plan B Two-Story, or even a completely different look such as a traditional farmhouse or a more modern style of home. Now is the time to guide your architect by selecting your desired overall style and options.

Finalizing that step will trigger your architect to begin locking in your design by assembling the rest of the design team and delving into the details within the design. This is commonly referred to as the *design development* phase. Remember, at this point, it's still possible to make revisions and establish options if they fall within the overall design parameters, style, size, shape, and location on the site.

Completing the first design step has allowed you to work with your design team. From conveying your ideas to making sure your designer listens to you and responds with relevant concepts, this is your chance to evaluate the design experience and its deliverables. Before lurching towards the next stepping stone, now is an ideal time to pause, gain your bearings, learn from the past, and look ahead to new obstacles.

2.130 LOCKING IN YOUR DESIGN

During the schematic design phase, the design process is more flexible and organic. Walls can be moved around easily, roof lines can be changed instantly, and kitchens can be at the back of the home one minute and at the front the next. However, the *design development step*—which is step two of the design process led by your architect—requires a more structured and disciplined approach. To move into this phase, you need to choose a design concept and options that you want your design team to further develop while being comfortable with the results of your budget checkpoint.

The design development stage represents a significant percentage of the overall design process that took up such a significant amount of time. Each step forward in the design development further entrenches the selected design and options. You may still make revisions and refinements, but during this step, it's important to avoid making significant changes like changing the architectural style, the size of the home, or where spaces are located. If you're still unsure about your choices, it's better to stop and go back to step one, because making significant changes later on could be costly in terms of design fees, construction start dates, and emotional stress.

2.131 THE OBJECTIVES OF DESIGN DEVELOPMENT

- Tailor the selected design and solutions.
- Select construction and finish materials for the exterior and interior.
- Visualize the exterior and interior with your materials.
- Finalize the materials, equipment, and scope of work specifications.
- Assemble the rest of the design team.
- Do your budget checkpoint and official estimating.
- Develop a set of plans suitable for approvals and estimating.
- Obtain early approvals from city jurisdictions and HOAs.

With a fully developed design, you can now visualize the design and options you selected along with the chosen materials. Suppose your project involves a new or expanded home. In that case, the structures on your lot have been given their final placements, further improving your visual capabilities. Ultimately, the goal is to have a comprehensive set of plans and specifications that allow you to visualize your new home and officially engage with city or county departments for early approvals and that will also allow contractors to perform actual cost estimates (vs. not being able to do so with earlier, less-specific budgets).

WHAT SHOULD HAPPEN
DURING DESIGN DEVELOPMENT

- The appropriate consultants are brought in early enough.

- A strong collaboration is occurring between all design professionals.

- The selected design is feasible from a construction and approval standpoint.

- The interior design work officially begins.

- Construction and finish materials are specified.

- You can visualize your new home and spaces with your choices incorporated into it.

- The scope of work and equipment are specified.

- A set of plans and specifications are generated that are suitable for more accurate and realistic estimating beyond the theoretical budgeting done in the discovery step.

As you can see from the list above, developing a design involves many aspects of architectural and interior design. I'll address each of these items within this section and beyond. First, here's a look at essential tasks that should be accomplished during the design development step. I've broken the tasks down into three categories: architectural design, interior design, and specifications.

2.132 ARCHITECTURAL RESPONSIBILITIES

An architect's responsibility reaches way beyond just supplying drawings—the crux of their responsibility is creating a feasible project by orchestrating multiple resources. This concerted effort continues in the second step of design as the architect takes proactive steps to verify elements of the new design with respect to your property and existing structures, coordinates multiple individuals and consultants, and prepares the plan pages that will culminate into your plan set so that you're ready for early and final approvals.

2.134 DESIGN CHECKPOINTS

Once a schematic plan has been selected, a prudent pause point is to validate the design before you take too many steps forward. I call these pauses design checkpoints. This quality assurance activity reminds the team to identify any assumptions that may have been made, double-check conformance to city and county regulations, and verify existing conditions and measurements.

ZONING AND MUNICIPAL CODE COMPLIANCE

As we progress through the design process and eventually the approval process, I'll present the functions of your city Planning department in Understanding Design Limitations on page 180. What's important at this particular design checkpoint is that the design you've selected does in fact conform to all rules and regulations documented in your city and county zoning ordinances and your municipal code. Your designer should have uncovered these during the schematic design phase.

You may recall that it's ideal for your architect to visit your local Planning department during the very first design step to ensure that *all* parameters are understood before diving into the design. If this does not occur or if the rules, regulations, and/or codes are misunderstood, a few unwanted things can happen, including some big ones that can disrupt the design process and delay the permit submittal applications. Let's dig into what complying with codes can mean.

SOME HIGH-LEVEL EXAMPLES OF CODE COMPLIANCE

- The methods used for floor area calculations (known as FAR) is one ordinance that can mandate the maximum size of your home. The FAR calculates the conditioned living space of your new home, and this can become complicated. For example, tall and vaulted ceilings can count as double the FAR.

- The methods used to calculate building heights can be tricky. Where to measure the height from and to where? This becomes all the more complicated as roof pitches and the grade around your house play a role.

- Some codes apply to the proximity of structures to easements throughout the property. For example, can a building be right on the easement line, or is there a setback requirement from the easement?

To put all of this into perspective, here's a real-life experience that surprised our design team late in the design process. Let's say your home is 8 feet from the side fences and 20 feet from the back fence. Your new primary suite expansion is aligned with your home's existing side and rear walls, which makes perfect sense. However, since the time when your home was originally built, the *setbacks* (the space you are not allowed to build in) have become more significant. It sounds ridiculous, but it wouldn't surprise me if the new addition had to be offset from the existing home to conform to the new rules.

The point is, did your designer check this or did they assume it could be aligned? This is an easy mistake to make and can potentially force a redesign. It can't hurt to ask about this kind of issue now. In the *Understanding Design Limitations* section, you'll learn more about setbacks and many other potentially problematic areas.

Understanding your zoning designation and more importantly how to interpret the sometimes confusing rules and calculations is always a challenge and opens doors to oversights. The larger the project is, the more difficult it becomes to tackle these rules and calculations on your own. Being able to depend on a qualified design professional to handle all of these issues is a core component of the value of said professionals. But still, you should be aware of possible snags, because it's possible to get caught up in the confusion. Even city planners get hung up on interpreting their own rules!

WHAT YOU CARE ABOUT IN THIS EARLY STAGE OF DESIGN DEVELOPMENT

- ✓ Has my architect reviewed the planning rules and regulations in detail?

- ✓ Does my selected design conform to all rules and regulations?

- ✓ Have specific steps been taken to ensure that my design can safely proceed?

I could go on, but I'll save more for the Understanding Design Limitations section. It's prudent to wrap your head around these limitations so that you can understand and circumvent common oversights and misunderstandings during the design development phase. The best scenario is to exhaust all efforts with the Planning department to minimize risk.

EXISTING CONSTRUCTION ASSUMPTIONS

When remodeling and expanding an existing home, your design team will inevitably make assumptions that will affect the design and engineering of your plans. A few critical and common assumptions could be the size and depth of the existing foundation you plan to build onto or the location of your property lines and where the house is situated within the property lines. Let's explore some specific potential assumptions and verifications.

FOUNDATION

This concrete structure under your house supports the floor, walls, and roof. The foundation can be constructed in several ways, from its depth, width, and height to whether or not any steel reinforcements are inside the concrete. When modifying an existing structure, new walls or load-bearing posts may be bearing on the old foundation. The architect and engineer will "assume" a specific minimum size and then decide how to design and engineer the solutions. But without verifying the size of the foundation (also called footings), they can't be certain about its specifications.

In my travels, I've seen foundations that only go 6 inches into the ground, have no steel reinforcement, and are undersized. Obviously, if engineers were assume that kind of foundation is an adequate size for expansion, they would be wrong. Verification can solve this if it's not too invasive. I often have someone dig at a couple of corners of the home to expose the size of the footing. It only takes a couple of hours to resolve assumptions about the size and condition of the foundation.

Assumptions can be categorized as resolvable or unresolvable. The extent to which assumptions can be resolved will depend on your design team's experience, professionalism, and diligence. If conditions of the home can be reasonably observed and evaluated without significant invasive methods, then these would be resolvable assumptions. In contrast, conditions that would require an inordinate number of invasive procedures to investigate (such as seeing inside walls without cutting them open) would be considered a typical unresolvable assumption. However, it's up to you to define how invasive it would be to resolve any perceived-to-be-unresolvable conditions. If you know to ask "What assumptions are being made and how could they affect the project design or cost?", then you're empowered to participate in the decision-making process.

VERIFICATIONS

Verifying the design's truth, accuracy, validity, and associated assumptions is paramount before completing the design development step. Those verifications are also often overlooked. The carpenter's adage of "measure twice, cut once" couldn't apply more to this situation, yet so many designers and contractors miss this one! What contributes to this oversight is a word that you'll see used throughout the remainder of this book: accountability.

Between architects, engineers, and contractors, the no-responsibility clauses cancel each other out, therefore leaving you in the middle. But initiating a verification process can uncover any issues early enough and thus leave you in the driver's seat. If the foundation has some problems, perhaps you won't design that two-story addition and will add on to the first floor instead. If the foundation is inadequate, the engineer can include the necessary retrofit design so that your contractor can cost out the project before your start rather than during construction, which would trigger those scary words "change order."

And so we're back to the question you should ask your design pro, albeit with a slight twist: "What assumptions have been made and what can we do to resolve them?" Asking that question means you've transferred the accountability back to your design team and have now positioned yourself to decide which assumptions you're willing to accept.

The objective of design checkpoints is to make you aware of potential and common oversights as early as possible so that you can ask the right questions to protect yourself from potential inefficiencies and delays in the design process.

2.136 CONSULTANT RESPONSIBILITIES

A large part of an architect's responsibility is to engage with the consultants who support their work. As you saw in the section about *understanding design professionals,* several consultants could be influencing the design. In some cases, they could be *significantly* influencing the design.

A prudent architect consults with a variety of design professionals early on and even hires them during the initial phase to better understand the site characteristics that can drive the design. For example, *surveyors and civil engineers* provide drawings that identify property lines, easements, slopes, drainages, and more. This data can influence a new home's design and location and even look. Bringing these consultants into the project early on minimizes any backtracking during the design development phase. A geotechnical engineer can undoubtedly build in some restrictions by identifying the stability of the soils, performing drainage analysis, and even finding earthquake faults that may affect where the home could be.

Although most architects and some residential designers have experience in the fundamentals of structural engineering, a structural engineer's expertise can still significantly impact the architect's design. During the schematic design step, ideally a structural engineer became involved to scrutinize design concepts for feasibility and value engineering. If this proactive step did not occur, then it's officially time to begin orchestrating all of the players during the design development.

It's not uncommon for design compromises to surface during this handoff as consultants attempt to blend solutions with the architect's concepts. Ultimately, it's your architect's job to be sure that the design details align with the plans and specifications each consultant provides. These proactive steps fall under the category of value engineering. Input from consultants during this phase could save you thousands of dollars, from site work to structural engineering and beyond.

Let's take a peek at the leading consultants that may apply to your project and the affected areas of design. At this stage of design, it's prudent to ask your architect which consultants will be involved and when they will begin their work.

CONSULTANT	IMPACT
Surveyors	Location of buildings relative to property lines, easements, and slopes. Data drives the location and orientations of new buildings.
Civil engineers	Location of buildings relative to slopes, drainages, utilities, and septic systems. Data helps refine the locations and heights of buildings.
Geotech engineers	Location of buildings relative to the structural supports of soils, ground water, and retaining walls.
Structural engineers	Comparison of the building design vs. the architectural design and potential compromises on concepts.

MEP designers/ engineers	Location of equipment and duct and plumbing raceways vs. the structural design; coordination of lighting design with other ceiling components.
Low-voltage contractors	Location of equipment; architectural design accommodations for systems.
Fire protection contractors	Location of equipment; coordination with other ceiling components and water main size.
Energy-efficiency experts	Design of floor, wall, and roof assemblies, window/exterior door products, insulation, HVAC equipment specs and locations, and water heating solutions and locations.
Solar contractors	Design of optimal roof plane orientations; location of equipment; coordination of roof penetrations, backup power solutions, and equipment.
Interior designers	Refinement of architectural design with interior details; locations of doors, windows, beams, cabinetry, and appliances.
Landscapers	Building orientations and heights relative to grade, door locations, decking and patios, privacy, and irrigation demands.

2.137 PLAN PAGES

Schematic-level designs are usually adequate for early consultants. With their input, the design development stage is off to a good start. Step two of design is when you'll see your designs develop into actual plan pages. Over the course of steps two and three, your architect will continue to build upon each plan page, ultimately ending up with a completed set ready to build with. I'll go deep into understanding plans in the section titled exactly that (see page 208).

By the time we reach the end of step two, many of your plan pages will be developed enough to allow more detailed cost estimating, which in turn will lead to you being able to make informed decisions before you finalize your project plans. Here's a quick look at what kind of information materializes within plan pages and specifications, what you care about, and the benefits of each specification.

SITE PLAN

The buildings will be placed on the site within a plan page called Site Plan for New Homes or Extensive Remodels. The objective is to orient the home properly by integrating the house plans with the survey and civil engineering plans.

KEY BENEFITS OF SITE PLANS

✓ These plans allow you to visualize your new home on your property.

✓ These plans provide suitable data points to engage with general contractors, subcontractors, and Planning and Building departments.

✓ These plans allow you to accomplish budget checkpoints and cost estimations.

FLOOR PLAN

The floor plan is the primary plan page of a project—it controls the multitude of subsequent plan pages. An example is finalizing the sizes, shapes, and locations of walls, windows, and doors. Ideally, things won't change going forward since making a window larger can snowball into more complexity than you would think.

KEY BENEFITS OF FLOOR PLANS

✓ These plans allow you to visualize space plans for rooms, sizes, windows, and doors.

- ✓ These plans provide suitable data points to engage with general contractors, subcontractors, and material suppliers.

- ✓ These plans allow you to begin collaborating with the interior designer.

- ✓ With these plans, you can also accomplish your budget checkpoint.

ELEVATIONS AND SECTION DRAWINGS

These supplemental drawings prepared by your architect or designer are to articulate more design details to you, to consultants, and to city/county departments. Think of *elevations* as you standing at the front of your home to see what it will look like and *sections* as being a doll house replication that slices through your home and lets you see the interior. Beyond being able to accurately visualize the home with the proper materials, consultants and staff who work in Planning departments are interested in the mass, scale, and heights of the home, which are commonly limited by codes and which affect the home's structural engineering. Your contractor and subcontractors will also look at these plan pages to accurately estimate costs.

KEY BENEFITS OF ELEVATIONS AND SECTION DRAWINGS

- ✓ These drawings allow you to visualize the exterior and interior of your new home by understanding the heights of ceilings and the proportions of windows, doors, and details.

- ✓ These drawings provide suitable data points to engage with consultants, general contractors, subcontractors, material suppliers, and Planning and Building departments.

- ✓ These drawings allow you to accomplish a budget checkpoint.

The detail level of elevations and section drawings from your architect can vary widely. Knowing you can and should participate in reviewing these drawings hits that nerve again about "knowing what you don't know."

HOW TO TAKE CHARGE OF YOUR EXPECTATIONS

✓ Ask to participate in the review of the drawings during design development and have your designer walk you through the details.

✓ Look at the overall size, scale, and mass of the proposed design. Although 3D modeling will help you much more with this task later on, don't forego trying to envision the full scope of the design at this stage.

✓ A big fancy word in the world of design is "fenestration." This is the arrangement of the windows and doors on your elevations. Look closely at their locations, sizes, and proportions. Are they centered? Do they *need* to be centered? (Spoiler: not always.) Do you want grids? How about a trim around the windows? What type of doors are on the patio? The more accurately the fenestration is represented, the lower the odds are that your contractor and suppliers will make mistakes, not to mention fail to provide you with accurate costs.

✓ Siding, exterior trim, stucco, masonry, and any material cladding on the outside of the home should be represented on the elevations. Performing a detailed review of the look and feel of your home empowers you to maintain control of the results. Be prepared for your observations to range from "That is not even *close* to what I want!" to "That's precisely the look I was shooting for!" It's better to review these details now than when the mason is installing the wrong stone on-site.

✓ Interior elevations are often absent from architectural plans, unfortunately. That's a mistake that can leave you open to false interpretations. Drawings of this nature are not required by Building departments, so they often get deferred to a later date…never to be seen again. Architects are certainly capable of providing these elevations, and the most qualified ones will indeed provide these crucial details assuming that you've authorized them to do so. *Not* enabling your architect to maximize the level of details they provide is a prime example of handcuffing your designer, only to pay a price later.

✓ Why are interior elevations so valuable? In order to have the best outcome, it's crucial to communicate intricate details and materials such as kitchen and bath design and architectural millwork so that they can all converge into one perceived interior through design work. If you were to ask a designer or architect "What are some of the most important aspects of your craft?", inevitably, you'd hear about scale, proportions, transitions, reveals, and details. The only way to pursue the proper solutions and make informed decisions is to explore the ideas and details within design work and drawings. Leaving this task up to your contractor is an irresponsible concession to make.

Qualified architects are fully capable of articulating their vision through their design tools, yet they often don't take their vision far enough. Why? For one of two reasons: the client (that's you) didn't think such details were needed (back to the concept of "you don't know what you don't know") or your architect wasn't interested in providing these details and therefore didn't even offer them. Note that interior designers can play a role when it comes to these details, too, which can be a perfectly fine avenue if initiated at the right time.

- ✓ Are you comfortable with the look and feel of the home based on the interior and exterior renderings? You want to be sure you're comfortable before anyone declares that the design development has been completed.

- ✓ Who will be responsible for showing you what the interior of your home will look like? Are drawings and details forthcoming?

MEP DESIGN CONSIDERATIONS

Although the MEP (or mechanical, electrical, and plumbing) plans are essential to a project, strangely enough, they're too often neglected. Now is your chance to participate in the design of your electrical, lighting, and heating and air-conditioning systems! Of course, you must depend on the pros to design the systems. Still, your contribution is sharing your lifestyle and desires so that the design can be tailored to you.

It's not uncommon for the architect to design the MEP plan pages for most projects. This can be adequate to cover the basics, but if you're dealing with a complex project such as a large custom home, then adding specific mechanical, electrical/lighting, and plumbing designers or engineers to the team is a thoughtful consideration.

KEY BENEFITS OF MEP DESIGN CONSIDERATIONS

- ✓ These considerations allow you to optimize your living experience in your new home with proper lighting and power where you need it. You'll also be comfortable with the appropriate design and equipment.

- ✓ These considerations provide design and data points to engage with consultants, general contractors, subcontractors, and material suppliers.

✓ These considerations obtain valuable input for value engineering and budget checkpoints.

EQUIPMENT LOCATION

A variety of systems exist to heat and cool a home, but delving into these is a topic for another book. For our exercise now, we'll assume a forced-air system. Identifying the location of your HVAC equipment affects three of the trades involved in the installation: mechanical, electrical (power), and plumbing (gas). Since costs are associated with each trade, specifying what equipment goes where will enable each contractor to include their HVAC-associated cost within their scope. This may seems basic, but assuming that this has been documented by your designer within your plans can lead to inferior installations and cost surprises.

DUCTING

Locating ducts that supply warm and cool air throughout the home can be challenging, especially if these locations weren't addressed during the design process. Structural components of the home such as beams, walls, shear walls, and foundations can significantly compromise the performance of an HVAC system, not to mention costs. Multistory homes in particular are very challenging when it comes to getting ducting to the proper locations. If ductways are not considered during design, compromises such as dropped ceilings, soffits, and closets being consumed with ductwork will occur.

ELECTRICAL CONSIDERATIONS

One of the most significant assumptions made in the purchase of a parcel and the design of a project is that power service exists and is adequate to serve the new buildings. However, this may not be the case.

- Many homes throughout the US are serviced by a maximum of 200 amps. Many older homes have 100 amps or less.

- Multiple homes are serviced by one power company transformer located on power poles or underground lines via a transformer placed on the ground.

- It's possible that a power company's transformer may need to be upgraded to serve your new home. Significant costs can apply.

Two interrelated components of power should be considered while developing a design:

1. The location and size of the power company's equipment.
2. The electrical load of the design.

The desires for and design of your home will eventually dictate the required electrical system. For example, a trend in residential construction is eliminating natural or propane gas by designing all-electric solutions coupled with solar power. On the surface, this sounds desirable as a way to reduce or even eliminate power bills, but the reality is that an all-electric design substantially increases the power demand, especially for larger new custom homes. Further challenging this all-electric direction of home building is the fact that equipment technology has not reasonably caught up to meet modern energy-efficiency standards. This results in more expensive equipment solutions.

During the development of your design, you *must* calculate the total electrical load of your home before finalizing the plans. An electrical engineer or qualified electrical contractor can perform load calculations based on parameters such as the electrical equipment loads demanded by appliances, HVAC, water heating, power, and lighting combined with occupant usage.

KEY POINTS OF LOAD CALCULATIONS

- ✓ What size power service do I need to serve my design?

- ✓ Where are the power utilities located?

- ✓ Will the existing power company's equipment serve my needs?

- ✓ Will the power company need to upgrade their equipment, and if so, how much will that cost? (It could be significant!)

Opening a conversation with your architect early in this phase and conferring with an electrical engineer or electrical contractor to determine the anticipated power requirements for your design will keep you ahead of the curve. Depending on the existing power service to your property, it's very possible that you may need to revise your design and even revisit your original discovery exercise. It's worth the effort! This valuable information allows you to remain in control and averts major surprises during construction.

POWER PANEL LOCATIONS

The main panel is where your power company connects power to your home. The power is distributed throughout your home using wire that originates from a main service panel located on the outside of your home. Beyond your main panel, there could be additional distribution panels or "subpanels" located throughout the home. Subpanels act as secondary distribution points; they're usually used in medium to larger homes.

WHY POWER PANELS SHOULD BE SPECIFIED ON THE PLANS NOW

- They provide accurate information for the electrical contractor to estimate costs.

- They allocate spaces and clearances within the floor plan per building codes that could affect room designs.

- They allow space for integrating solar power equipment and panels.

- They address home technology considerations such as smart power panels and the corresponding required spaces.

- They integrate power backup systems such as generators or battery storage.

- They influence circuit design in terms of considering the length of distribution, backup requirements, and future-proofing needs.

SOLAR PV SYSTEM INTEGRATION

Generating electricity from the sun is becoming a standard for new construction and extensive remodels. Addressing the design of a photovoltaic system at this point in the design development offers many benefits and influences other systems.

WHY YOU SHOULD ADDRESS A PV SYSTEM NOW

- The orientation of roof panels may affect the architect's final roof plane design.

- The roof structural design can be affected by the additional weight of panels.

- The locations of roof penetrations such as skylights, plumbing vents, and attic ventilation can be modified for optimal performance and aesthetics.

- Power backup system requirements can affect equipment space allocations and the location of power panels.

- Exploring PV options/requirements allows you to include these costs in the budget.

BACKUP SYSTEMS

Power backup systems continue to become more popular, especially in suburban and rural areas. Traditionally, generators fueled by natural or propane gas have been used, but more recently, battery backup systems supplied by a photovoltaic system on the roof have been gaining in popularity.

WHY NOW *IS A GOOD TIME TO ADDRESS A GENERATOR BACKUP SYSTEM*

- Clearances required to buildings, property lines, building openings (windows, doors, vents), sound mitigation, and screening all influence where generators are placed.

- The location of the generator relates to fuel supply and thus cost minimization.

- The location of power circuits to be backed up influences the design and location of power panels.

- Exploring your generator options allows you to include these costs in the budget.

LOCATION OF OUTLETS

You may have specific needs for plugging in equipment, such as home offices, audio-video equipment, home networking panels, device charging stations, kitchen appliance needs, bathrooms, lighted mirrors, garage equipment, or outdoor outlets for landscaping or yard maintenance. Or you might simply want locations where it would be convenient to plug in a lamp. Identifying these locations on the plan page will ensure accurate costs and installation.

DEVICE STYLES

Choices abound regarding the types of outlets and switches, ranging from various materials and colors to exposed or concealed screws. All of these affect material and installation costs. It's easy for a designer to specify a "standard device" without even asking what your preferences would be. Understanding your options ahead of time leads to a quality experience.

LIGHTING

Recessed lighting is a standard method for illuminating rooms today. Conveying your lighting desires to your designer gets you off to a good start! The location of fixtures within each room and how and where they're controlled covers the basics.

PLUMBING CONSIDERATIONS

The P of ME**P** identifies the water, waste, and gas systems: where they enter the home and how they're distributed throughout the structure(s). Identifying the systems, fixture locations, types, quantities, and specifications completes the information your contractors will depend on to estimate and install each system.

WATER SERVICE

Just *assuming* that the water service to your property is adequate for your new design can upend a project during construction and can once again provoke unplanned costs. Performing a plumbing load calculation early on during the design development step is prudent in order to remain in the driver's seat.

KEY QUESTIONS FOR PLUMBING LOAD CALCULATIONS

✓ Will my project require fire sprinklers?

✓ What size water service do I need to serve my design?

✓ Where are the water utilities located?

✓ Will the existing water company's equipment serve my needs?

✓ Will the water company need to upgrade their equipment, and if so, how much will that cost? (It could be significant!)

✓ Will I have to replace the water line on my property?

FIXTURE TYPES AND LOCATIONS

Since one method a plumber uses to estimate the cost of a project is based on the number of fixtures, the plans must reflect this number accurately. Frequently, a designer may have plopped a standard tub into a bathroom with one sink when in reality you wanted two sinks and a shower and didn't mention it. It's best to get it right the first time! The proper way to do that is to have *all* of your fixtures selected and placed on the plans and within your scope of work and specifications.

WHAT TO SPECIFY WITHIN THE PLAN PAGES NOW: WATER AND WASTE

✓ Quantity of sinks

- Baths and kitchens
- Outdoors, garage, shop, craft room, bar

✓ Fixture types at tubs and showers

✓ Exterior hose bibs

✓ Irrigation valve location(s)

TYPES OF WASTE SYSTEMS

There are basically two types of waste systems: a septic system located on the property or a municipal system served by your city or a separate service district.

DESIGN CONSIDERATIONS FOR A
SEPTIC WASTE SYSTEM

A septic system is either designed by a civil engineer or designed and constructed by an excavation contractor. A septic system consists of a multichambered tank near the house and a leach field. The latter is a large area of land beyond the tank that the tanks drain into, thus returning the processed waste back to the earth.

Septic systems can be designed in numerous ways and are influenced by:

- The size of the structures (based on the quantity of bedrooms).

- The slope of the lot (potentially requires a pump system).

- The availability of an area for a leach field and a secondary backup leach field.

WHAT TO ASK ABOUT SEPTIC SYSTEMS

✓ Has a place for the tank and leach field been considered with the proposed layout of buildings?

✓ Have the clearance requirements from property lines, easements, trees, and buildings been considered?

✓ Have the clearance requirements from artisan wells, springs, and domestic water wells been considered?

✓ Has an area been allocated for the required backup leach field?

✓ Will my septic system require pumps due to my sloping lot or limited spaces for leach fields?

✓ How can I obtain an estimate to include in the budget?

DESIGN CONSIDERATIONS
FOR A MUNICIPAL WASTE SYSTEM

NEW HOME _____

- ✓ Where is the connection point to the system? At the property line or beyond? Is this indicated on the site plan?
- ✓ What are the fees to connect to the system?

REMODEL PROJECT _____

- ✓ Where is the connection point to the municipal system? Is this indicated on the site plan?
- ✓ Where is the connection point to the house and does the new design affect the location?
- ✓ What is the condition of the waste line to my existing house?
- ✓ Do I need to replace the main waste line?
- ✓ Are there cleanouts installed at the property line and near the house?

GAS

Just like power and water consumption, appliances and equipment draw a certain amount of fuel based on the Btu specified at each piece of equipment. During the development of your design, the total gas load of the home must be calculated before the plans are finalized. A plumbing engineer or qualified plumbing contractor can perform load calculations based on the equipment Btu parameters. (For example, loads demanded by appliances, HVAC, water heaters, and pools or spas.)

✓ What size gas line do I need to serve my appliances and equipment?

✓ Where is the gas service located?

✓ Will the existing gas company's equipment serve my needs?

✓ Will the gas company need to upgrade their equipment, and if so, how much will that cost? (It could be significant!)

WHAT TO SPECIFY WITHIN THE PLAN PAGES NOW

✓ The size and location of gas service point(s) of entry to building(s).

✓ The specifications and locations of appliances, fixtures, and equipment that require gas.

- Kitchen appliances

- Outdoor kitchen equipment

- Outdoor heating equipment

- Water heater type and location(s): tankless, standard tank

- Boilers

- Furnaces

- Fireplaces

- Fire pits

- Pool and spa equipment

LOW-VOLTAGE DESIGN

Low-voltage work can be as simple as installing a few phone and internet lines or as complex as installing lighting controls, whole-house networks, power management systems, and on and on. LV goes hand in hand with the MEP design since they're interrelated. The more you're interested in smart home solutions, the more likely you'll be to need a separate low-voltage design and a low-voltage contractor.

Subcontractors often perform the design-build method since they're current with the most innovative technologies and solutions. Still, this part of the team inevitably needs to be brought in earlier. Low-voltage work is highly customizable and tailored to each homeowner's desires, so bringing this person in during the design development phase is vital. Their solutions can influence the electrical design and house structure because you want those automatic blinds that disappear into the ceiling.

KEY BENEFITS OF BRINGING IN A LOW-VOLTAGE DESIGNER NOW

- Learn about the possibilities of home automation and make informed decisions.

- Prepare and coordinate LV plans and specs with other plans for the best installations.

- Obtain valuable input for the budget checkpoint.

SOME IMPORTANT CONSIDERATIONS IN THIS PHASE OF DESIGN

- Defining the POE (point of entry) of the services to the home informs the LV contractor of the distances to the network distribution hub.

- Telecommunications

  - Telephone

  - Data network: This includes wiring for computer networks and related equipment. Identifying areas where the network wiring will terminate into a dedicated panel or rack requires space, power, and ventilation. Identifying a network closet or room during design is ideal as this area could house many of the equipment solutions listed above. The more space, the better.

- Cable and satellite
- AV systems
  - Audiovisual systems
  - Entertainment system design and equipment
  - Distributed audio
- Security
  - Alarm
  - Video monitoring, cameras
  - Gates
  - Intercoms
  - Window and door automation
- Home automation
  - Lighting and power control; smart switches and receptacles
  - Window blinds: Specifying automated blinds can trigger design modifications to walls and ceilings for the best solutions. Addressing this too late during construction equates to instant compromises.
  - HVAC system control
  - Smart appliances
  - Voice control
- Monitoring and management systems
  - Utilities: Smart meters and equipment for power, water, and gas. Special power smart panels monitoring

your electric consumption sometimes require additional space for equipment.

- Solar: Inclusion of a photovoltaic system (solar) combined with a battery backup system requires physical space for equipment and may influence the structural design of your roof.

- Indoor air quality

- Irrigation: Sensors, landscape, and agricultural aspects.

GENERAL CONSIDERATIONS FOR LOW-VOLTAGE WORK

The layout of any ceiling-mounted systems such as distributed audio can conflict with other items such as recessed lighting, decorative fixtures, sprinkler heads, and decorative beams. Your architect can overcome undesirable results by coordinating all of the consultants' design work into what's called a reflected ceiling plan or RFP (see Understanding Plans on page 218). An RFP depicts all items expected to coexist on the ceiling. Careful coordination archives the best symmetry between all components.

Fortunately, the nature of low-voltage cabling is such that it can be routed just about anywhere, so it's more about the physical space where the equipment will be located, how various elements will interface with each other, and how the work of other tradespeople may be affected, such as electricians, plumbers, and HVAC contractors.

So there we have it! Your architectural plans are beginning to take shape—hopefully you're visualizing your new home more and more. But we aren't quite done yet! The design development phase is the time to see the interiors of your home evolve and is usually led by an interior designer. The linchpin of this step is finalizing the specifications. These include materials, equipment, and the scope of work. You need all of these resources to progress with planning your project, so let's be sure that you have a clear understanding of what your project is comprised of by the time you complete this step.

2.139 INTERIOR DESIGN

Whether it's a significant new custom home, an expansion of your existing home, or a kitchen remodel, the scope of your project combined with your level of experience will determine how much an interior designer will be involved. Regardless, in order to estimate and then build your project, decisions and plans must be developed. Bringing in an interior designer as early as possible will optimize the design solutions and inch you towards step three of the design process.

Not unlike what your architect has provided for you, an interior designer has deliverables that you'll use throughout the planning, bidding, and building process. This begins with a floor plan view dedicated to precise kitchen and bath designs, material specifications, and other interior elements not necessarily provided by your architect. Detailed interior design drawings will empower your builder to meet your expectations. If you deprioritize this crucial information, be prepared to compromise and accept the consequences. And don't blame anyone but yourself! Let's look at the ideal interior design plans and specs you should have by the end of this step.

FINISH FLOOR PLAN

These plan pages are a bird's-eye view of your home wherever finish materials are specified. They're often imported into your designer's software (provided by the architect) and are used to identify kitchen and bath design configurations, specific equipment, flooring materials, and millwork such as built-in cabinetry.

KEY BENEFITS OF FINISH FLOOR PLANS
- Coordinate interior design solutions with architectural designs before finalizing the plans.

- Begin the material, fixture, and equipment selection process.
- Clearly communicate to contractors the location and specifications of materials and installation details.

INTERIOR ELEVATIONS

Interior elevations offer many benefits to you, to material suppliers, and to subcontractors. These pages focus on kitchens, baths, cabinetry, millwork, fireplaces, etc. Designers will provide detailed dimensioned 2D and 3D drawings depicting the selected cabinetry door style, countertops, appliances, plumbing fixtures, door and window trim, and beyond. This information is an excellent way for you to visualize the specifics of your kitchen, *and* it can also influence the accuracy of electrical, lighting, plumbing, and even HVAC plans.

KEY BENEFITS OF INTERIOR ELEVATIONS

- Coordinate interior design solutions with architectural designers and consultants before finalizing the plans.
- Continue with the material, fixture, and equipment selection process.
- Depict actual materials and fixtures within drawings.
- Provide dimensioned drawings to enable contractors to install their systems in the correct places.
- Engage with material suppliers and contractors to perform your budget checkpoint.

Other plan pages will be developed behind the scenes by your architect and won't require as much of your attention. You can learn more about pages such as the existing plan, demolition plan, roof plan, reflected ceiling plan, and schedules and details in the Understanding Plans section on page 213.

2.140 SPECIFICATIONS

As homeowners get deeper into the design process and begin seeing their dreams come closer to reality, they can fall prey to excitement and assume that the details are in the plans, the materials and equipment are specified and available when needed, and the contractors understand the proper installation methods. This common delusion is one of the top causes of unsuccessful projects, and it begins by asking a contractor to provide an estimate on a project that has inferior plans and specifications. The resulting inaccurate estimates lead to dissention, because contractors then must unfairly absorb costs and/or issue change orders for you to shell out unexpected cash. All of this snowballs into schedule delays.

By now, architects, draftspersons, junior architects, consultants, and interior designers are all contributing to the design. It is your architect's job to assemble this pile of jigsaw pieces into one completed puzzle. A designer's primary medium to document a project is their plan set, which is consumed with drawings and details. The challenge here is that the puzzle table usually isn't big enough to hold all of the assembled pieces and thus have the full picture that's needed to obtain estimates and manage the construction process successfully. One solution to this challenge is to supplement the plans with a set of specifications in the form of a printed book or other progressive technical tools. Tragically, this doesn't happen often enough. But when it *is* done correctly, plan supplementations protect you by spreading accountability throughout the design team and enabling them to meet your expectations. Now you know!

A comprehensive plan set begins empowering you to officially engage with contractors to obtain accurate estimates. However, you're not done yet. The ultimate objective of documenting a project is to be able to hand off a plan set supplemented with detailed information for builders, subcontractors, and suppliers. This information specifies materials, equipment, and methods of installation to meet the big goals of estimating costs, staying on schedule, and accomplishing high-quality construction for an overall great experience.

For the remainder of this section, I'll be outlining a method for understanding specifications and the essential elements of each one. Because specifications are so important, I dive deeper into them on the TAH site—there, you'll find additional information and tools.

THE THREE COMPONENTS OF SPECIFICATIONS

1. Materials

2. Equipment

3. Scope of work

Think about the scope of work as telling someone "I want new flooring throughout the house" or "I want a tile backsplash in the kitchen" and think of material specifications as being telling them what exact *material* you want for the flooring or backsplash. The material can be as detailed as providing an exact make and model (for example, Mirage, Model 2356 Dusky Gray Engineered Flooring) or as general as saying "prefinished hardwood flooring." Equipment is much the same—it could be an on-demand water heater, the exact model of the furnace you want, or what your architect and contractor suggest. The more precise the specifications are, the more accurate your plans become to integrate the equipment. Also, the fewer pricing issues you'll have with your builder and the better your chances will be that the materials and equipment you expect will in fact be installed correctly.

At this critical stage of design development, you must decide who is responsible for building the project specifications. A common approach is to distribute responsibilities between the architect and interior designer. As plans are being developed, contractors can also be invited to participate in solutions, specifying products and equipment and linking in outside resources such as specialty subcontractors and suppliers. The latter can be immensely valuable when they integrate their input into the plans and specifications.

2.141 BREAKING DOWN SPECIFICATIONS

Since this entire process can be overwhelming, now is a good time to introduce you to a term: *work breakdown structure* or *WBS*. A WBS helps everyone get a handle on the information that follows a project all the way through to the end of construction. Bank this WBS information—it will resurface throughout the upcoming sections!

A WBS is a list of construction categories that almost always go into a project. If you break your project down into a list, that can help you gain an understanding of the different elements that go into the project so that you can organize your specifications. My intention here is to enlighten you on how contractors think about a project. Or, to use our catchphrase, to help you know a little about what you don't know.

The list on the following page is organized by how a construction project would progress along with the material providers and subcontractors who would be involved. Categories requiring decisions and specifications are marked with a ● for construction items and a ■ for finishes. This helps identify the design team members responsible for helping you select materials.

BENEFITS OF A WORK BREAKDOWN STRUCTURE
- Provides a format to identify and organize specifications.
- Offers a format to obtain estimates.
- Provides a format to compare contractor candidate estimates.
- Is a reference when entering into a contract with a general contractor.

CAT#	CATEGORY DESCRIPTION	MATERIAL SPECIFICATION	
	SCOPE OF WORK	CONSTRUCTION	FINISHES
		Architect	Interior designer
22	Site preparation	●	
23	Demolition and disposal	●	
24	Concrete	●	
25	Rough carpentry	●	
26	Sheetmetal and waterproofing	●	
27	Roofing	●	
28	Siding and exterior trim	●	
30	Skylights	●	
31	Windows/patio doors	●	
32	Exterior doors	●	
33	Stucco and masonry	●	
34	Plumbing and fixtures	●	■
36	Electrical and fixtures	●	■
37	Low-voltage elements		■
38	Mechanical	●	
40	Fireplaces	●	
42	Insulation	●	
43	Drywall		■
44	Interior doors, trim, and millwork	●	■
45	Stairs	●	
47	Cabinetry		■
48	Hardware		■
49	Tile		■
50	Slab and stonework		■
51	Solid surfaces		■
52	Flooring		■
57	Appliances		■
60	Glass		■
65	Painting		■
68	Landscaping	●	■
90	Specialty	●	■

- Is a reference to establish construction scheduling.

- Is a reference to structure milestone progress payments to your general contractor.

- Is a reference to organize project information such as estimates, orders, and invoices.

As you can see, a WBS has many functions and is a valuable tool for wrangling all of the project information into one framework. The next time you'll see this system pop up will be in the upcoming Understanding Contracts and Estimating Your Project Cost sections on pages 306 and 285. For now, let's get back to understanding specifications.

2.142 MATERIALS

CONSTRUCTION

A significant milestone of a home remodel or new construction project is when the drywall is completed. This stage represents a time in the construction when your contractor shifts gears to finish mode, which is more about interior aesthetic materials. The best way to think about construction materials is that they're everything that went into the home *before* this stage—in other words, the materials built into the walls and attached to the exterior of the walls. Some good examples are windows, doors, skylights, fireplaces, roofing, siding, and masonry.

Your architect is the key person who will work with you by proposing construction materials to complement the home's design. Still, you'll also participate by researching materials, understanding options, and making final decisions. This participation could even include meeting directly with suppliers during the design process. A big one is windows and doors since your final selection could affect the architectural design and accuracy of the final plans that go to your builder.

FINISH MATERIALS

Think of the materials stuck to the walls, floors, and ceilings that make up the look of the house's interior: the cabinetry, tile, stone, floors, moldings, paint, appliances, fixtures, and hardware. Depending on their experience and how much available time they have, some homeowners tackle this part of a project independently.

Selecting all of the finishes of your new kitchen or entire home is fun and rewarding, but it can also get super overwhelming. When your contractors ask you what tile you want in the bathrooms, you beeline it to the tile store and can't believe how many options there are. You also scramble to attain the knowledge you need to figure out what you want and how everything goes together. If you have an interior designer, this is their wheelhouse. The fact that interior designers have knowledge of materials and resources and a deep understanding of you, your style, and your priorities is worth a lot. Your interior designer will commonly create ensembles geared specifically for you, with options that meet your style. This helps narrow down the selections. They can think about your entire home holistically and incorporate appropriate options into their storyboards and design work. All of this usually helps you lock in your decisions.

Not only can your material selections affect your home's look and feel, they can also swing the costs substantially. When you're in budget checkpoint mode, you want to be realistic so that you can make informed decisions. In the TAH Planning and Building Workbooks, I introduce a comprehensive list of materials organized by standard categories of the materials you'll have to specify.

2.143 EQUIPMENT

Home systems are supported with equipment that's primarily tied to the mechanical/HVAC, electrical, low-voltage, and plumbing categories mentioned in the Consultants section (see page 94) and the Understanding Plans section (see page 208).

There are two ways to approach specifying the equipment in your new home. First, you can rely on the subcontractor for that category seeing as they presumably have experience and knowledge in their particular trade. Second, you can have a more objective and qualified consultant specify the equipment and then use those specifications to obtain quotes from subcontractors. This decision will depend on a few areas, such as the size and complexity of the project, your knowledge, and the level of interest you have in each respective category.

For example, suppose you're building a large net-zero all-electric 5,000-square-foot home with a well and septic system. In that case, you may need consultants to analyze the design in detail to propose proper water filtration, electric heat pump systems for your heating and air conditioning, the correct electrical service size and design, and so on. Implementing a hybrid consultants + subcontractors model is also beneficial for large projects. In that case, you would bring together your MEP engineers and qualified subcontractors to provide input and validate the specifications that the engineers develop. On the other hand, if you're simply remodeling your home and adding a little square footage, having your HVAC contractor educate you and propose heating and cooling equipment options is not the wrong choice.

Your equipment is your home's infrastructure—it's the heart and brain of your house. Educating yourself and carefully considering which products and solutions align with your expectations is a prudent path.

2.144 SCOPE OF WORK

All the pretty lines on the plans certainly help you visualize your home, but do they tell the mechanical contractor that you want all new ductwork in the older portion of the house or the plumber that you wish for a new on-demand water heater? Do the plans tell the roofer to re-roof the entire house and not just the addition?

Someone must define and document *all* of the work you want and need. The plans created in step two should be your primary framework for this—they should be a tool to specify the scope and an accountability mechanism for your contractor candidates to include in their proposals. Remember, you'll use the plans to open dialogues with builders to provide proposals. But not all the information made it into the plan pages, and this is where a separate scope of work document comes in.

Unless the plans are packed with information and narrative related to the scope of work and specifications, contractors are destined to provide incomplete estimates. Consequently, a scenario often goes like this: you told Ace the Builder to include all new ductwork but forgot to convey your request to John, the Contractor. You get your bids and John's is cheaper, so you go with him. Construction starts and you're so excited! Ductwork goes in, but it's not what you expected. You confront John about this. He says you never told him what you wanted. Away we go with conflict on your project! This lack of thorough and consistent information is a classic problem that constantly happens in this business. Fortunately, it can be prevented with a little know-what-you-don't-know preparation.

Identifying the scope of work on your plan pages and distributing them to your potential construction teams equitably ensures that you'll receive comparable bids from one contractor to another. That sounds ideal, but depending only on the plans to capture the entire scope is unrealistic. Incomplete information stems from deferrals and exclusions of specifications, insufficient space within the plan pages, and too much information crammed onto one page, which fosters inattentiveness.

A consequence of inadequate information is having to issue multiple revisions through new plan pages. Revising via the plan pages can quickly become difficult to track and can lead to confusion during the estimating, contracting, and construction phases. I've tried addressing this conundrum in many ways over the past thirty years and have settled on supplementing the plans with a scope of work and specifications system.

Defining the SOW as organized by The Awakened Homeowner's WBS system completes the specifications of your project. It allows you to include materials and equipment and creates a vehicle for narrative and direction to areas that aren't specific to material or equipment, thus ensuring that your contractors will include costs and installations. Lastly, focusing on specifications and creating a SOW will prompt a thorough plan review, which will certainly lead to a fortuitous advantage because missed expectations will be averted.

Design development is a massive milestone in the design process. At this stage, you practically have a set of plans ready to build the project. This enables you to begin formal discussions with contractor candidates, refine your budget, begin formal estimating, consult with Planning departments (as needed), and direct your design team before completing your plans in step three, which centers on the construction documents. I recommend that the completed design development plans be labeled as such so that if you ever have to refer back to them, it'll be clear when you officially called the step "completed." It'll also be clear as to what's included in the plans and specifications.

2.145 BUDGET CHECKPOINT #2

The interdependencies of a completed plan set and specifications are quite different from a completed schematic plan. At this point, you now have adequate information to do one of two things: make the decision to refine your budget or move beyond the hypothetical basis of a budget and into the official estimating process. Your decision will depend on whether or not your plans and specifications are complete enough. If they aren't, then it's time to determine why. Perhaps you're not as far along as you think.

ESTIMATING OR BUDGET CHECKPOINT

Unlike a budget—which is more hypothetical and based on square footage and some hard facts—an estimate is a cost that your contactor determines based on your final plans and specifications. Your goal by the end of step two is to be able to obtain hard dollar estimates. This real-life number will empower you to make final decisions on the scope of work and adjust your choices before the plans are finalized in step three.

At the end of step two, it's possible to initiate the official estimating process provided that your choices have been made and documented to a reasonable level within the plans and specifications. It would be productive to review the Estimating Your Project Cost section on page 306 if you're considering beginning the estimating process at this point. Otherwise, within the Planning Workbook, you would perform the estimating towards the end of step three. If the project isn't quite ready for the official estimating process, then you should review and refine the budget to ensure that you're still on the right track.

CONTRACTOR SEARCH

An added benefit of beginning the official estimating process at the end of step two is that it naturally initiates the search for a contractor.

It's like killing two birds with one stone: can you afford it *and* who will build it?

During the design process, you or your architect may have invited contractors in to collaborate with you. This offered an opportunity to work with each one and begin your contractor qualifying process early. Now would be the time to narrow down your candidates (assuming there's more than one). Otherwise, the end of the designdevelopment phase is your first opportunity to begin the search for contractors to execute your plans and specifications.

The motivating forces for a contractor to respond to your inquiry are how close your project is to starting, whether or not you have thorough plans and specifications, and how reasonable you are as a homeowner. We'll get into the details of hiring contractors in a bit, but there's one big opportunity at this juncture, and that is this: if you can locate one or more contractors, they may be able to assist in performing your budget checkpoint beyond the TAH system.

STEP TWO: DESIGN DEVELOPMENT CHECKLIST

DESIGN AND PLANS		
PLAN PAGES	RESPONSIBILITY	RESOURCES
3D renderings of your home on-site	Architect	Surveyor and civil engineer
Site plan	Architect	Surveyor and civil engineer
Floor plans	Architect	None
Elevations and sections	Architect	None
Structural plans (progress)	Architect	Structural engineer
MEP plans (mechanical/ HVAC, electrical/lighting and plumbing)	Architect	MEP designer/ engineers and interior designer

PLAN PAGES	RESPONSIBILITY	RESOURCES
Low-voltage plans and specifications	Architect	LV contractor or consultant and home automation specialists
Solar power plans and equipment	Architect	Solar power contractor or consultant
Interior design finish plans	Architect and homeowner	Interior designer
Interior design elevations	Architect and homeowner	Interior designer
SPECIFICATIONS		
Materials	Architect or homeowner	Interior designer and homeowner
Equipment	Architect or homeowner	MEP engineers, LV consultant, and contractors
Scope of work	Architect, homeowner, and agent	

WHAT TO FOCUS ON NOW

- Doing an early search for and qualifying of contractors.

- Having another pair of eyes to scrutinize the plans and specifications.

- Getting preliminary estimates for a more accurate budget checkpoint.

- Getting final cost estimates if the plans and specifications are ready.

2.150 STEP THREE: COMPLETING YOUR PLANS

A lot has occurred during step two of the design development! It felt like a whirlwind, with many people getting involved, ideas being tossed back and forth, materials being researched, and multiple meetings being held.

The purpose of doing budget checkpoints was to determine if you're prepared to continue with the final step in design as planned or if you need to make modifications to achieve your desired results. You may have decided to break the project into phases or options or abandon part of the project, but either way, now is the time to choose a definite path forward.

Step three initiates the process of completing your plans and specifications into written materials known as construction documents. You're now cementing all of the work done throughout the previous steps into a completed plan set and specifications for building permit applications and construction. From a time perspective, your design team may have spent the least amount of time on the construction documents, but they're the most important documents to have on hand as the project scope and plans are formalized.

THE OBJECTIVES OF CONSTRUCTION DOCUMENTS

- ✓ Finalize the design decision options, alternates, and phases.
- ✓ Complete the specifications: materials, equipment, and scope of work.
- ✓ Compile the plans suitable for permit submittals.
- ✓ Prepare for the construction launch.

DECISIONS THAT MUST BE MADE BEFORE THE PLANS ARE COMPLETED

✓ Selection of options and alternatives

✓ Selection of phases

✓ Scope of work and specifications finalization

✓ Final directions to your design team

With this huge milestone behind you and the completed plans in front of the design team, your architect goes into action and begins assembling the construction documents.

STEPS TO ASSEMBLE CONSTRUCTION DOCUMENTS

1. Revise and clean up the design and plans per your final choices and directions.

2. Complete any architectural and structural details on the relevant plan pages.

3. Complete any plan pages not previously mentioned, such as existing and demolition plans, roof plans, reflected ceiling plans, schedules, and architectural details. (See Understanding Plans on page 208 to expand your knowledge of plans.)

4. Insert compliance information for local and national building codes into the plan sets.

5. Compile all plan pages, consultants' pages, and supporting information into a "submittal set," which then goes to your Building department.

For the most part, as the homeowner, you should not need to participate much in step three other than to monitor the progress. That's because there could be changes you should be aware of because of the final construction documents step. It will be tough for you to pick these out on your own but not tough to ask your architect, especially since the buck stops with you. It doesn't take much for a designer to slip in one final construction detail that could cost you thousands, so ask, "Could you point out the things that have changed from the completed design development step to now? Especially the ones that could affect the cost or how something may look." Asking the questions you didn't know to ask is all about managing your expectations and holding those you hire accountable. Not to mention holding *yourself* accountable.

If you've followed the steps I've outlined to this point, then not only are you ready to submit your plans for a permit, there's a good chance you know who your contractor will be. If you still need to pin that person down, though, now is when you need to reach out to your candidates and obtain final proposals. Otherwise, this is the time to convey significant changes to your contractor candidates, obtain revised costs, and make final decisions. If nothing else is blocking your choices and the permitting process hasn't spurred any expected substantial changes, you can contract with your contractor while permitting occurs. But! *Before* you take this leap, refer to The World of Construction on page 261 to learn all about contractors and contracts and also read Understanding Design Limitations on page 180. It's a deeper dive, but it's paramount to understand what you may be up against.

DESIGN PROCESS REVIEW:
THE STEPPING STONES OF DESIGN _____

The goal here is to build your primary tools: a comprehensive design and detailed plans and specifications.

STEP ONE: CONCEPTUALIZE YOUR DESIGN
- ✓ Pursue your discovery exercise within your designer's creative process.
- ✓ Visualize your new home or remodel.

✓ Perform the budget checkpoint.

STEP TWO: LOCK IN YOUR DESIGN

✓ Select your plan and dig into the details.

✓ Put the entire design team to work.

✓ Specify materials, equipment, and the scope of work.

✓ Perform budget checkpoint or estimating.

STEP THREE: COMPLETE YOUR PLANS

✓ Provide final direction to your design team.

✓ Compile your plans and get them ready for permitting.

✓ Engage with your contractor candidates to finalize cost.

✓ Make an appointment to submit your building permit application.

———————————————————————————————————————

Now that you have a better understanding of design professionals and the design process, we'll shift gears and dig deeper into how design agreements are structured and what options you have in terms of entering into an agreement with your designer. The world of design continues! We'll also explore design limitations you may be up against and go into understanding plans in more detail, and we'll take a closer look at how to go about obtaining approvals and permits from your city or county.

2.200 DESIGN AGREEMENTS

Finding the right design professionals who fit you and your project begins to build the foundation of you having a successful experience. (For more details, see *Building Your Team on page 341.*) Your team will be your designers, consultants, and contractors. There are two common paths to take as well as some alternative routes. But before we get to hiring your team, you'll learn about the different methods that architects use to charge for their services. These options will matter to you when the time comes to select a design team! With this information in your knowledge bank, you can move into more details of the design world and the work products of architects. Let's delve into the framework of a design agreement and the various agreement methods: hourly, fixed fee, and percentage.

2.201 DESIGN AGREEMENT FRAMEWORK

The costs associated with project design are directly related to each step within the Design Process section on page 110. The proposals often break out the costs for each step: step one is schematic design, step two is design development, and step three is construction documents. There are also ancillary services your architect can provide (listed below), such as construction administration and building permit submittal.

Here's an example of how a design agreement framework could look:

DESIGN PHASE	FEE	PAYMENT SCHEDULE	AUTHORIZATION
Discovery mapping (optional)		Retainer	
Step one: schematic (flat rate)		Begin schematic drawings	
Step two: design development (flat rate)		Begin design development	
Outside consultants (flat rates; see schedule)		Submittal to client	
Step three: construction documents (flat rate)		Begin construction drawings	

Building permit submittal (optional*)		Submittal to city	
Construction administration (optional)		During construction	
TOTAL ESTIMATE * Not including city permit fees			

As you can see, each design step within the table can have a value in each Fee field. The "outside consultants" row is a placeholder for the consultants who may apply to your project. Understanding how your architect prefers to handle consultants is worth a conversation.

Here's an example of how a consultant's breakdown could look:

CONSULTANT	COST	ADMIN FEE	FEE TOTAL
Land survey (proposal)		25%	
Civil (proposal)		25%	
Geotech/soils (proposal)		25%	
Structural engineer (estimate)		25%	
MEP engineers		25%	
Fire suppression		25%	
Energy		25%	
Landscape (TBD)		25%	
Arborist (TBD if needed)		25%	
Other		25%	
TOTAL ESTIMATE			

Based on their individual proposals, each consultant has a value in the Cost field. It's not uncommon for an architect to facilitate the consultant process for many reasons, mostly related to their relationships and the coordination that needs to occur. In this example, the architect has added a 25% fee to the consultant's proposal to cover all of the time required to interface with the consultant.

The two optional steps of building permit processing and construction administration may or may not apply to your project, or you may elect to have them within your agreement. In the Approvals and Permits section on page 242, I uncover the building permit process. You must decide if you can facilitate this process; if you cannot, I recommend that you have your design pro handle it. Construction administration is an option for involving your design pro during the estimating and the construction progress. There can be real value there! I explore this further in the bonus content on the TAH site.

2.202 AGREEMENT METHODS

The most common arrangement for engaging with an architect is captured within three options: fixed fee, hourly, or percentage of construction. Each has its pros and cons, but all depend on the quality of the information you provide to obtain proposals. If you can articulate all of the information outlined in our first exercise (see *Dreams, Realities, and Focus on page 30)*, your architect or designer will love you and that will influence how they craft their proposal. Even though designers make a big part of their income based on the time they spend on a project, the passion comes from hitting the mark for their clients as early as possible, leading to an effective and efficient outcome. Your architect will be one of your best advocates as you move through the design and even construction process! Let's look at the three typical business models:

HOURLY

An hourly agreement pays your architect the set cost per hour stated in the declared rate schedule (see example below).

POSITION	RATE PER HOUR	DESCRIPTION
Architect/principal	$250	Lead architect or principal (often the owner of the firm or the individual who holds the license)
Designer	$175	A designer who may have a degree in architecture but does not have a license; the designer assists the principal with design activities
Design/drafting	$125	Responsibilities include assisting architects and designers by drafting and formatting plans

On the surface, an hourly agreement with anybody can seem scary—a client can equate an hourly deal as requiring them to have their checkbook be permanently open, with a never-ending experience in front of them. However, an hourly agreement can be very beneficial to the homeowner.

AN HOURLY AGREEMENT MAKES SENSE FOR...

✓ A client with extensive experience in home building or remodeling.

✓ A client who provides solid guidance with a clear focus on the style, specifications, and overall requirements for the design.

✓ A client who has plenty of time to spend on the project during the design process.

✓ A client for whom the cost of design is not the highest priority.

A homeowner who has those attributes enables the architect to focus on their core skills instead of moving the target multiple times by starting and stopping the design with numerous revisions. In theory, this can achieve a timely design process and accomplish design goals. An architect agreement would identify this method along with established billing cycles and payment policies.

RECOMMENDATIONS FOR CLOSING THE FEAR GAP

✓ Request that an estimated allocation of hours be attached to each step's hourly fee.

✓ Identify a "not to exceed" value for each step. The architect can gauge this request based on your profile, project type, complexity, etc.

✓ Request regular statements, including the hours spent on each step.

✓ Request a status update on how the progress is going. Ask "How are we doing?" and "Are we on track?" and "Is there anything I can do to keep us on track?"

FIXED FEE

Identifying a dollar cost for each design step can be a safe way to make both the architect and the homeowner comfortable. In our example, a dollar value would be placed in each row and you would pay at specified milestones. It sounds simple, but the relationship can wind up being degraded if the two parties aren't working closely together. In addition to the client attributes mentioned above, projects that could work under a fixed fee could be minor ones, including interior remodels, small additions, kitchens, and baths.

- A client with minimal experience in home building or remodeling.

- A client who has a high level of comfort and trust with the design team.

- A client who's willing to allow enough time for the design process to occur.

- A client who's willing to invest in design fees to achieve a superior design, plan set, and specifications.

- A client who's genuinely interested in having a quality construction experience.

A homeowner who has these attributes enables the architect to approach the project holistically, knowing that the client trusts them to handle things. The architect's creative mind is then empowered to begin the design process because the architect knows what the expected level of detail is. A fixed fee agreement can be a solid way to go if there are predefined limitations.

WHAT A FIXED FEE AGREEMENT MAY SET FORTH

- ✓ Limits the amount of design concepts.

- ✓ Limits the number of revisions before step two of the design process begins.

- ✓ Declares which plan pages will be included by the architect in the plan set (see Understanding Plans on page 208).

- ✓ Provides clear language on who provides interior design information.

- ✓ Provides clear language on who is responsible for documenting the specifications.

✓ Includes an understanding of which services will be included beyond the three steps: consultant coordination, permit processing, and construction administration.

PERCENTAGE OF CONSTRUCTION COST

At first glance, placing a value on design services relative to the construction cost can seem suspicious to a homeowner. You proclaim, "How is it that if my materials cost more, I pay my architect more??" The time spent on design time directly reflects the project's type, size, and complexity; therefore, those determine the design cost. For example, suppose you prefer a high-end window manufacturer in Italy instead of a local standard vinyl window maker. In that case, your architect will spend excessive time learning, detailing, and specifying the design, plans, and installation methods for the high-end window product. Multiply this by a hundred for higher-end projects, and you have design fees that surpass the standards. Somehow, the architect should be compensated to achieve your desires. That compensation could be hourly or it could be based on a percentage of the material and labor costs.

A PERCENTAGE OF CONSTRUCTION COST MAKES SENSE FOR...

✓ A client who prefers innovative and upper-end designs, products, and solutions.

✓ A client with limited time to spend on the details.

✓ A client who prefers to have one person see the project all the way through construction.

✓ A client with a project that's large in scope and size, such as a new custom home, a major remodel, or a tear-down.

A homeowner with these attributes gives the architect a clear design focus without being concerned about hourly or fixed price restrictions. This method can relieve a design professional of administrative accounting, plus it simultaneously builds in a certain level of accountability to an overall budget that's declared and that fees are based on.

In my experience, the percentage can range from 7% to 12% of the total construction cost, which includes the general contractor's cost for labor, materials, and subcontractors associated with the plans and specifications within their contract. This fee does not include the consultants' hard cost but rather the time needed to coordinate each consultant. If you did your homework and built a budget in the early discovery phase, you'll have a better idea of what your design costs could be. If you're thinking about going this route, you can dig deeper into the content regarding agreement methods on the TAH site.

Regardless of the method your architect proposes when requesting design proposals, however, you must understand *all* potential costs.

PRIMARY DESIGN COSTS TO CONSIDER WHEN MAKING DECISIONS

- Architect's fees (including staff)
- Consultants' fees
- Reproduction and technology expenses
- Permit processing (for Planning and Building departments)
- Construction administration

INTERIOR DESIGNER AGREEMENTS

Involving an interior designer in a new home or remodel project can close your expectation gap. The timing of this engagement can also influence an architect's proposal if they're aware that you plan to have a person assist in the interior aspects of the design—then the architect knows they don't need to allocate time for this area. Interior design is so important that interior designers may be staff members at the architecture firm. If they are, then open up a conversation about including them in the process. When beginning your search for an interior designer, know that some high-level skills should be in their coffers.

- Have the ability to design and draft floor plans, elevations, and details.

- Are skilled in space planning.

- Have the ability to provide 3D renderings of your spaces.

- Have the ability to articulate their proposed materials and fixtures in a format that helps you visualize them.

- Are knowledgeable about local and online resources for materials and fixtures.

A common theme you may have picked up on by now is that selecting and documenting *all* of the materials, fixtures, and equipment for the project is crucial. Making these choices in a timely manner results in thorough design, realistic cost estimating, and adherence to the construction schedule. Your interior designer can play a pivotal role in selecting and documenting these essential elements. In fact, doing so should be part of their services.

The arrangement with your interior designer can be more simplistic. Because they aren't starting with a blank canvas the way architects do, their scope of work is more straightforward to determine. For example, an interior designer is usually brought in once step one of the design process has been completed. This means everyone knows there's one kitchen, three bathrooms, and a fireplace, and there's also an aesthetic direction. Having this level of insight can enable the designer to provide a fixed price proposal for the project or allocate a realistic number of hours for an hourly agreement. In either case, be clear about what you want your interior design work to achieve.

WHAT CAN BE INCLUDED IN AN INTERIOR DESIGN AGREEMENT

- Collaborating with the architect.

- Assisting with selecting colors, materials, and fixtures.

- Presenting the proposed materials in a storyboard format.

- Providing floor plans, elevations, and details that identify the configurations and products.

- Providing 3D models that depict a reasonably realistic representation of the proposed materials.

- Documenting the product specifications within a scope of work document suitable for distribution to material suppliers and contractors.

Another option to consider is that if your project is on a smaller scale (such as a kitchen or bath remodel), a qualified interior designer may be all you need. During the course of my design-build business, I employed many interior designers to handle all aspects of designing, composing plans, and even obtaining permits. I found this to be a good fit for interior remodel projects.

2.300 UNDERSTANDING DESIGN LIMITATIONS

This may surprise you, but just because you own a piece of dirt doesn't mean you can do whatever you want on your property. Even in rural counties, there are rules as to what you can build. So unless you're in an extremely remote location like Mars, understanding design limitations will become very critical as you consider purchasing a property or if you have big plans to remodel a home you already own.

WHAT WE'LL COVER _____

- ✓ Evaluating your property

- ✓ City and county rules and regulations
- ✓ Homeowner's associations and design rules
- ✓ Project classifications and why they matter
- ✓ How property taxes play a role

2.301 PROPERTY EVALUATION AND ACQUISITION

Various outside forces can influence a project, whether you're purchasing a home to renovate or a lot to build on or you're remodeling your current home. Suppose you fall in love with a lot—the view, the size, the solitude. But have you thought about the utilities? Where are they and how much will it cost to get power a mile down the storybook tree-lined driveway? Where's the water service located? And what about potentially having to plow snow down a steep driveway?

Emotions can cloud the decision-making process and lead to unknown consequences. (Ben and Jane fell victim to this classic homeowner mistake in our prologue.) Say you're thinking about purchasing an existing home and you have visions to expand the house. But *can* you? How do you know? How much can you add? Are there easements, limitations, and so on? Does your realtor know? Do they really care? Who *truly* has your best interests in mind? Real estate agents, developers…who do you turn to?

An architect can provide tremendous value when considering purchasing land or modifying an existing home—their skills in placing structures on a parcel and their knowledge of local rules and regulations are invaluable. A contractor can supplement these factors with construction-related experience to balance out the information. Involving design and construction professionals as early as possible is what kicks off the Awakened Homeowner's guiding principles. Ultimately, whether or not you proceed will be a judgment call based on your experience and knowledge, and gaining both is what TAH is all about—I want to help enlighten, empower, and protect you! In that spirit, before you purchase that dream lot or lock in on your ideas for expanding your home, let's examine some often-overlooked information that could constrict your possibilities.

2.302 CITY AND COUNTY REGULATIONS

Each city and county has documented rules and regulations, often in the form of the municipal code. This is usually accessible online through the city or county website via their Planning department. If your property is located within a homeowner's association (HOA) area, you might have an additional set of rules and regulations that your architect must understand before design work begins.

Thoroughly researching these parameters *before* any design work begins is prudent but is also easily overlooked, deferred, misinterpreted, or assumed to be unnecessary. Qualified design professionals are well-versed in these typical design constraints and commonly take it upon themselves to understand these parameters before beginning any design work. That said, there are thousands of stories where a project was submitted to the city...only to be declined because it did not comply with criteria outlined in the municipal code or even deeper within outlying regulations, where criteria are not immediately visible.

2.303 PLANNING DEPARTMENTS

Within your city or county, government departments regulate the design and construction of buildings. To determine what's possible on your property, the Planning department will be your first stop. Think of this department as the entity that cares what your home will look like from the outside. City planners live by The Book of Zoning. Their job is to regulate the look, mass, and scale of a home by using the various documented ordinances established within the municipal code. They don't care about the inside, so if you're doing an interior remodel with no expansion or effect to the exterior, then I doubt you'd be dealing much with the Planning department if at all. But if you're planning an expansion or a new home, you'll be immersed in Planning department procedures to obtain the necessary approvals. For this exercise, we'll assume you're building a new home or doing a large-scale renovation.

Understanding and conforming to the zoning ordinances will be your path of least resistance when designing a project. It seems logical to understand these outside forces early, but homeowners and design professionals fall flat on their faces more often than you might think. Common causes of denied applications are ignoring the due diligence required, not taking preliminary steps to understand how to apply the ordinances to a specific site, assuming that the same rules apply from city to city in your area, mistakenly not conforming to standard ordinances, misinterpreting the rules, and/or intentionally exceeding the ordinances.

THREE PRUDENT STEPS YOU OR YOUR DESIGNER CAN TAKE TO SMOOTH OUT THE PLANNING APPLICATION PROCESS

1. Research the city/county Planning department website to gain as much knowledge as possible and highlight the confusing areas that are difficult to interpret.

2. Coordinate a pre-design meeting with a city planner to better understand the ordinances and how they apply to your specific parcel. Ask the questions that I've peppered throughout these sections.

3. Coordinate a pre-submittal meeting with a city planner to informally review what you intend on submitting.

Here's an outline of the criteria that your city Planning department will be referring to. Get up to speed on these *before* you begin designing your dream home!

2.304 ZONING DISTRICTS

Knowing the zoning district of your neighborhood within your municipality will be the first step to understanding the limitations imposed on your property. Again, these zones can often be found on your city website. The Zoning department posts zoning maps of the city or county and identifies each district with various categories and colors. Residential neighborhoods are often segregated by lot size and therefore have different rules. Here's a sample of a zoning map and the districts within a city:

Visit theawakenedhomeowner.com to see samples.

This sample is a snippet of the zoning map of the city of Saratoga, California. On the right is a legend defining each zoning district. In this case, Saratoga represents residential districts with "R-1" and lists a numeral corresponding to the minimum and maximum lot size, usually expressed in square footage or acreage. Here, the light-orange color identified as "R1-12,500" is a single-family lot greater than

10,000 square feet and up to 12,500 square feet. This information is essential as the rules for an R-1-10,000 lot differ from an R-1-12,500. These rules primarily dictate setbacks, floor area ratios, heights, and allowances (or not) for second stories. More on these crucial terms soon.

With these basic principles in mind, look up the zoning map for your own city and then investigate the rules governing your proposed project. These will be within the municipal code with the Zoning category. All of this municipal data is typically aggregated within a third-party website accessed through your city or county Planning department. Many cities use the same provider, which makes it easier to navigate through various codes. Here's a sample of a municipal code and its relevant sections:

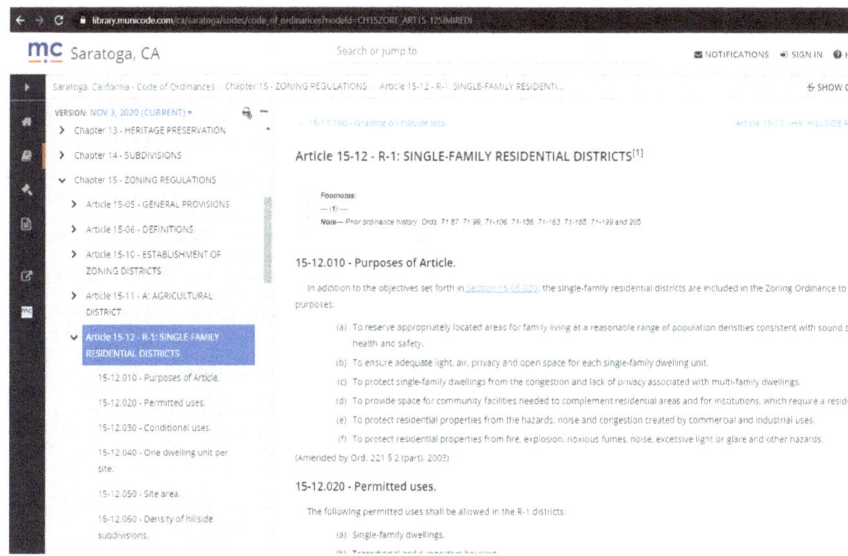

Visit theawakenedhomeowner.com to see samples.

I quickly found this site after searching for "city of Saratoga municipal code." I then navigated to the section titled Zoning Single Family Residential districts and ultimately scrolled to the appropriate R-1-12,500 district to learn my limitations. I could continue to drill down into each sub listing, but at the cost of losing you in the weeds... My goal here is to inform you of how to obtain the information so that you can intelligently converse with your design professional or research the design limitations yourself.

Once you and your architect have researched online tools for your city and have come away with a good understanding of the design constraints, you need to take *one* more step to ensure that your design pursuits are as productive as possible: physically visit the Planning department. This is prudent because in reading the municipal codes, there's always room for interpretation. This investigation especially applies to complex formulas used to calculate how large your home can be or how close it can be to the property line (the latter is known as a setback). You want to discover as much as possible about your property! Occasionally, supplemental rules to specific neighborhoods are not identified within the standard municipal code—instead, rules that supersede the standards within the published code could be attached to parcels and recorded.

Here's a real-life example that affected a project and ended up causing a redesign after plans for the project had been submitted to the Building department. There are historical districts within San Jose, California, with "secret rules" on setbacks. In the case of me and my client, the documented front yard setback was 20 feet from the property line. Unfortunately, in the 1940s, an extraordinary setback was recorded for this one-block neighborhood, indicating that the front yard setback was 25 feet from any portion of the structure, including overhangs. That effectively increased the front setback by 7 feet and drastically impacted the proposed design. This requirement was not documented within the code but instead was buried in a city archive that the Planning department uncovered during the submittal process. A visit to the Planning department after having researched the codes—accompanied by some prodding before designing—would have theoretically circumvented this issue. Interestingly, we *did* visit the Planning department and still got blindsided. That leads me to a supporting point.

A visit to the city Planning department is only as good as the person you meet with. Understanding the qualifications of the person seated behind the counter should influence how you tailor your questions. Planning departments typically have a hierarchy of administrative personnel: associate planners, senior planners, and department heads. It's common to begin your experience with an associate planner. That's okay if you go in knowing that this person needs to be better versed in interpreting the code and may require assistance as you dig into more complex issues.

Documenting your visit is essential! Take the business card of the person you meet with and others above this person. Record notes on the day and time of your visit. Encourage the planner to reference the municipal code and take note of the relevant sections. Ask "Is there anything specific to my site or neighborhood outside the code's bounds that could affect my project?" Take as much time as you need and as many notes as possible. Follow up with an email to the planner, and as required, CC the department head if you notice a discrepancy between what you were told and what is documented within the codes.

2.305 ZONING ORDINANCES

Once you've determined the zoning district and the location within the municipal code where you can learn about the rules and regulations, becoming familiar with the terms and calculations is your next task. Ordinances related to zoning districts are designed to protect the integrity of residential neighborhoods. From the size and scale of a home to even its paint colors, each community will have its own codes. That said, communities often have similar terms and restrictions. Let's explore many that you'll likely encounter.

2.306 FLOOR AREA RATIO (FAR)

In most cases, the size of your home is limited by your local Planning department. A handful of rules and methods dictate the size and scale of a house, theoretically achieving a responsible design for the neighborhood. It can be painful, but the goal is admirable. Have you ever lived in a neighborhood with some horrible gigantic pink palace plopped into a classic neighborhood? FAR is supposed to eliminate that. Each city and county has adopted rules with similar descriptions and methods. The first is how much living space you are allowed.

- FAR calculates your living area square footage as it relates to your lot size square footage, also known as the site area. As an example, let's say your home with a proposed addition is 2,300 square feet and the lot is 6,000 square feet. If you were to divide 6,000 by 2,300, you would get a 38% floor area ratio. A caveat: interpreting how your city defines "floor area" is essential. In many cases, it's *not* just the interior of your home. Some examples that increase the percentage are:

    - Attached garages or other structures can contribute to the structure's size and scale. Many cities include this in their FAR calculations, thus substantially increasing your FAR. If you include the typical 400-square-foot two-car garage in your FAR calculation, your proposed project is now at 45%.

    - Enclosed porches and patios exposed to the outside could be included in your FAR. Good examples are covered porches and patios with a roof that's integrated with the home and two or three walls. The logic is that these elements contribute to the size and scale and *could* be enclosed, thus increasing the living area. So if you have a front porch with walls on three sides that measure eight feet wide by five feet deep, this adds 40 more square feet to your calculations, taking you to 46%.

- Tall ceilings can double the FAR calculations. Vaulted and raised ceilings are common elements in homes today—entries, foyers, and living rooms often have two-story voluminous ceilings. As you enter the foyer, for example, you can look up 18 to 20 feet above you to see the suspended chandelier and the balcony overlooking the living room. Having to count that area twice is likely the price you'll have to pay for it. Bear in mind that this rule may apply when calculating your FAR! Sticking with our current example, let's say that you hoped to have exceedingly high ceilings in the entry and living room. You decided not to pursue the living room during the design process but still desired to accomplish having a high ceiling in the 50-square-foot entry area. This decision triggers the inclusion of another 50 square feet in your FAR calculation, taking you to 47%.

- Lot size matters. The allowable FAR on your lot can range from as little as 30% to not usually over 50%. Cities have zoning ordinances that establish the exact percentage allowed. A typical city postage-stamp-sized lot may be defined as R-1-6, meaning a residential single-family parcel up to 6,000 square feet. Within this zoning, the city may allow up to 45% FAR. Other neighborhoods in your community may have R-1-10, meaning lots up to 10,000 square feet with a FAR of 40%. More in-depth calculations determine the FAR, which you can learn about by visiting your city Planning department online or in person.

- "Net site area" is a term you may see that can also affect your home's size. That's because easements play a role in your FAR calculations. For example, if at the rear of your lot you discover a 5' wide by 60' long easement for a utility company to work on the overhead power lines or under-ground water service, you may have to deduct this area from your lot size to determine your net site area. This would mean that instead of a 6,000-square-foot lot to base your calculations on, it would be 5,700 square feet.

- Sloping lots can reduce your home size. Many communities built on sloping terrain have a formula that triggers a reduced FAR allowed relative to the slope percentage. Retaining a civil engineer or land surveyor will be required. Those two professionals will determine the average slope and percentage, ultimately reducing the allowable floor area. This nuance is a perfect example of how the principle "know what to ask" can possibly influence your purchase of a lot and will certainly influence the design of your expansion.

2.307 HEIGHT RESTRICTIONS

Limitations on the height of your new home are often embedded into the municipal code, which can relate to single- and two-story homes. Once again, this is to limit the mass and scale of a structure. So, what is "height," exactly? It sounds simple, but where do you begin the measurement and where do you end it? Each jurisdiction will handle this differently. Understanding exactly how to measure height early on in the process circumvents any costly redesign needs.

Many urban and suburban communities have 6,000- to 12,000-square-foot lots on city-paved streets with curbs, gutters, and sidewalks. The height measurement could begin from the top of the curb and then go up to the highest point of the roof peak. No big deal, but be careful! On many lots, the curb is lower than the grade around the house, indicating whether your driveway slopes up from the street. Determining the height from the curb to the roof peak can be difficult. This measurement can be accomplished in several ways, but doing so lies outside the bounds of an inexperienced homeowner. A survey of the property with a topographic map is one way (more on this later); using a laser transom (a fancy level) to establish heights is another way. It's best to consult with your architect about determining height measurements—then you'll better understand how to proceed.

To give you one example of how tricky this issue can get, in the case of a particular client I worked with, the curb was 2½ feet lower than the grade (dirt) around the house. Given a height limitation of 25 feet, the home height had to be reduced to 22½ feet off the adjacent grade to comply. With a proposed two-story home, the height calculation began to restrict the design—this usually affects the heights of ceilings on the interior and the roof slopes. So if you start combining the FAR for the first and second floors, the setbacks for the first and second floors, *and* any relevant height limitations, you can now see how your city is going to control the design of your home to a great extent. Understanding all of this information *before* starting the design process is paramount to setting realistic expectations.

2.308 LOT COVERAGE

This one can sneak up on you late in the design process! Awareness of this not-so-popular restriction early on in the design process may influence your decisions. Lot coverage commonly refers to *any* buildings on the property, including your home, attached or detached garage, shop, barn, covered roofs, extended eaves, sheds, etc. Lot coverage is a percentage of the lot size, much like the FAR calculation mentioned previously. So although the FAR calculation of 45% may allow you to build a 2,700-square-foot home and garage, the lot coverage calculation could be 50% to 60% of the lot's square footage. If you have existing outbuildings or want some in the future, you may need to decrease the size of the home. Designing or modifying a house on a small lot can quickly become challenging.

2.309 IMPERVIOUS COVERAGE

Impervious coverage is any surface that prevents water absorption from precipitating into the earth. If you have a detached garage, covered patio, pool, concrete walkways, and/or any patio, these areas need to be calculated much like the FAR, which is to say as a percentage of the lot.

Historically, cities allowed drainage into the municipal storm drain system. This allowance has changed, however, and the preference now is to keep water on-site to recharge groundwater aquifers. Therefore, there needs to be a certain percentage of the area on a lot that can absorb water. Pervious products and design solutions exist to achieve this requirement, like concrete and pavers that allow water to permeate.

2.310 SETBACKS AND PROPERTY LINES

Setbacks are dimensions required from the outside walls of your home to your property line; these influence the size and scale of the house just as the FAR does. Assuming that fencing has been placed precisely on the property line is a frequent mistake made by homeowners and design professionals alike. A prime reason why? Particularly in older neighborhoods, fences have been improperly replaced over the years. But here's what's even worse: assuming that the existing home is within the current setback requirements. That is a recipe for disaster! Establishing property lines is paramount to understanding boundaries and is the benchmark for establishing setbacks.

Fortunately, there are a few steps you can take to gauge your proximity to the original property lines.

Let's create a likely scenario by taking a quick look at the county assessor's website. You've established that your rectangular lot size is 60 feet wide by 100 feet and has 6,000 square feet. You measure along the back fence from the center of each neighbor's fence, and you're at 60 feet. Okay, you're good there. You do the same thing along the front, and it's very close. You then measure from the back fence towards the front of the lot and stop at 100 feet. In your case, this is where the sidewalk begins.

Overall, you've established that the fencing locations are pretty accurate. Next up, you measure from the side of the house to the fence at the front, which comes to 5 feet. You then move to the back of the house and come up with 4½ feet. *Huh?* Wait a minute! How could this be??

A few things could be happening here. First, the fence has a bend; second, the house is not parallel to the property line. Third, your lot is not in fact a rectangle as you assumed it was. All of these conditions will affect the design of your new primary suite addition that you expect to align with your house. Researching the setback requirements with your city will tell you if you can align your new addition with the old house.

Zoning dictates the FAR and also determines the setbacks. Often, the smaller the lot, the smaller the setback. You quickly learn that the setback requirement is 5 feet on each side, 20 feet at the front, and 25 feet at the back. So now you're stuck with 4½ feet at the side towards the back of your home. If you extend the primary suite out another 20 feet, it becomes clear that the house is not parallel to the property line. Now you're in big trouble, because unfortunately, your contractor uncovered this during the construction of the foundation.

Hiring a land surveyor or civil engineer is the way to mitigate risk and any assumptions your designers could make.

2.311 EASEMENTS

A legal right of way granted to another person or entity to gain access to a portion of your property is an easement. Technically, you cannot use easement areas to build on, whether it's a structure, swimming pool, or patio. A typical example of an easement is a PUE or public utility easement, where the power company has reserved the back 5 feet of your property to install and maintain the overhead power lines. Likewise, your water company may have a main water line running along the front of your property you never knew about, and so on. Although these elements are part of your 6,000-square-foot lot, you have granted your utility company the right to use these portions forever. A not-so-common easement can be an easement given to a neighbor behind you to gain access to their property. Landlocked lots are an excellent example of needing these easements, and often, property owners are unaware of said easements until the time has come for their neighbor to gain access. In older communities, underground pipelines can dissect a property right down the middle. Because it's not visible to you, these can go unnoticed until the day comes to plan a new home or expansion. You may be wondering how this impacts the project.

WHAT TO UNDERSTAND ABOUT EASEMENTS (AND WHAT TO ASK QUESTIONS ABOUT)

- Easements can affect the size of the lot when calculating the FAR. Each city will handle this differently, plus site specifics may affect how or if this deduction is applied. For example, if you have a 5' side by 60' long 300-square-foot easement along the back of your property, you'll need to reduce the calculation from 6,000 to 5,700 square feet to determine the size of home you're allowed. This adjustment is known as the net site area.

- Setbacks are not typically affected by easements, but I've seen occasions where road easements can affect setbacks, so this point is a little more precarious. For example, if you have a side setback requirement of 10 feet and a ten-foot easement for your neighbor to gain access to the property behind you, the question arises of "Can I build right on the easement line?"

Below is an example of how an easement can affect your buildable area. This two-acre parcel is dissected by a ten-foot-wide PUE (public utility easement) as shown in red. The easement is for underground power, cable, and phone utilities from the street to the neighboring lot. You would never have known this by simply walking along the site. As you can see, this reduces the size of the buildable area by cutting off the right section of the lot—a home cannot extend into that area. Furthermore, the dashed line set 20 feet from the property boundary is the setback where no structures are allowed.

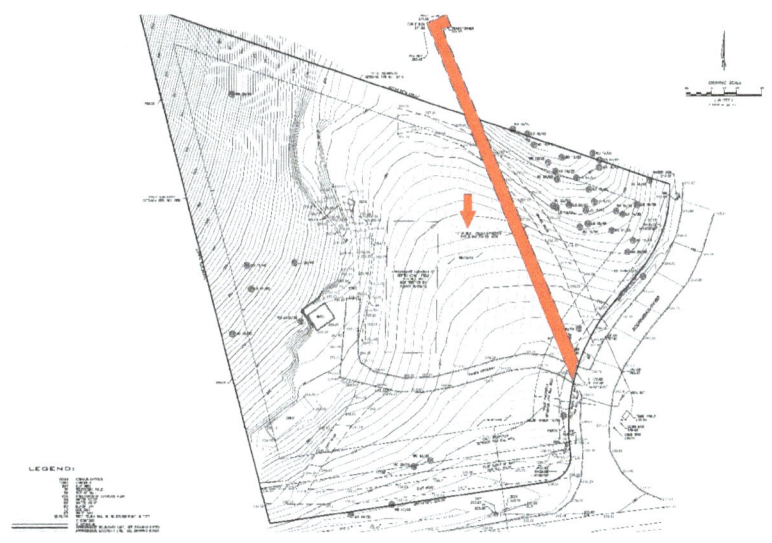

When you purchase your home, easement declarations exist within your purchase documents and title reports; these are recorded by the county. Understanding how your city and county deal with easements is an intelligent step. Your design professional should be aware of all these parameters, but here comes that word: *assuming* that they're aware opens you up to considerable risk.

2.312 TWO-STORY HOMES

Putting the squeeze on two-story homes is the objective for many cities, especially in existing urban and suburban neighborhoods. Two main factors control the size and scale of a house: 1) The FAR is calculated similarly, but be aware that many jurisdictions only allow a percentage of the downstairs square footage to be allocated to the second floor, so if you have a home that's 1,500 square feet on the first floor, you may only be able to add up to 750 square feet upstairs. 2) Setbacks for the second floor could also be handled differently by your town. Many cities require a more considerable side setback for the second floor than the first floor to reduce mass, promote design interest, and be sensitive to neighbors. Consequently, you could have a five-foot setback on the first floor but a seven- to eight-foot setback on the second floor.

2.313 PARKING

The closer you are to an urban area and the larger the city is, the more parking restrictions there are. Homeowner's associations are also known for mandating parking requirements. While designing your new home or significant remodel, don't let this one slip you by as you get deeper into the design process!

I can unfortunately speak from firsthand experience when it comes to this issue—I once had a project that the homeowner and I took too far down the path only to have to turn back and redesign it. In the homeowner's community of small urban lots with homes dating back to the 1940s, many homes had detached and attached one-car garages. The client wanted to design the project with a one-car garage, and my design staff thought that would be acceptable given the existing homes. Once we had a design concept together, we visited the city. They said it was OK, apparently without checking the code. We proceeded with the process, completed the design and plans and engineering, and submitted documents for the building permit. Then the dreaded day arrived in our inbox: the city told us that the home had to have *two* covered parking spaces. Our jaws dropped. Lesson learned.

Parking regulations exist to prevent congestion on your neighborhood street. Typical requirements are the width and depth of parking spaces found inside a garage or carport. Some cities will only require one covered space and one uncovered space, but beware! Placing a parking space in a property setback is not usually acceptable.

2.314 TREES

If you live in an urban or suburban area, to some degree, trees can be a player when the time comes to expand your home. Terms such as "heritage trees" and "protected trees" with their corresponding sizes will dictate how you must address their involvement. The primary triggers that force a homeowner to engage in the tree process are:

- The width of the tree trunk at a specified height from the ground indicates the approximate age of the tree.

- Many cities publish a list of trees that are "protected" by dint of their species. This can trigger compliance requirements.

- The tree's condition will also play a part in whether or not you get an approval to remove it.

For example, let's say that you're planning on adding your primary suite 20 feet into the backyard and you're facing different scenarios.

Scenario One: *A tree is right smack in the middle of the addition. The circumference and species of the tree define it as a protected tree.*

Scenario Two: *There's a protected tree within five feet of the new addition, so theoretically, it could stay. But can it?*

Projects involving protected trees have a laundry list of required steps with policies that range dramatically from city to city and county to county.

- Arborists represented by the city and homeowner must participate in the assessments. They compare notes and decide what is the best course of action.

- Tree protection plans are required and created by your architect or arborist if you plan to remove a tree close to your project.

- Replacement of removed trees elsewhere on the property is a common stipulation of approval. Another is contributing to a city fund to replant trees elsewhere within the city boundaries.

- As you're preparing your design and assuming you'd like to keep that heritage oak tree in your backyard, consider a few dynamics of trees that can bite you during the approval process and construction costs. I am not an arborist, but this info stems from experiences I've had on various projects.

  - The tree canopy forms a drip line that your city building department may find unacceptable to build underneath.

- The tree roots are within the canopy *and* beyond it. These can impede the foundation of the new expansion. Alternative foundation design can mitigate this, but at a cost.

2.320 FLOOD ZONES, RIPARIAN SETBACKS, SEISMIC ZONES, AND FEMA

Restrictions related to local and federally declared hazard zones that are not buildable or severely restrict possibilities could apply to your parcel. For example:

- If your parcel is adjacent to a creek, river, or drainage and your existing or proposed home is near this body of water, then additional rules will inevitably apply. Such restrictions can affect where and how you can build or remodel your home. If you have an existing home in a FEMA flood zone and desire to expand, you may be required to elevate the new portion above your existing home. As you can imagine, this could present complex design challenges.

- A state or federally declared fault zone may be located within your property or be close enough to restrict development.

- If your home is on the coast, researching what hazard zones your parcel may be in is prudent before purchasing a property or planning a new build or remodel. FEMA can drastically restrict the size of your project and the engineering of the home, which drives cost and feasibility considerations.

2.321 WILDLAND-URBAN INTERFACE

Known as WUI, this designation identifies properties prone to wild-fire risk nationwide. A proposed project in the WUI comes with design criteria to combat damage to structures in the event of a fire. Once again, this can affect the methods and materials used to build or remodel your home and will inevitably affect the cost. Knowing these criteria as early as possible will influence your design or perhaps prompt you to reconsider purchasing a property.

To research parcels that may be affected, visit:

https://msc.fema.gov/portal/home

https://www.fema.gov/sites/default/files/2020-07/fema_p213_08232018.pdf

http://silvis.forest.wisc.edu/data/wui-change/

2.322 HISTORICAL PROPERTIES

Across the nation, cities, counties, and states have established historic neighborhoods and buildings to protect the integrity of neighborhoods and the heritage and history of our country. These neighborhoods are often identified and recorded within the local jurisdiction by an acting entity such as a historical society and are recorded within the Planning departments of city and county offices.

In rare cases, a home could be on the National Registry of Historic Places, which is an entirely different governance level. You likely discovered this identification when you purchased your home, but if you didn't, it's worth checking to see if there's any chance your home is in a historic area. At first glance, these neighborhoods are usually identifiable as older neighborhoods (pre-1940s) featuring historic architecture such as Victorian and Craftsman styles. However, other factors can come into play, such as buildings designed by a famous architect, inhabited by a famous person, or home to a significant historical event. Regardless, inquiring about potential historic designations at your local Planning department is prudent before beginning the design process.

Historic buildings can pose extremely demanding design constraints. These rules aim to protect the aesthetic integrity of the structure's exterior. Depending on the level of historic classification and city enforcement, a designation could mean that modifications on the exterior are not permissible unless the proposed changes match the existing structure. For example, a town in my area—Los Gatos, California—dates back to the 1800s. Many neighborhoods and homes within the core downtown area are from the Victorian and Craftsman eras, with unique architectural designs and features. I once had a renovation project that involved replacing rotting windows within this Victorian neighborhood. My team and I were mandated to replicate the existing windows, which were very custom—they had arched elements, custom-milled moldings, and other unique features. This forced us to work with a custom mill workshop in Oregon to build the windows. The cost was four times the price of a typical double-hung window. To add even more requirements, the original redwood siding profiles had to be replicated to maintain the house's integrity. Once the project was completed, you would never know we had touched those windows.

Working within a historic district can complicate things during the design steps. Conforming to the rules is one aspect, but factoring in the time needed to obtain approvals is another. Most cities will not accept a building permit application until the historic arm of the Planning department has approved the project, adding weeks and even months to the timeline of designing and obtaining building permits. As I mentioned earlier in the section on zoning (see page 184), a visit to the planning office is prudent. And don't expect to uncover all of your possible restrictions unless you ask a lot of questions!

2.323 HOMEOWNER'S ASSOCIATIONS (HOAS)

Knowing your neighborhood or the community you plan to build in will likely play a big part in whether you want to purchase a home or a lot in your selected area. That's because many planned communities have established guidelines that can dramatically direct the design of your home, even dictating the architectural style, exterior materials, heights of buildings, landscaping elements, and on. These guidelines are often rolled into the HOA and are controlled by a design review committee, usually composed of your neighbors who will scrutinize your design. If you're purchasing a new home or lot in a planned community, reviewing these documented HOA guidelines is vital before you follow through with the purchase.

Thousands of folks have fallen in love with a lot and purchased it on the spot...and then come to find out they were heavily restricted in terms of what size and style of home could be built. Complying with HOA design policies can be a steep part of the path to your new home. If you don't thoroughly review such policies *before* your purchase or design, your new home could be the disappointment of a lifetime.

Architects seasoned in custom home design and renovations within planned communities could be your best go-to person to decipher complex rules. I say *could* be because if an architect has not worked in your community before—or worse, not dealt with HOA design review committees before—there's a higher chance of getting eaten alive by the board.

Remember that the first mandate of HOA design review guideline committees is to protect their members' investments and foster an aesthetically pleasing community. On the flip side, HOAs with relaxed guidelines or enforcement can also be a bad thing. I've been in many communities where high-end homes all look alike, and I've seen others where the styles, colors, and sizes of homes are so dramatically different that there's no resemblance between them. I bet you've seen those areas as well. Finding a balance is the key.

Let's pause for a moment and take a breath. We just went through many obstacles that came at us from all sides, particularly in terms of design parameters that are often overlooked and misinterpreted, thus potentially sabotaging a project. Ensuring that you're in the right hands boils down to having the knowledge to suss out the level of experience and professionalism your designer has. If a licensed, experienced architect were to read the previous list of potential design limitations, they would probably say "Obviously!" But it's easier than it seems to fall prey to the multiple drivers that push you towards the home you desire even if that path is going to be rocky or even impossible. In the interest of smoothing your own path, we're going to look at just a few more potential blindsiders you need to be aware of.

2.340 PROJECT CLASSIFICATION

It seems strange, but your remodeling and addition project may be considered a new home in the eyes of your city. This section sheds some light on how your project gets classified, which in turn directly impacts the requirements of the Planning and Building departments.

It's pretty straightforward in part: if you have an empty lot and plan to build a home, your project classification is "new." But what if your project involves a significant renovation and expansion where you plan to keep a portion of the home intact but demolish part of it, add space, replace all the windows and siding, and have a new-*looking* home by the end of the project? This dynamic matters, because if your remodel project is classified as a "new" home, then all of the rules, ordinances, and building codes that would apply if you were starting with an empty lot are now in effect. Note that this determination varies across the country; in some areas, there's no such thing as a classification process.

So, what can affect your project if it's considered to be a new home? Here's a short list that could apply, and then we'll look to see how this classification is defined in many urban and suburban areas.

- ✓ The Planning department approval process has to be followed as if it were a new home.
- ✓ The project must conform to all zoning ordinances (such as setbacks) even if your existing home does not.
- ✓ The entire home must comply with building codes.
- ✓ You must have fire suppression systems such as sprinklers.
- ✓ Green building requirements will apply.

Each city will have a way to classify a project if an applicable policy is in place. We're about to explore a few such possible policies to enlighten you and protect you from getting an unwelcome surprise deep in the design process.

2.341 THE 50% RULE

The project could be a new home if your new design increases the living area by more than 50%. So if you have an 1,800-square-foot home (not including the garage) and you increase the home to 2,700 square feet, *BAM!* A complete set of additional rules could apply to the project. The city figures that above 50% of the entire home is impacted, so therefore the structure must be upgraded to meet current codes. Safe to say, this will increase the cost of the project. Being aware of this possibility can empower you to take charge early on and ask the right questions, because we know who the buck stops with...*you!* Once you understand a rule like this, you can remain in the driver's seat.

COMPLEX CALCULATION RULE

In northern California, cities have made this classification determination even more difficult. Rather than just looking at the 50% rule, they want to understand better how much the existing structure will be affected. Understanding this interpretive rule ahead of time is ideal. Cities will look at the square footage and lineal footage of materials that will be removed or impacted—for example, siding, roofing, exterior walls, interior walls, flooring, etc. Calculating this can take some time and it's best that your design professional handles such calculations.

Why does this matter? In our previous scenario, we added 50% more than the existing home. However, with this method, you could only add 450 square feet but wind up remodeling the entire house, thus impacting the abovementioned materials. Although the home will look new, you're actually only increasing the square footage by 25%.

This complex method can get incredibly involved, so I'll leave things there. By asking the right questions, hopefully you'll become aware of and be in front of this potential limitation. Here are a couple of tips:

✓ Clearly understand how the 50% rule is applied. Does the city include the garage? Does lot coverage play a factor? If so, then...

✓ Consider intentionally designing the project to fall under the 50% rule. Instead of a 2,700-square-foot home, for example, you may be able to live with a 2,650-square-foot home.

✓ Take a closer look at what you think you may be saving by keeping a portion of the home intact. It may surprise you that a complete demolition is an option should you desire to keep the house at 2,700 square feet or beyond.

✓ Become aware of how the county tax assessor will treat your project if it's classified as a new home.

2.342 HOW YOUR DESIGN AFFECTS PROPERTY TAXES

One last factor to be aware of is how property taxes can impact your ideas. If you have property taxes in your state or province, it's safe to say that when you're building or remodeling your home, the Tax Man will find you, reassess the value of your home, and establish your new annual property taxes. I bring this to your attention now as this could influence your overall budget before you move into the design phases.

In my experience, reassessment is inconsequential if a project renovation stays within the "four walls" and no additional square footage increases the living area. But once you expand the home's total square feet, add bedrooms and bathrooms, and increase the property's value, you'll likely trigger a reassessment. Each county has its formulas to establish the value of a project, so I won't delve into specifics here, but know that they will base it on per-square-foot of new space and existing space that has been affected. Usually, a typical renovation and room addition is not highly impactful to property taxes, but what can blindside you is if your project is so large that it pushes itself into a different classification.

DESIGN LIMITATIONS REVIEW

Whether you've purchased your property yet or not, understanding what you may be up against begins with knowing that restrictions may be lurking around the corner. Visit with your architect and Planning department to understand *exactly* what those may be. Here's a quick refresher on the concepts we've covered:

✓ Zoning district and ordinances

- A set of predetermined rules and regulations based on lot size.

✓ Floor area ratio (FAR)

- The allowable living area relative to lot size.

✓ Height restrictions

- The height of your new home is measured from a point dictated by the city.

✓ Lot coverage

- The allowable footprint of structures on the site based on lot square footage.

✓ Impervious coverage

- The lot area is covered with buildings and materials that water cannot penetrate.

✓ Setbacks

- The distance the home can be from the property lines.

✓ Easements

- Others have rights to the property, which influences the design.

✓ FEMA hazard zones

- Flood zones and other restrictions can affect the design and cost of your home.

✓ Wildland-urban interface

- Being in a WUI-designated area will affect the design and cost of your home.

✓ Parking

- Mandated parking requirements can reduce the buildable area.

✓ Trees

- Coveted tree species and sizes need to be addressed.

✓ Historical properties

- Your home must comply with the historical aims of the city.

✓ HOAs

- The earlier you understand the rules, the better off you and your project will be!

✓ Project classification

- An extensive remodel could be considered to be a "new" home, which would then drive code requirements and costs.

✓ Property taxes

- The Tax Man may reassess your home upon completion and increase your taxes.

2.400 UNDERSTANDING PLANS

This section takes a deep dive into understanding plans. I intentionally placed this section *after* the design process because I wanted you to first understand the players, the design process, and design limits before you get bombarded with even more details. As you embark on designing your project, I recommend referring back to this section to gain a deeper understanding of each page of your plans. And don't worry too much when the time comes to review those plans—I have an arsenal of tools and checklists that cover everything you're about to learn.

Due to the size and complexity of plan pages, it's virtually impossible to visually demonstrate plans within a book. Therefore, I have assembled a sample plan set at the TAH site, where you may join the community, view the samples, and harness learning opportunities.

WHAT WE'LL COVER _____

- ✓ What are plans?
- ✓ The composition of plans
- ✓ Architectural pages
- ✓ Civil engineering plans
- ✓ Structural engineering plans
- ✓ Energy compliance
- ✓ Interior design

WHAT ARE PLANS?

Historically, plans were referred to as "blueprints," but in recent times, they've become known as simply "plans" or "plan sets." The final plan set is the work product of your architect, designers, and consultants. Your design team will tap into their knowledge, professionalism, talents, and skills to create drawings, details, and specifications depicting your new home. Your plan set will be the number-one accountability tool for you as the homeowner to convey the project's design, technical information, and construction methods to your contractors. Lastly, your plans coupled with a set of specifications empower you to obtain final and accurate costs.

After the huge milestone of completing the plan pages, they're compiled into construction documents. These are the final work product of your architect and design team and are combined with the specifications and the scope of work that was used to obtain permits. Bear in mind that your final construction documents convey the work that's to be performed by your contractors and the materials that are to be provided. Ultimately, these factors determine the final cost of your new home.

Understanding what plans are, how they're organized, the work that goes into them, and who will be doing the work empowers you to make informed decisions as you interview design candidates, monitor your design progress, and interview potential contractors. To get started, let's dig into a typical plan set for a single-family residential project. Then when you're ready to see more examples of these pages, you can visit the TAH website and join the TAH community.

2.401 THE COMPOSITION OF PLANS

SIZE AND SCALE

The plans are 24" x 36" size sheets of paper (known as D+ size in the industry). Other sizes could be used, but this is the most common size for residential projects. Architects and designers draw in scale, which means they've reduced the size of your home down to fit on the paper size and have correctly proportioned the pictorial representation of your home. This is Design 101, but I wanted to at least touch on this subject to help you interpret drawings and communicate with your designer and builder.

A quite common scale your architect will use is this: one-quarter of an inch equals one foot (¼" = 1'), primarily used for floor plans. Other scales are used for more detailed drawings, such as one-half of an inch = one foot (½" = 1') or three-eighths of an inch equals one foot (⅜" = 1'). Scale rulers are available to purchase; these are a staple in any designer's studio. This implement allows you to simply measure a room and then know that the 4-foot-wide room would be 16 feet at the scale of ¼" = 1'. Plan pages (also referred to as sheets) commonly indicate the scale used to prepare the drawings. Professional designers and architects usually have a designated area on every page where the scale is stated.

2.402 PAGE DESIGN

On each page, you'll see a border detail around the perimeter of the page. This is often referred to as the title block. On the right-hand side (the 24-inch edge from bottom to top), you'll commonly see the Page Label, Job Name, Scale, Date, and Drawn By fields. The next two areas could be in either order but usually include the Design Firm and Project Info fields. Lastly, the box at the top right is the Revision Date field. One of the most important fields in the border is the Dates To Track their revisions.

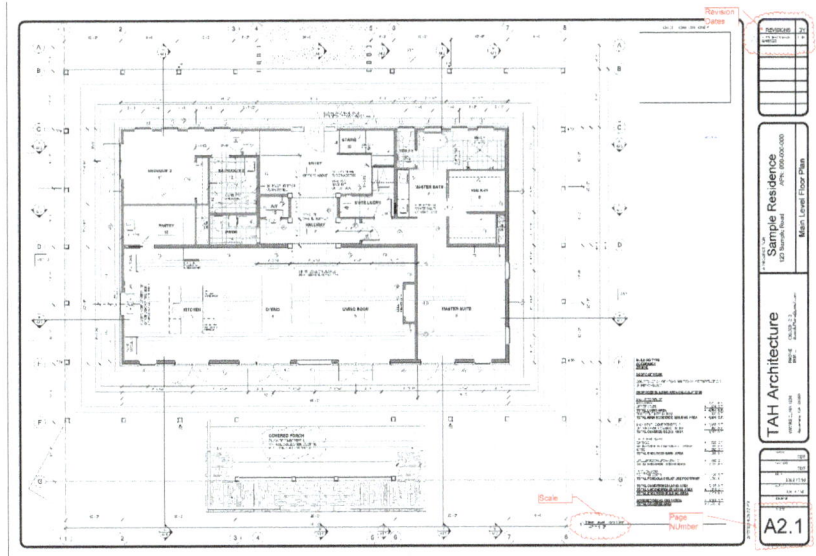

Sample architectural floor plan page
Visit theawakenedhomeowner.com to see samples.

ORGANIZATION AND LABELING

It's important for you to understand how plan sets are organized so that you can communicate intelligently with your design team and your contractors when the time comes to hand off the plans for estimating and construction.

Just about every set of plans includes a way of organizing and identifying the pages. Each plan page will be labeled with acronyms organized by various portions of the project and the discipline of each design team member. To demonstrate this kind of labeling, I'll identify each sheet using the letter-number system you'll likely see used in a similar way when you begin your project.

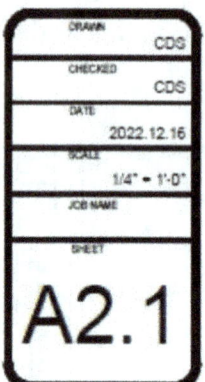

In this example, the page number is A2.1. The A stands for "Architectural," the 2 represents the pages associated with floor plans, and the .1 is a secondary level created to organize the pages.

Here's a close-up of the legend of all of the pages; it's located on the title page,

ARCHITECTURAL

A1.1	Site Plan
A2.1	Main Level Floor Plan
A2.2	Upper Level Floor Plan
A2.3	Basement Floor Plan
A2.4	Roof Plan
A2.5	Detached Garage Plans
A2.6	Cabana
A3.1	Exterior Elevations
A3.2	Exterior Elevations
A3.3	Garage Elevations
A3.4	Cabana Elevations
A4.1	Building Sections

Understanding this organization method will help you locate and refer back to pages as you interact with your designers and builders.

The size and complexity of the project often trigger variations of this organizing and labeling system. The sample project I'm using, for example, depicts an extensive new custom home.

Although this isn't a course on how to prepare plans, I hope that the insights I've provided here will help you better understand your architect's methodology and where information is located within the plan set. Knowing this empowers you to communicate intelligently with your design and construction team.

PLAN PAGE DATING

The revision dates that are often located in the upper right-hand corner of the title block often get ignored, which confuses everybody. For example, revisions may have been made between the bid set and the final plan set...but no dates were entered in the field. Without a proper way to track revisions, your builder could inadvertently be working off the older bid set, causing mistakes to occur. Guess who gets to pay to redo the work? You. As plan sets are issued to you and your construction team, I highly recommend that you monitor this Revision Date field on your plan pages to ensure that the plans that have been issued are dependable.

2.410 ARCHITECTURAL PAGES AX.00

Your plan set will begin with the drawings and details prepared by your architect or residential designer and be followed by a compilation of consultant's drawings coordinated with the architect. In the following section on understanding plans, I'll outline the common plan pages within a plan set accompanied by some examples. Since it's impossible to display every page within a book format, I've assembled a plan set at the TAH site for your perusal.

Usually, the first pages of the plan pages created by your architect are the title page and site plans. With remodel and addition projects, it's important to show both the existing home and the new home at certain locations in the plan set, so you may see a reference to both. This can help others disseminate between new and old and the scope of work that's required. But don't assume that the latter will be included in your standard plan set! Within the A sheets of the plan set, a variety of drawings are often included. Let's look at the typical ones.

TITLE PAGE

The first page of the plans is called the title page; it's also called the cover sheet because it captures the project summary information. Common inclusions in this page are a visual representation of the project, a scope of work narrative, a map pinpointing the address, project data such as square footage and site calculations, a list of all design professionals involved in the project, a table of contents listing page labels and descriptions, and legends that define acronyms, labels, and drawing details.

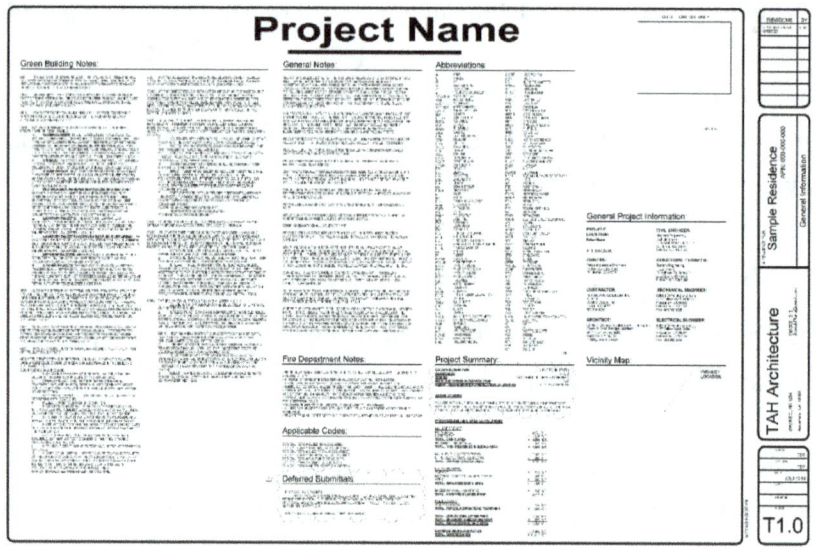

Visit theawakenedhomeowner.com to see samples.

SITE PLAN AS.00

A documentation of your entire lot with the home situated on the site—that's the simplest way to describe what a site plan is. It coordinates the surveyor's data obtained during step one of design (schematic design) with your architect's design of the home placed on the site, which in turn is eventually finalized with input from the civil engineer. You'll learn about the latter in this section.

Site plans are required by city and county Building and Planning departments and are especially scrutinized by the Planning department to ensure compliance with all of the rules and regulations. If you're embarking on an extensive remodel and expansion project or demolishing the existing home, then demonstrating the existing conditions and new project graphically within a site plan can enable the Planning department to fully understand the scope of the work. A site plan that includes information pertaining to a remodel also assists your contractor and subcontractors when the time arrives to introduce them to the project.

THE MAIN ITEMS REQUIRED ON A SITE PLAN AND HOW THEY CAN BENEFIT YOU

- Property lines: Locating the property lines as opposed to simply assuming you know where they are elevates the accuracy of the design, reducing the risk of building on portions of your site that aren't allowed and allowing you to correctly calculate the lot area.

- Easements and setbacks: Graphically identifying the easement and setback restrictions positions your design team to consider them fully while conceptualizing your new home. Between setbacks and easements, all too often one or both are either not considered or misunderstood, leading to wasteful design time that costs you-know-who.

- Utilities: Spotting the location of the utilities entering the property is valuable when communicating with your design team and eventually your contractor. Locating the POE (point of entry) to the site is the first step. In the case of a remodel or expansion, identifying where the utilities enter the building is the next step. Examples of utilities you'll benefit from pinpointing are water, sewer, gas, electricity, and communications. Identifying the precise locations of each will provide the kind of information that's too often missing and thus will allow you to nail down the costs associated with connecting various utilities to your home. Trenching distances and other relevant obstacles are prime examples of which elements can be exposed early on that can potentially affect the design. Knowing these means you can dodge an unknown cost bullet—otherwise, your contractor might tell you, "I had no idea that the electrical service was across the street! That'll be another 10K, please."

- Obstacles: Trees first come to mind. At a minimum, identify any trees in the path of your project and/or trees that the city or county might require to be protected during construction. Although county requirements can range widely, at a minimum, trees must be spotted on the lot and their diameter or circumference and species must be noted. For example, any tree with a diameter of 12 inches will likely need to be documented on the site plan to ensure that they're addressed by the Planning department and identified as being protected or not protected. Rock outcroppings can be a nemesis since you don't know what might be lurking beneath the surface. Identifying where rock outcroppings are on a plan can influence the placement of your new home or addition and potentially save you thousands of dollars—dynamite and blasting are a real thing in some areas and don't come cheap.

- Buildings: Accurate placement of *all* buildings within the boundaries of the property serves multiple purposes. Knowing where structures such as the main residence, garage, shop, and shed are with respect to setbacks and easements empowers you to know what complies and what might not. Older properties that have been built up over the years are prime candidates for nonconforming structures blindsiding you when the city planner declares that your garage is in a setback and must be torn down. Precisely understanding the square footage of your structures shines a light on your lot coverage and how much you can expand or build; it's a valuable tool for identifying structures in the path of your project that must be removed.

- Hardscapes, pools, driveways, and roads: Locating all of these on a site plan has an immense value, from the design phase to bidding exercises. Although it's often overlooked, specifying the area of hardscape that's to be removed and/or installed protects you; on the flip side, lacking this information leads to misunderstandings and inevitable change orders from your contractor. Remember lot coverage? One of its elements is the hardscape. Calculating impervious coverage is quite easy if it's documented within the site plan.

- Topography: Sloping lots can insert another level of complexity into a project for a variety of reasons. Cities almost always require a land surveyor to document the terrain of your lot, especially for new homes or large projects. First and foremost, determining the slope percentage of a lot directly impacts the size and scale of the building by limiting the floor area ratio, heights, and especially your interpretation of the home. The slope will also influence the magnitude of the foundation design, from the amount of the excavation to the dimensions of your footings. Identifying heights and locations of retaining walls to stabilize your site is crucial and unfortunately frequently omitted from plans, potentially leaving you positioned for a big surprise when your builder says, "How are we going to hold up the hill by your driveway?" Once again, you're blindsided and wind up confronting your design team. Conflict invariably ensues.

You have two avenues for obtaining the information that your architect needs to develop a site plan:

1. Your design team can retrieve any information available from the county assessor's office and title reports, then measure existing structures and relevant hardscaping and place those on the plan.

2. You can hire a civil engineer or a licensed land surveyor to gather this information.

Whether you're doing a major remodel or building a new home, if you're working on a larger-sized project, the second option is the preferred path. These professionals will document everything I've mentioned and more, and they'll often provide software files for your design team to import into their programs, thus adding another layer of protection. Smaller-scale projects such as remodels with small additions can sometimes be completed in-house by your design team. For example, if you're on a flat lot and you're adding a master suite that's nowhere near the setbacks or lot coverage limitations, then it's possible that your architect can create the site plan in-house. But a caveat! It just takes one nosy neighbor to ask the Building department, "Is that house too close to my fence?"

2.420 FLOOR PLANS

These are the drawings of your home—both new and old—as viewed from above. Floor plans depict all of the rooms and the fixtures inside each area. You'll see locations of windows, doors, cabinetry, and plumbing fixtures as well as room labels and dimensions. Some architects will implement a room-labeling numbering system and will also identify windows and doors within a system. This is helpful when communicating with contractors, suppliers, and designers. Floor plans will be multiple sheets in your plan set. Every remodel, addition, and complete tear-down starts with a plan.

A1.00 EXISTING FLOOR PLAN

- The existing plan depicts your home before you've done any remodeling or rebuilding. The big differentiator between an existing site plan and an existing floor plan is that the site plan simply shows the outline of your home, whereas in the floor plan, the roof is removed and all walls, fixtures, doors, and windows are displayed.

  - New design impact: Being able to interpret the impact of the new project compared to the existing structure provides invaluable information for potential builders or anyone who's unfamiliar with the project. Once these design studies are completed, your design team should be able to articulate the implications of the project within a plan sheet by overlaying the new design over the existing home. This assists in understanding the scope of work and ultimately allows for an accurate cost analysis.

A1.10 DEMOLITION FLOOR PLAN

- Dedicating a sheet to define the demolition scope of work required by the impact of the new design provides a vehicle to communicate to contractors. The size and complexity of the project usually dictate the necessity of having (or not having) a dedicated sheet. In the case of smaller and simpler projects, you may see an architect combine both the existing and demolition plan on one sheet. That's perfectly acceptable assuming that the quantity and quality of the needed information has not been compromised.

- Hatching is a customary practice used to identify the areas that will be affected and removed. Hatching is simply drawing a series of diagonal lines across walls, rooms, the roof area, windows, doors, etc. The purpose is to clearly differentiate between affected areas that will be demolished from the areas that will remain.

- Labels and notes are also utilized to further elaborate on the hatched areas. The quantity and clarity of these notes are crucial, so be sure that your contractor includes these in their cost.

Always remember that plans are your main tool for setting expectations and holding others accountable! Plans can be backed up with a narrative in your scope of work document.

A3.00 NEW FLOOR PLANS

- Normally drawn at one-quarter inch per foot ($\frac{1}{4}$" = 1'), these sheets represent the new design and space plan in two dimensions as viewed from above. As we delve deeper into the plans, the more detailed they become. Depicting the new floor plan and layout of the home is the obvious objective, but this comes with much more detail (or at least it should). Let's peek into a typical floor plan page:

  - Walls: We all know what walls are, so when viewing your plans, first try to understand where the existing walls are as compared to the new walls. Architects accomplish these depictions in a variety of ways, but the bottom line is that you need to understand their methods. (Unless you're building a new home, in which case this comparison won't exist.) A common way to depict the walls is to identify all of the existing walls as "hollow"—i.e., two parallel lines with no shading between them—and new walls as solid or shaded. This makes it very clear to anyone which walls are to remain and which are new. To further understand the modifications being made, many designers will place a lighter version of the existing floor plan underneath the new floor plan. This adds clarity and provides everyone with a better understanding of the plans. Embellishing the floor plans this way will also add clarity for a contractor when they're disseminating the scope of work based on the plans.

- Windows, doors, passages, skylights: Openings are placed in the walls and ceilings that have obvious designations. The sizes of each of these openings are clearly labeled for quick understanding. For example, a window that's six feet wide by four feet tall is labeled as 6'0" x 4'0" and the label often specifies whether the window is a slider, casement, or double-hung. Doors are labeled in a similar manner: a 36-inch wide by 80-inch tall door is labeled as 3'0" x 6'8" and the direction the door swings is noted. It's unfortunate, but many mediocre designers simply plop in a standard window symbol during design and never return to it and edit the label. Perhaps you don't want double-hung windows and you miss seeing that double-hung windows are on the plans. Your contractor orders $10,000 worth of windows and you're once again blindsided. You are now forced to make compromises or take a financial hit. Accountability is fuzzy in the world of building homes! That's why I'm trying to enlighten you on so many issues. But I digress... Professional architects and designers will place identifiers on each window, door, and opening that requires a product to fill the hole. I've seen a variety of lettering and numbering systems used that usually link to a schedule (list) of materials. You'll find these kinds of details very helpful when you're trying to communicate with window suppliers and contractors.

- Rooms: It can be helpful to have each room identified so that communications during the design and construction process have less room for errors. For example, label the bedrooms as Bedroom #1, Bedroom #2, Bedroom #3, etc. instead of just saying a generic bedroom each time. If you don't, the following scenario is likely to occur: you want to add some recessed lighting in *one* of the bedrooms, so you call your contractor. He calls the electrician and supposedly explains which bedroom the light should be in and the rest is history—now you have recessed lights in *two* bedrooms and you're paying for both. In contrast, simply stating "Add four recessed lights in Bedroom #3" leaves no room for error. At least, we hope... Regardless, in that case, you aren't paying for eight lights, but only four.

A3.10 ELEVATIONS AND SECTIONS

Elevations are two-dimensional drawings that are developed to help illuminate the exterior and interior of the home while viewing the walls from each side. Elevation drawings convey information to Planning/Building departments during the permit application process, plus you and your builder also benefit from better and more accurate visualizations, material specifications, and construction methods.

Drawings known as sections are similar, but they're more like a slice of your home. Dissecting the plans in a section format helps see how floors, walls, ceilings, architectural details, and equipment fit into the overall structure.

A3.20 ROOF PLAN

Providing a two-dimensional overhead diagram of how the roof planes intersect with one another is the responsibility of the architect. This plan is used to convey the intention of the design as it's handed off to the structural engineer for analysis and generation of technical drawings that will be used to construct the roof. Carpenters use roof plans to understand the design and roofing contractors use them to build estimates.

A3.30 REFLECTED CEILING PLAN

This can be a valuable tool for studying feasibility and potential conflicts as the home systems come together. Think of an RCP as the ceiling reflected onto the floor plan—ceiling details like structural beams and elements, skylights, lighting, HVAC supply, return registers, decorative beams, audio-video equipment, and fire sprinklers are key components that all converge on a ceiling, and if all of them are *not* explored thoroughly, that can lead to serious compromises in the design. You may want your kitchen island centered on the skylight that's well above it, for example, or you may want the fire sprinklers centered between decorative beams. Perhaps you *don't* want the surround-sound speakers installed an inch away from a recessed light. A professional designer will overlay the MEP pages over the S page floor plans (more on that in a minute) to refine the design. Moving a beam or ceiling joist six inches can add to an overall quality perception that you may not be able to exactly pinpoint but that will contribute to a pleasant visual experience.

A4.00 MECHANICAL, ELECTRICAL, AND PLUMBING

Known in the industry as the MEP plans, you'll find these pages labeled and organized in different ways depending on who prepared the design. Because it's not uncommon for an architect to prepare the MEP information, it'll often be included under the architectural pages beginning with page A4.00. If your project involves separate MEP engineers, then it's common for the plan pages to begin with M; you'll see corresponding page numbers such as M1.00, E1.00, and P1.00.

For small- to medium-sized projects, you may see all of the MEP information on one plan page. For larger projects such as custom homes, you might see the MEP information disbursed over multiple pages. One crucial objective for your architect is to coordinate the three MEP disciplines with the architectural design to create a well-planned home.

PRINCIPAL ELEMENTS INCLUDED IN PLAN PAGES

- Specifications of system equipment and installation provisions.
  - For example, actual make and model numbers.
- Allocation of spaces for specified furnaces, air-conditioning, and ventilation equipment.
  - Spaces designed for main and ancillary equipment.
  - Installation diagrams. This ensures that enough space is allocated and that each space is coordinated with electrical and plumbing plans.
- Correlating locations and routes for ductwork within the structures.
  - Dedicated spaces for air supply and return ductwork that do not disrupt the floor plans prepared by your architect.
- Locations of air supply and return registers.
  - Critical coordination with the electrical and lighting plan!

- Prudent coordination with architectural floor plans and reflected ceiling plans. This ensures that conflicts won't undermine the design quality.
- Coordination of special equipment such as radiant in-floor or wall heating.
  - Location of boilers or on-demand heating equipment.

MECHANICAL PAGES

The primary objective of the mechanical pages is to instruct contractors about what, where, and how HVAC equipment is to be installed throughout the home. Within the pages, you should see symbols, notes, legends, and diagrams of your heating, ventilation, and air-conditioning systems.

I must emphasize that incorporating mechanical systems within a set of plans is often neglected by designers. A common scenario is shifting responsibility to the HVAC contractor to design the system, resulting in inferior system performance and undesirable aesthetics. The number-one objective is to blend the system design with the architectural design to avoid unintended consequences.

ELECTRICAL PAGES

Unless a concerted effort is initiated by your design team, the E in MEP can stir up a lot of challenges during construction. An electrical plan *not* tailored to your desires or coordinated with the big picture usually equates to cost overruns and an inferior living experience.

Like the mechanical plans, your electrical pages will include symbols, notes, legends, diagrams of receptacles, and designations of switching, lighting, and main power locations. Your contractors will utilize these plan pages to estimate and install the systems. Additionally, your city will scrutinize this information prior to issuing a building permit.

The electrical scope of work on a project can be split into two categories: power and lighting. Let's look at the important components that should be indicated on the pages.

POWER

- Size of power service to the buildings, i.e., 100 amps, 200 amps, 400 amps.

- Location of power point of entry and main service panel to the buildings.

- Location of distribution panels within the main and accessory structures.

- A load calculation document with circuitry design (for larger projects).

- Location of backup generator or solar battery systems.

- Locations of general power receptacles on floors, walls, and ceilings.

- Locations of special power receptacles for personal needs.

- Locations of power receptacles for appliances and MEP equipment.

- Locations of power receptacles for home automation and networking equipment.

LIGHTING

- Locations and specifications of recessed lighting fixtures and switches.

- Locations and specifications of decorative lighting fixtures and switches.

- Specialty lighting fixtures and locations.

- Recessed ceilings, closets, cabinetry, attics, crawl spaces, and lighted mirrors.

PLUMBING PAGES

As the last part of the MEP design, the plumbing pages will include symbols, notes, legends, diagrams of fixtures, and designations of waste, gas, water, and gas main locations. Your contractors will utilize these plan pages to estimate and install the systems. Additionally, your city will scrutinize the information prior to issuing a building permit.

The plumbing scope of work on a project can be split into three categories: water, waste, and gas. Let's look at each of the components that should be indicated on the pages.

WATER

- Size of water company's meter.
- Size and material type of water line to the entry point of the house.
- Location of fire sprinkler riser equipment (if applicable). This will impact the size of water line.
- Location of whole-house water filtration systems (if applicable).
- Location of domestic well equipment (if applicable).
- Location and specifications of water heating equipment.
- Accurate locations of all plumbing fixtures within the floor plan.
- Diagram and sizes of hot- and cold-water line routes.
- List of plumbing fixture specifications.

WASTE SYSTEM

- Location of sanitary sewer system waste line at the property line.
- Location of septic tanks and leach field (if applicable).

- Location of sewer line at the point of exit at all buildings.

- Location of all fixtures that require a waste system (same as plumbing fixture locations).

- Diagrams and sizes of waste line routes.

GAS

- Type of gas available to site (natural or propane).

- Size (diameter) of gas line servicing the property.

- The gas point of entry location to all buildings.

- Accurate locations of all appliances and equipment that require gas.

A4.20 LOW-VOLTAGE PLAN PAGES

Dedicated low-voltage plan pages aren't necessarily common in residential projects, but not because they aren't important. This area is frequently overlooked or deferred to later…which is often in the middle of construction. Not a good idea for a variety of reasons.

Many aspects of the low-voltage category can involve more than one subcontractor and bleed over into others. The primary installers of LV who will depend on your plans and specifications are home automation, security, networking, and electrical professionals. It's very possible that one subcontractor can perform all of these aspects of LV but not necessarily specialize in all of them.

Identifying the scope of work, products, and installation specifics of low-voltage solutions can affect the electrical and lighting plans and even the architectural and structural plans if you have very specific requirements such as hidden window blinds, power management and monitoring systems, and lighting controls—these all require dedicated spaces, ventilation, and so on. Building a set of specifications accompanied with plans that identify the locations of equipment and the installation specifications will optimize the accuracy of the plans, provide well-designed solutions, and provide data to obtain costs during the estimating process. It will be up to you to prioritize and invest time during the design phase to protect your experience.

I will talk more about low-voltage considerations and how to go about consulting with someone about the possibilities. Depending on your level of interest and detail, it will be up to you to pose the questions to your architect as to how and who will help pull together the plans suitable to hand to a LV contractor for estimating.

A6.00 SCHEDULES

No calendars involved with these schedules! Instead, visualize a list in a table format that identifies materials such as windows, doors, and skylights. Because numerous variables apply to these materials, it isn't realistic to include them all on the floor plans or elevations. Instead, most professional architects and designers create schedules that list out every single window and door with all of the distinct options specified, such as window type (casement, slider, double-hung, etc.), color, hardware, glass type, grids, and so on. A thorough and accurate schedule can be of immense value to your suppliers and builders, from helping them order correctly to making sure they construct the proper opening sizes. Still, despite the importance of these schedules, they're all too often missing or ignored, which leaves the door wide open for mistakes to be made.

Taking schedules a step further, architects will create schedules for the interior and exterior finishes by utilizing the room and area label nomenclature established earlier in the design process. These valuable schedules can include items such as wall finishes, paint colors, floor materials, moldings, locations and specifications of tiles, cabinetry, countertops, etc. These kinds of schedules aren't seen as frequently as typical window/door schedules are—they're usually a product of very professional architects who have been compensated to create them. I could argue that compensating an architect to generate these details may save you money, time, and aggravation in the long run.

AD7.00 ARCHITECTURAL DETAILS

Floor plans, elevations, and sections can only accomplish so much. Architectural details (often referred to as AD on plan pages) are larger-scale, close-up drawings of how the architect wants something constructed. This better articulates the design vision and technical instructions regarding assembling materials. I don't necessarily suggest that you try to interpret these drawings. If you are interested, however, asking for some explanations may whet your appetite of curiosity.

2.430 CIVIL PLANS

A civil design and set of plans addresses crucial elements that impact the performance and sustainability of your home. The design of a new home or extensive remodel project extends past the boundaries of the structures! Think of civil plans as covering the areas of your property that surround your new home up to your property lines and beyond.

Civil improvement plans prepared by a licensed engineer are the keystone of a well-planned project. These directly correlate with the work of your architect and soil engineer—the civil design begins with importing the survey and topography map, disseminating the soil engineering report, and incorporating your architect's proposed designs.

PRINCIPAL ELEMENTS OF CIVIL PLANS
- A hardscape plan: This identifies the pervious and impervious surfaces throughout the site; these all contribute to drainage calculations.

- A driveway or road plan: This designs and specifies the entrance to the property and the property's encroachment into city or county roads to meet both your preferences and the city's regulations.

- A grading plan: This identifies the portions of the parcel that need to be cut down or filled to accommodate the buildings. It also identifies drainage solutions and the locations of retaining walls that will support slopes.

- A utility plan: This identifies the locations of underground power, water, communications, and sewer systems.

- A storm drainage plan: This designs a drainage system to collect and direct runoff from the property and its buildings.

- An erosion control plan: This specifies locations and methods for controlling erosion during construction.

- Septic system design: Location of leach fields and equipment specifications.

As you can see, many facets of civil design may apply to your project. Suppose you're building a new home on a sloping lot in a rural or unincorporated area. In that case, most of the items listed above will apply, potentially significantly impacting the project's overall cost.

2.440 STRUCTURAL PLANS

If you're planning a new home or substantial remodel project, a separate structural engineer will likely get involved. In the Consultants section (see page 93), I introduced what a structural engineer is; in this section, I'll introduce how they contribute to your plan set.

The structural plan pages are very technical and specific to the foundation and framing of the home as well as the essential information that your contractor will depend on when estimating and building your project. I'll briefly touch on each of the plan pages that will become part of your plan set. When you're ready to explore further, know that I've prepared a primer and a series of presentations that will enable you to understand the basics of residential structural engineering. You can access these documents on the TAH site. Meanwhile, let's look at an outline of what your engineer will produce and ultimately include in your final plan set.

Figure 1: Three-dimensional structural engineering drawings.

Your home skeleton—the S sheets of your plan set—are a necessity that's prepared by a civil or structural engineer. These sheets supplement the architectural pages. Although licensed architects in many states are allowed to prepare these pages, architects often farm this vital task out to specialists. The more complicated a project is, the more likely architects are to delegate these details to others. With their knowledge of structure, your architect or designer will concentrate on the creative and compliance aspects of the project; once the schematic design has been approved, they'll engage with a structural engineer during the design development phase.

I call these the S sheets because the industry standard acronym is S (for "structural"). These sheets are identified with a single-decimal numbering system. The numbering system behind the S may vary between engineers, but it'll give you a good idea of how the information is organized.

While you're attempting to gather costs, you may hear a contractor ask if you "have all the structurals." They're looking for the S sheets. Reputable contractors will *not* provide a firm cost without your structurals—be aware!

Due to the technical and complicated nature of structural engineering, no one expects a layperson to comprehend the highly technical aspects of the drawings and details within a plan set. Instead, the goal is for you to understand their purpose, what the standard pages convey, and how the drawings and details are organized so that as discussions occur, you'll be empowered to ask the right questions.

You should become more familiar with structural plans before you engage with a contractor. Again, on the TAH website, I have more information and examples of each of these pages as well as a primer on the basics of structural engineering.

S0.00 GENERAL NOTES AND DISCLAIMERS

This page is filled with text that acts as directions for the contractors as to which materials to use and what methods to use to build specific details of the project. Disclaimers are important to read! The engineers may require certain observations and directions on specifications for your project.

S1.00 FOUNDATION SHEETS

These pages direct the construction of the foundation of the home and are correlated with the soils and civil engineers' data.

PRINCIPAL ELEMENTS OF FOUNDATION PLANS_____

- Dimensions and depths of the concrete slabs and footings.

- Reinforcement materials and locations to be embedded into the concrete.

- References to corresponding detail pages for specific areas of the foundation.

S1.10 FLOOR AND WALL FRAMING

I've been using the term "framing" throughout this book. It simply refers to building the structure with wood and steel framing materials such as joists, studs, rafters, etc. It's common for each floor of the home to have its own dedicated page. For larger projects, the plans will further break out areas, such as delineating the floor structure from the wall framing.

WHAT EACH STRUCTURAL PAGE OF THE PLANS DEPICTS

- The types and sizes of solid and engineered wood and the steel materials used to construct the skeleton of the home.

- The hardware used to connect the materials together down to the exact sizes of nails, bolts, and nuts.

- Specific instructions on the placement of materials and fastening hardware.

- References to corresponding detail pages for specific areas of the foundation.

S2.00 CEILING AND UPPER FLOOR FRAMING

Your typical flat ceilings rest on top of your walls and are constructed using ceiling joists. A ceiling in a two-story home could also be acting as the floor framing for the second floor. In this case, the ceiling is called a floor joist.

- The types and sizes of solid and engineered wood and the steel joists and beam materials.

- Locations of ceiling details: vaulted, raised, coffered, etc.

- Locations of beams supporting structural components above, such as a roof or walls.

- The hardware needed to connect the materials together down to the exact sizes of nails, bolts, and nuts.

- Specific instructions on the placement of materials and fastening hardware.

- References to corresponding detail pages for specific construction methods.

- Instructions as to what extent joists or beams can be modified for systems such as HVAC ducting, electrical wiring, and plumbing.

S3.00 ROOF FRAMING

Constructing a roof structure can be the most detailed and time-consuming element for a designer and contractor. This plan fully details all of the structural members needed to build the roof. These are known as rafters or manufactured roof trusses.

PRINCIPAL ELEMENTS OF ROOF FRAMING PLANS

- The types and sizes of solid and engineered wood or of steel rafters and ridge beams.

- The types and sizes of the sheathing covering the rafters and beams.

- The pitch of each roof plane.

- References to corresponding detail pages for specific construction methods, such as connection hardware.

S4.00 STRUCTURAL DETAILS

Structural details are crucial for your contractor to have to construct your home per the specifications. These details provide visual graphic diagrams to ensure that your home is built correctly. Think of such details as close-up views of where materials are connected.

PRINCIPAL ELEMENTS OF STRUCTURAL DETAILS

These drawings are increased in scale in order to communicate the specific methods to be used to connect structural components, including which wood, steel, and hardware materials will be used.

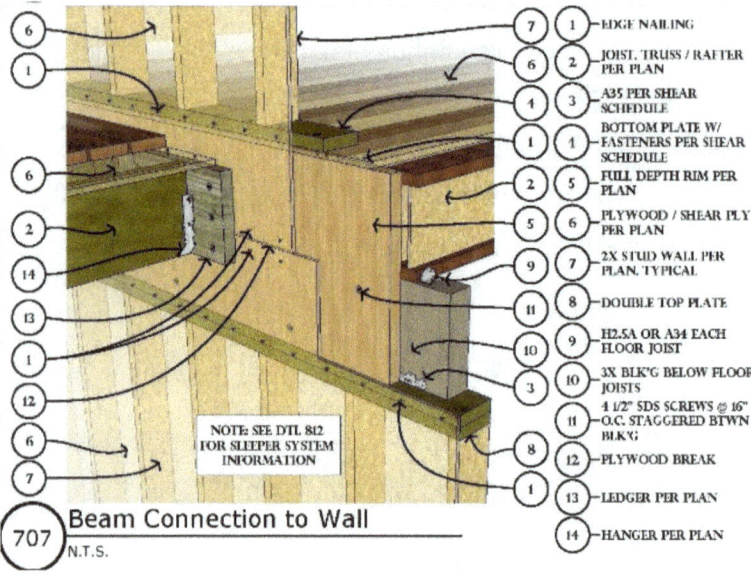

Figure 2: Structural detail sample

2.450 ENERGY PAGES EX.00

Energy compliance documentation consists of plan pages and specifications required by most Building departments to ensure that the building is conforming to current energy codes. This one gets quite complex, but it's good to understand a few key points.

- Roofing underlayment, material reflectivity, and performance specifications.

- Window, skylight, and exterior door minimum performance specifications.

- Locations and types of insulation and air-sealing methods, including minimum performance specifications.

- Specifications of HVAC (heating, ventilation and air-conditioning) equipment.

- Lighting fixture specifications and energy consumption maximums.

- Water heating product specifications.

2.460 INTERIOR DESIGN PAGES IX.00

Interior design pages of your plan set can be labeled in a similar manner as the architectural and structural pages. In our example, we'll use the letter I for "interior" then a decimal number to organize the pages.

A qualified interior designer not only provides assistance in selecting materials, colors, and fixtures, they also cross over into documenting these choices within detailed plans and documents.

HOW INTERIOR DESIGNERS CONTRIBUTE TO A PROJECT

- ✓ Enable you to visualize your home with the actual materials you've selected.

- ✓ Help contractors understand the installation of materials and the preferred methods of installation.

- ✓ Provide visibility and instructions for subcontractors to install their systems in the proper locations.

In the descriptions below, I'll show you some examples of this kind of work. If you desire to learn more, check out the resources on the TAH site.

I1.00 FINISH FLOOR PLAN

An FFP begins with the architectural plan stripped of irrelevant information and supplemented with information related to interior materials. If your architect recommended that you involve an interior designer for kitchens, baths, and other areas, most professional architects will request to review the plans provided by the interior designer and then will include the necessary drawings and information within their plans for the sake of consistency. Unfortunately, this does not always occur, so you'll need to micromanage this step to be sure that your expectations are met.

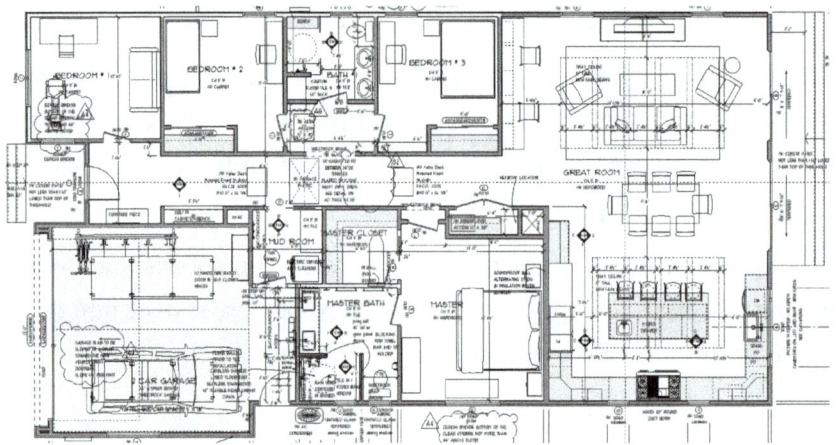

Visit theawakenedhomeowner.com to see samples.

VALUABLE INTERIOR DESIGN INFORMATION FOR YOU AND YOUR BUILDER

- The kitchen and bath layouts accurately representing the proper fixtures and appliances; all should be located, sized, and dimensioned.

- Locations of all built-in cabinetry.

- Furniture layout.

- Flooring materials identified in each room, including all sizes, thicknesses, and orientations (i.e., which way is the hardwood floor going?).

- Interior window and door molding specifications.

- Closet, pantry, shelving design, and materials.

- Wall finishes placed within a schedule specifying products, colors, and sheens.

- Interior material specifications such as tiles, stones, countertops, cabinetry, hardware, and so on.

12.00 INTERIOR ELEVATIONS

Interior views of the walls where a lot of materials converge are a necessity to properly convey the specified materials, installation locations, patterns, and overall look. Kitchens and baths are a prime example of this—in those rooms, just about every tradesperson who's involved appreciates as much detail as possible. For example, your interior designer will create detailed 2D views of your kitchen walls with cabinetry, appliances, countertops, backsplashes, fixtures, and hardware. Dimensioning these plans makes these drawings invaluable for just about everyone involved.

Here are some interior design drawing examples of a remodel project my team and I designed and built. These drawings were prepared by our in-house interior designer:

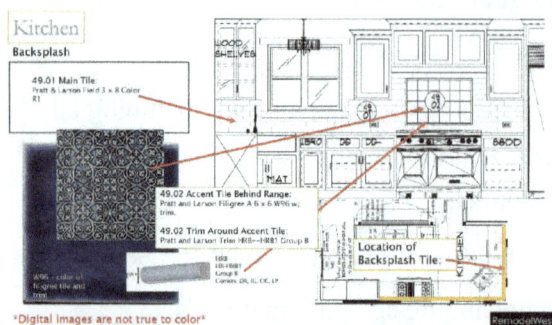

Figure 3: Detailed elevation drawings of the kitchen in two dimensions with material specifications.

Figure 4: The same project as in Figure 3, but in a 3D-rendered drawing depicting the materials to be used.

And just for fun a picture of the final project

Visit theawakenedhomeowner.com to see samples.

Numerous people benefit from interior design pages, such as your contractor, your subcontractors, and you!

- Your cabinetmaker or supplier can easily interpret what size and configuration you desire along with any interior fittings.

- Visualizing the hardware style and placement can help you be more decisive.

- Your tile-setter will love you, because the intricate tile backsplash detail you desire in the kitchen doesn't leave them playing any guessing games. Also, with detailed interior drawings, your tile supplier can participate in the design process and order material correctly. Getting the correct material the first time is a common challenge in this business.

- Your countertop fabricator will understand the edge detail you want and where you may want a stone backsplash instead of tile.

- Your plumber will know where to place your shower valves, how high you want your showerhead to be, and where you want that high-end wall-mounted faucet to be installed.

- The electrician is thrilled because you selected the light fixtures already and your designer dimensioned the elevations for the proper height.

UNDERSTANDING PLANS REVIEW

Plans are comprised of many pages provided by designers and consultants that are then compiled into a completed plan set that's ready for permits and construction. The plans accompanied by your specifications are the only tools you have to obtain accurate costs, hold all those involved accountable, and ensure that your expectations are met.

- ✓ Title page
- ✓ Site plan and civil plans
- ✓ Architectural with consultants
- ✓ Structural
- ✓ Energy
- ✓ Interior design

2.500 APPROVALS AND PERMITS

Approvals and permits are primarily processed at your city or county public offices via an application process. Obtaining a building permit can be one of the most feared and dreaded processes but also satisfying at the same time. Each city or county department operates in similar ways when it comes time to submit your application. The Planning department and the Building department are the two components of a city or county bureaucracy that govern the construction of projects within their boundaries. The larger the scale of the project is, the more likely you are to be dealing with both departments (but not necessarily concurrently). At the end of this section, I'll present a graphic representation of the inner workings of the approval process.

As you begin the design process, there may be one other entity that impacts the possibilities of your new home or remodel, and that's a homeowner's association or HOA. Back in the Homeowner's Associations section (see page 202), I introduced HOAs and their inner workings. In this section, I'll share an example of an HOA approval process that you should become aware of should your property fall under the scrutiny of a design review committee.

2.501 HOMEOWNER'S ASSOCIATION APPROVALS

Homeowner's associations typically have a formal application process that begins with giving you a documented set of design guidelines for your designer to follow. The submittal materials required for the design review committee's consideration are a survey/topo, a site plan, floor plans, elevations, color schemes, and a preliminary landscape plan. I've found that 3D renderings can significantly help committee members visualize the project and therefore can instill an elevated level of credibility for your application.

Early on in the design process (usually at the end of step one of the design process, which is the schematic design), you or your architect submit an application to the HOA accompanied by the required materials. The committee—which is usually formed of residents within the community—establishes regular meeting dates and slates your project for review and hopefully approval. The architect attends these meetings to address questions posed by the board or other community members. I would also recommend that the homeowner participate in the process to ensure complete visibility and also to do some PR work. Meetings can sometimes be contentious, as subjective reasoning will inevitably infiltrate your design. Don't be surprised if revisions are needed to appease the committee members, and be prepared to do some political maneuvering to accomplish your approval.

Once the submitted materials have been approved, the design review committee will provide a written letter formalizing the approval and laying out the steps you'll need to take to move forward. Because your community is within an HOA, the city or county Planning and/or Building department will require this document when you submit your documents for their Planning and Building department permit approval.

2.502 PLANNING DEPARTMENT APPROVALS

Back in Understanding Design Limitations on page 180, I first introduced you to what a Planning department is and how they govern projects in your jurisdiction. The larger the project is, the more involved the Planning department becomes. Your Planning department will be your first interaction with municipal authorities when the time arrives to begin the design process and eventually obtain approvals.

During step one, hopefully your design team researched the parameters mandated by your local city or county Planning department and reviewed your homeowner's association design guidelines before any concepts were created or developed. If they skipped this step, you're already behind the eight ball. Regardless, it can't hurt to ask your design team if any research has been done as you begin the design process.

Although the official Planning department approval process comes at the end of step three, making a *pre-submittal* visit to your Planning department *before* you lock in the design is an intelligent step to take. Some jurisdictions have a formal process for pre-submittal; others have an informal process. Taking this proactive action early in step two of the design process gives you a chance to confirm that the proposed design is compliant and allows you to revise the design if necessary. This proactive step circumvents wasting time and money.

Obtaining early approvals can be a smooth process *if* your design professional is knowledgeable and conscientious of your city's rules and regulations. If your project involves expanding your home, renovating within a specially designated historic district, or building a new home, restrictions could impact the design of your project, and those restrictions sometimes aren't immediately understandable or visible. Unfortunately, a designer can push, misunderstand, or overlook boundaries, causing a nightmare before you even begin construction.

If your property is located within a homeowner's association, initiating the formal approval process as early as possible entrenches your design and plans early enough to allow you to build upon them and prepare them for a Planning department application.

Depending on the project's complexity and the comfort levels of you and your architect, plans can progress while you're waiting to get planning approval. Whether or not to pursue this strategy is a judgment call made by your design pro. Another good productive step to take while waiting for planning approval is to delve into the many other decisions that must be made on a project, such as choosing interior materials, finishes, and fixtures, none of which are affected by the Planning department's approval criteria.

After a submittal is taken by the Planning department, the approval process begins. It usually takes four to six weeks for a planner to review your plans. Typically, the planner provides comments to your design professional, asking for clarifications and compliance modifications. Your architect then responds to these remarks and resubmits the plans. The city could take two or three weeks to review your materials and then ideally issue an approval.

As you can see, the timeline of this process means that it could take a minimum of two months to obtain approval. It can stretch out for many more months, too, depending on the city's workload and the quality of your application. If your architect's due diligence has led to a quality, professional submission, the planner will likely move your project closer to the top of their pile and thus give you a quicker response. On the contrary, if your design comes across as unprofessional and nonconforming, the application will bounce around the department for months, only for you to eventually receive a ten-page document full of corrections. This starts the project off on a bad note by unnecessarily extending its timeline.

Beware! One other element of a Planning department approval process could surface: the dreaded public hearing. A handful of project details can trigger an opportunity for the public to chime in on your application. Let's take a look at the most common ones:

- New homes
- Projects that are designed outside of the standard zoning parameters. For example: building into setbacks, increased height, increased floor area.

Public hearings are a process where the Planning department notifies your surrounding neighbors of your application. A set amount of time is established for the public to review your plans, and then a date is set for a meeting at the department office for the public to voice their concerns. It's best for you and your design team to attend and be prepared to answer questions and dispute any unreasonable requests. After having been involved in several public hearing meetings, I strongly discourage you from opening yourself up to this level of scrutiny if at all possible...and you can do so by responsibly designing your remodel project to conform to the rules. In the case of a new home, it's best to respect the neighborhood you plan to live in, design a project that fits like a glove within the established parameters, and hope for the best.

The extent of information that your Planning department requires will depend on the project scope. Below is a sample list of primary required information for a custom home application. The list could be shorter or longer depending on the specific jurisdiction and project type:

✓ Site plan: Including the zoning and the size of the lot in square footage or acreage. The plan must provide the new home's footprint as well as any outbuildings, streets, driveways, setbacks, easements, slopes, and utilities.

✓ Floor plans: Including all rooms and the square footage data for the living areas, high-ceiling areas, outbuildings, and lot coverage. This data must comply with departmental regulations.

✓ Elevations: Depicting the home as viewed from the exterior, including heights that must conform to departmental regulations.

✓ Perspective or 3D drawings: Presenting the overall look of the home, materials, and colors on the site.

With the Planning department's approval behind you, you can then move forward to develop the design feeling productive and safe—you will have avoided getting a dreaded denial *after* getting deep into the design.

2.503 OBTAINING BUILDING PERMITS

As an essential step in the planning and building process, abiding by the Building department's permit application process can either go smoothly if handled correctly or add time and aggravation if not handled properly.

Homeowners often question whether a permit is required for their projects, especially minor ones. For instance, if you're planning a kitchen renovation that involves replacing the cabinets, counters, appliances, and plumbing fixtures and there are no structural changes like moving a wall or window, it seems like you wouldn't need a permit. However, updating a kitchen or bathroom in an older home will likely require having electrical work done to conform to the demands of the new appliance, and whenever you touch an electrical or plumbing element, you must apply for a permit. The permitting process for a nonstructural kitchen remodel can be much easier than larger projects and can often be obtained on the same day. Many cities have adopted online permitting processes that further streamline their applications.

A building permit is accompanied by an inspection process. This involves another pair of eyes—a building inspector who's employed by your city—to show up at various intervals of the construction progress and confirm that the project is being built according to the plans. It's worth remembering that a building permit is designed to ensure that a project conforms to mandated building codes, which in turn aim to ensure the safety of the home and its occupants. Moreover, documenting all of the work performed on the house adds a layer of protection and removes any possible conflicts during the sale transaction if you plan to sell your home someday.

HINT!

There are usually several inspections during the project; the one at the end is called the *final inspection*. Have your contractor tie some of the progress payments to the city approvals of each inspection. This builds in an accountability component for your contractor and offers peace of mind for you.

It's also true that a project with a permit undoubtedly adds complexity and time to the project. That's why it's tempting to do a project without one. But there are consequences! Some are obvious and some are less obvious. A project being constructed without a permit removes a layer of accountability from those performing the work. This mistake can lead to cutting corners and inferior or even deficient work. From the city's or county's perspective, some consequences can severely impact the project timeline and cost.

A "red tag" is a term that many jurisdictions use to identify a project that isn't compliant, such as one without a permit. If your project is red-tagged, you must stop construction and obtain a retroactive permit. This is a miserable experience—you must now visit the city with your tail between your legs, provide acceptable plans, and pay the fees and penalties. The kicker is how far along you were in the construction before you were shut down. If the electrical and plumbing are behind you and the walls are closed back up and the cabinets are going in, you could be in a world of hurt. Why? Since no inspections have occurred, the city has been unable to see if your modifications meet code requirements and are safe. Expect to be asked to remove the cabinets and open the walls so that building inspectors can examine essential areas…and of course you'll have to close them back up, too. As you can imagine, this will cause delays and cost overruns and even foster a contentious relationship with your contractor. Hence, it's essential to think seriously before starting a project without a permit. If you do, be prepared to pay the consequences.

Let's get back on the reality train and assume that you prefer *not* to be miserable and that you'd rather hire a contractor who has some level of integrity. We'll also assume that your project is on a larger scale, such as an addition or a new home.

BUILDING CODES

A Building department's job is to ensure that the documented building code has been applied to your plans. Each department doesn't create its codes—rather, it begins with the IRC (International Residential Code) and adopts and amends the IRC codes to tailor its own building codes. This code refinement starts at the state level, and then some communities add more restrictive measures that apply to their civic dynamics. In California, for example, we have the CBC (California Building Code), which each city and county are mandated to enact.

I share all of this so that when you hear the phrase "build to code," you know the code isn't just some arbitrary set of rules that your city came up with—the rules go deeper than that and are consistent across your state and even the country. Much like the municipal code, the building code consists of many chapters addressing all aspects of what goes into a building. Think of the municipal code as the outer-layer aesthetics of your home and the building code as the skeleton and organs of your home.

The code is a complex set of instructions used to build your home, and each consultant you hire will refer to their respective sections. If I were to go deeper into the weeds, I'm afraid I'd lose you, but know that your building permit is driven by a code that's there for good reasons!

2.504 BUILDING PERMIT APPLICATIONS

Let's get your expectations dialed in for the permitting process. We will make a few assumptions: your project is more extensive and you've hired design professionals and consultants as needed to complete the plans and specifications. If your project is smaller (such as a kitchen remodel), the process will be much easier.

Submitting plans to the Building department is an accumulation of all the time and work put into one of the significant milestones of a project: the construction documents (see The Design Process, Step Three: Completing Your Plans on page 110). Many cities are genuinely interested in taking in a "clean application," so to speak, and offer a worksheet (commonly aggregated into a checklist format) that summarizes the materials that are required to apply for a building permit. This list can be intimidating even to a design professional, not to mention a layperson. A productive and efficient strategy for a design professional to tackle this list is to have the city requirements on the list at their fingertips as the construction documents are being developed. The really smart ones have this document ride along for the entire time while the full design process is proceeding and growing.

This proactive step removes the daunting task of preparing the plan for a permit, which is not necessarily the most creative and desirable portion of a designer's job but can be a significant contributor to the value they provide. (I say "can be" because again, it's better to keep the permit requirements in mind throughout the process.)

Your pursuit of a building permit will begin with filling out an application form that asks for information like owner name, architect name, address, project scope, project valuation, contracting method, and contractor information, including proof of insurance. Pretty straightforward. Secondly, you'll be asked to provide multiple copies of the plan pages, which have been compiled into a complete plan set, including all of the pages I outlined in the Understanding Plans section. Let's sum all of this up in a checklist.

SUBMITTAL CHECKLIST FOR THE APPLICATION
REQUIRED PLANS AND INFORMATION

- ✓ Architectural pages: Stamped and signed by the design professionals.

- ✓ Structural pages: Stamped and signed by the engineer.

- ✓ Structural calculations: A separate document provided by engineers.

- ✓ Roof truss design and calculations: Provided by truss company.

- ✓ Energy pages: Provided by consultant.

- ✓ Green building (if applies) and waste disposal programs.

ADDITIONAL PLANS AND INFORMATION REQUIRED
FOR LARGER OR NEW HOME PROJECTS

- ✓ Planning approval documents (if applicable).

- ✓ Civil engineer: For grading and drainage.

- ✓ Tree protection plan: Provided by arborist.

✓ Fire sprinkler design: Provided by fire sprinkler contractor.

✓ Solar power design: Provided by solar contractor.

There are a few options for making the handoff to the city. Which one you choose will depend on the way you've approached design. Did you piece it together yourself or did you hire a design professional to facilitate the entire process? Or somewhere in between? Remember, the more you're in the middle, the more responsibility you'll take on and possibly the more stress and aggravation you'll experience. A Building department can eat someone alive if that person is unprepared. I equate an inexperienced homeowner submitting a building permit application to hiking in the jungle with no trail and no means of defense from the wild animals lurking in the bushes.

Each Building department has their own way of taking in a project. Some will be an administrative process where someone at the counter checks the application and collects the fee; some will take appointments and perform a cursory review of your materials; others offer express plan checks to review your plans right in front of you. More recently, cities are moving to an online submittal system. This can be efficient if you provide a quality application, but if you don't, your plans will disappear into the abyss.

Here are two steps to take along with a few suggestions that you should consider in conjunction with your project type and what kind of arrangement you have with your designer. Even if you have no plans to participate in the permitting process, try taking these steps to protect yourself and stay as informed as possible.

1. Contact the Building department, explain your project type, and ask what the procedure is to apply. Does it simply entail being a delivery person with a checkbook or does the application include someone from the city doing an in-person, live, detailed review of materials while you or your architect is present and wherein questions can

arise? Once you know what the procedure is, adjust your thinking as follows.

2. Ask your design professional if they will be applying for the application.

- If the city will be doing some level of review of the materials and questions might possibly come up, then I recommend that your architect be present to immediately address any such questions. You can then decide if you would like to attend. You can learn a lot about your project and its requirements that otherwise may never get fed back to you. Or...

- If the application is a simple handoff, then perhaps you'd like to handle that yourself rather than pay someone to do it for you. Just be careful here, though, because if you're inexperienced, questions still might come up that you're not able to answer.

- If filing the application is an online process, I suggest that your design professional handle it, *but* they should include you as a contact so that you can monitor the progress and be aware of any questions that may arise.

2.505 THE INNER WORKINGS OF APPROVALS

Say you've completed the application process by unloading those 20 pounds of plans and paperwork or you've had a sense of closure after clicking the Send button. Either way, you've reached a big milestone of the design steps and you're that much closer to getting your project started. Now what happens to your plans and what should you do in the meantime? It can feel like you've fallen into a black hole after sending in your application, but don't fret—the Building department's inner workings will kick into gear and the department will begin processing your application. During the application process, the department asked for multiple copies of the plan sets: three copies of architectural, two copies of structural, and two copies of energy. Each city has its own requirements, but multiple copies should be expected because they'll be distributed to different departments behind the scenes. Let's look at the process more closely so you'll be a bit enlightened.

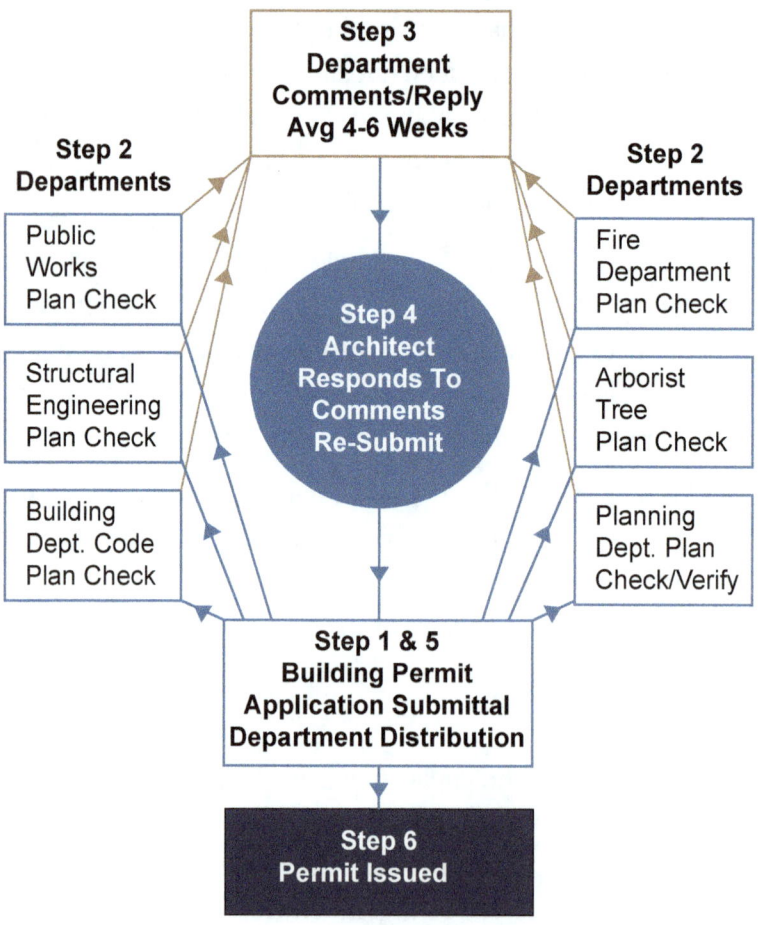

The chart above represents a simplified graphic presentation of the inner workings of a Building department. Essentially, multiple departments are tasked to review your plans by comparing them to the established codes and policies.

Step 1: An application is completed and the appropriate materials are submitted to the Building department along with your first payment. This is usually called the plan check fee. The person in charge of the intake distributes the plans to each department, sometimes simultaneously; that's why multiple copies are needed. Then the clock starts ticking.

Step 2: Each department reviews the plans against their respective codes, ordinances, and policies. The Building department will use the city's codes to ensure that your plans meet their standards. At the same time, structural engineers (usually in-house employees or sometimes engineers outsourced to independent firms) review the plans purely for structural purposes, which are also part of the code. The Public Works department oversees the water and sewer system and the property immediately adjacent to your home, such as the sidewalk, curb, gutter, and street. Their job is to be sure that your project is not impacting these areas. Public Works staff will become involved if it's a new home on a vacant lot or an extensive renovation where you're tapping into city systems or increasing services on an existing home.

The Fire department will review your plans in terms of its size and scale to determine if any additional provisions are required. How projects are classified is important and is also the primary trigger that determines requirements. For example, if your project is a new home from the ground up, a fire sprinkler suppression system may be required, but if your home is a remodel and addition, this system may or may not be required. It all depends on the magnitude of your project, which ties into a documented method used to define your project. The proximity and capacities of fire hydrants could also play a role.

The Planning department also has to sign off on the project. The classification of the project will determine what level of scrutiny will occur. As outlined earlier, if your project is more extensive and classified as a new home or significant remodel, hopefully you've already obtained the city's approval for it. The Planning department will review and compare your final plans to the plans that were approved earlier. You may have to obtain a lengthy review and reapproval if there are substantial changes. If you skipped the pre-planning approval or elected to do a concurrent submittal, this will all occur simultaneously. Good luck! That's the riskiest way to submit a project.

Step 3: Upon completing their own departmental review in approximately four to 12 weeks, each department will document their findings in a plan check comment format. Specific questions, clarifications, and required changes will be outlined and returned to the person who took your application. These documents will then be submitted back to you for revision. The level of changes is specific to the project classification and is a direct reflection of the quality of your plans and your knowledge of the code, ordinances, and policies. Said changes could be as simple as a few minor notations or they could mean a significant redesign. All the steps we have taken within the TAH mission are to avoid the latter.

Step 4: Your design professional receives the plan check comments and makes revisions. Although you may not fully understand the required revisions, it's wise to have at least some visibility into the revisions to know how they might impact the scope and cost of your project. You may have already obtained costs from your general contractor or subcontractors, and the required revisions could affect those costs. If those potential impacts are not addressed, your contractor and subcontractors may not become aware of the revisions until the project is underway, thus placing everyone squarely behind the eight ball. So absolutely ask your architect, "Do any of the revisions that the city requires affect the cost of my job?"

Step 5: Revisions are completed by your architect and then returned to the Building department for final approval and processing. This could take two weeks or more.

Step 6: You'll receive a notification to pay the remainder of the permit fees and pick up the plan set that's been stamped and approved by the various departments. Also included in your permit package is an inspection card used by the inspector to approve each inspection or request corrections before an approval and sign-off can occur. This important record will follow the project through to the end of construction and should be retained by you as long as you own the home.

PART TWO CONCLUSION

Our first foray into building your knowledge was about the world of design. I began the section on understanding design professionals by presenting all of the players you may have to engage with and how their agreements can be crafted to suit your comfort. In gradually unpacking the intricacies of the design process, you learned about a series of procedures that experts use to shape concepts into design work, enabling you to witness your new abode materialize.

The section on understanding design limitations aimed to spare you from experiencing chronic problems in design by bringing potential challenges to the forefront early enough to prevent impossible ideas from being pursued. With this wealth of knowledge in your coffers, we went even deeper and boosted your knowledge by exploring how to understand plans. Now you have a better understanding of your project and can intelligently communicate with those involved. Also as you now know, a primary objective of the design realm is to prepare your project for construction. This process culminates in approvals and permits. Fortunately, now you're more familiar with what those entail since you've gained insights into the intricacies involved in obtaining building permits from your city.

"I can't say enough good things about Bill Reid. Throughout my remodel, Bill was very visible and gave me weekly updates and kept me on task for my own responsibilities for the project."

- Viki B.

PROJECT BY BILL REID
OF REMODELWEST

"Construction and design are interdependent—one without the other leaves our dreams abandoned."

W.W. Reid

3.

THE WORLD OF
CONSTRUCTION

THE WORLD OF CONSTRUCTION 3.

3.0 INTRODUCTION

The output of the design process sets expectations and establishes accountability for your construction team. They're the ones who will be responsible for implementing the plans and specifications. Once your plans and specs are ready, you can enter the construction world and begin engaging with contractors.

Hiring an independent general contractor is the most common way for homeowners to have their projects built off the plans their architect created, but hiring a GC is not necessarily the only option. This section pulls back the veil of the construction world, the many players who are involved, and most important aspects of contracting your job to a builder. Once you couple your construction knowledge with your design knowledge, you'll be empowered to study the various options you have for hiring your team.

WHO YOU NEED

- **Understanding contractors:** Learn about who will build your project, the value they bring, when to engage with them, how they can contribute early on, and how to hire them.

WHAT YOU NEED TO KNOW

- **Understanding contracts:** Learn about contract types, the intricacies of said contracts, and how best to protect your experience.

- **Managing risk:** Understanding insurance and liens.

- **Plans, specifications, and permits:** These are your primary tools for building your project. They also form the basis of your project cost and are an accountability tool for all involved.

- **Construction proposals:** How to facilitate the process of obtaining cost estimates and proposals from contractor candidates to build your project.

3.000 UNDERSTANDING CONTRACTORS

You may have heard the word "contractor"—perhaps your friends have said, "I'm meeting my contractor to pick out windows tomorrow." Contractors are skilled people who own and work at companies of various sizes who hold licensing in the construction industry. They can also be the people who lead a team to construct a project. When your friends referred to "my contractor," they were likely referring to their general contractor, but actually a subset of contractors makes up the entire team.

WHAT WE'LL COVER _____

- ✓ What contractors do
- ✓ The various types of contactors
- ✓ The value of hiring a general contractor
- ✓ The attributes of a quality contractor
- ✓ How contractors make a living
- ✓ How cost is determined within the estimating process
- ✓ Contracting methods to understand and select

3.010 WHAT CONTRACTORS DO

Contractors are professionals skilled in interpreting plans and specifications and physically building structures and installing systems, equipment, and finishes such as cabinetry, tile, stone, and flooring. There are two types of contractors: general contractors and subcontractors. Both possess knowledge, experience, licensing, and insurance.

3.011 GENERAL CONTRACTORS

A general contractor oversees the construction process by orchestrating a team of employees, subcontractors, and suppliers to build your project. Also called GCs or builders, general contractors come in various forms, but it always boils down to this: one person holds a license issued by the state that your project is in.

A GC could be one person who hires out all aspects of a project or a GC could be working within a larger company with multiple employees, locations, and levels of management. Because creating a home is so custom and personal, a GC is usually a blend of the two—likely they work for a small business that can cater to a homeowner's needs. From constructing the house framing and setting windows and doors to installing siding and finishing carpentry elements, a typical small- to medium-sized custom home builder often handles all of the carpentry aspects, with its employees representing a significant and essential part of the project. The remainder of the project is usually assigned to a team of subcontractors brought in by your GC who specialize in the necessary trades needed to complete the team. In rare instances, a GC can perform all of the work associated with a project...but that's not necessarily a positive attribute due to the ol' cliché that goes "a jack of all trades is a master of none."

Acting as a general contractor comes with significant liabilities, from the project quality and costs to the safety of the people involved.

I emphasize this because many contractors who are not the best at estimating or reading plans tend to "share the love" of liability with the client by structuring their costs and contracts accordingly. Ask yourself, "How thorough and accurate are my plans and specifications?" The more thorough and accurate they are, the less risk you're taking. The more thorough and accurate they are, the more accountable your contractor becomes and the more reliable the project costs are.

Accurately estimating the cost of a project is vital for all involved, and it begins with your GC disseminating the project plans and specifications through numerous channels of subcontractors and suppliers. Your builder will take the provided plans and specifications, review them in detail, and build the project in their head. This amazing visualization expertise allows a builder to accomplish many things: assemble a list of materials, identify the subcontractors needed, identify problem areas, and translate the plans to subcontractors, employees, and materials suppliers to obtain accurate costs.

It's important to note that not all general contractors are created equal. There can be significant differences between actual qualified contractors and people *posing* as qualified contractors. That basic starting point is then combined with and compounded by different business models. Let's compare two contractors, Fred and Ace, to illustrate the importance of selecting the right contractor for your project.

3.012 A TALE OF TWO CONTRACTORS

Construction companies and contractors come in all shapes and sizes and have varying levels of expertise and knowledge. To narrow things down, know that generally speaking, there are two varieties of GCs. Both can be successful if matched to the right customer and project, and neither one needs to know absolutely everything. It's best to choose whichever GC can assemble the best team relative to your project.

Let's say you're about to meet two different contractors. First, you shake Fred the Builder's hand. It's as rough as a granite boulder. His truck is in the background; a barking dog is pacing back and forth in the bed that also has lumber piled high above on the racks. Fred is hands-on and has been building homes for 30 years. His dad was a builder; Fred remembers digging ditches during summers when he was ten years old. Dad was hard to work for, but he taught Fred how to build a home from the ground up. Fred is now in his 50s and has a few employees and longstanding subcontractors. Guys like Fred often have a strong grip on the structure of the building and how to construct the foundation and framing. They're proud of how fast it can be done with a reasonable level of quality. "Fred is my guy," you think. He's down-to-earth. You need what Fred can provide, although sometimes that's at the expense of other crucial elements of a complex building process, such as all of the aspects of project management and new innovative products and systems.

Next, you meet Ace the Builder. He may be younger than Fred. He's wearing a button-down shirt and his truck doesn't have a speck of dirt on it. Ace didn't spend as much time in the ditches as Fred did—instead, he worked for larger builders and gained experience in construction management, scheduling, and hiring. Ace understands construction and keeps up with the advances in materials and methods and leverages technology to manage a job. You love this because you feel an elevated level of professionalism emanating from him. Contractors like Ace often have a hierarchy of team members in construction and design who provide quality service. In fact, on occasion, guys like Fred may end up working for Ace because they just want to build and not be bothered with paperwork.

The reality is that you need Ace *and* Fred. If you can pull that off, it's the best of both worlds. Ultimately, your choice will come down to a balance between the type of project you have and the candidates you're considering. If it's a master bath addition, perhaps Fred is a good fit. But if you need to design and build a 5,000-square-foot house, then Ace may be the ticket, with his employees like Fred in charge of the foundation and framing.

ATTRIBUTES OF A GENERAL CONTRACTOR

- Interprets and disseminates your plans and specifications to the construction team.

- Prepares cost estimates, contracts, and payment schedules.

- Manages the construction schedule and budget, ensuring timely project completion within the specified cost constraints.

- Coordinates with employees, subcontractors, suppliers, and vendors to procure necessary materials and services for the construction project.

- Oversees the construction process from start to finish.

- Ensures that construction complies with plans, specifications, building codes, and regulations.

- Conducts regular site inspections to monitor overall progress, the quality of workmanship, building inspections, and adherence to safety standards.

- Addresses any issues or concerns that arise during the construction process, making necessary adjustments or modifications as needed.

- Communicates regularly with the design team and client to provide updates on the construction progress and address any questions or concerns they may have.

- Ensures that the completed home meets the client's expectations and complies with all relevant building codes and regulations.

- Provides post-construction support and assistance, including addressing any warranty issues or maintenance needs that may arise after the project is completed.

As one of my customers once so aptly said, "I just need one throat to choke." After I caught my breath, I realized they were right: a GC orchestrates it all.

In the next section, I'll delve into how to hire design pros and contractors and pinpoint the best time to start engaging with potential builders. Before we get to that part, though, it's worth mentioning a few more key points here. A GC can be a valuable participant as early as back in the design process—including a GC at that juncture means you can begin an early search for the GC who will ultimately helm your project. Here's how a GC can help early on:

- ✓ Design checkpoints: Having a construction mind be a part of the team and perform verifications and feasibility studies as the design evolves is invaluable.

- ✓ Budget checkpoints: A contractor can help you surpass the theoretical budgeting numbers and provide preliminary estimates.

- ✓ An added benefit: Bringing in contractors early allows them plenty of time to qualify and build relationships. Then when the time comes to obtain official estimates, they'll be ready to go.

However, all of that said, I must mention one reality that may interfere with early contractor engagement: because contractors must spend many hours of work to provide you with an estimate, they may not initially appear to be highly motivated to give you a quote. If your architect has a group of contractors they work closely with, this usually overcomes their aversion to spending time doing what could turn out to be unpaid labor. If you're looking for a contractor on your own, offer to compensate potential contractors for the time they would be spending at your side during the design process.

3.013 SUBCONTRACTORS

Although a general contractor is the primary person in charge of constructing your home, they're also responsible for assembling a team of people and companies who specialize in construction trades that your GC does not provide. These are known as subcontractors. Think of subcontractors as the actual people on-site who are performing a specialized skill set.

"Subs," as they're called, play a vital role in the construction world, from excavations and foundations to plumbers, electricians, drywallers, and multiple folks who participate on the team. These subs require licensing and insurance and contract directly with your GC. They focus only on one trade, such as tile-setters or roofers.

Here's a look at the typical subcontractors who are involved with a residential construction project and whom a GC will have on their team.

SUB	SCOPE OF WORK
Excavation	Land clearing, grading, drainage, utilities, septic, foundation excavation
Concrete	Foundation, flatwork
Rough carpentry	Framing
Roofing	Roof coverings

Stucco	Exterior wall finishes
Masonry	Stone exterior cladding, columns, patios, etc.
Mechanical	HVAC systems
Electrical	Power, lighting, generators
Plumbing	Water, waste, and gas systems
Solar	Photovoltaic power systems
Low-voltage	Security, network, audio-video, home automation
Fireplaces	Built-in fireplaces and woodstoves
Insulation	Insulation systems
Drywall	Interior wall finishes
Stairs	Specialty installs of stairs and railings
Tile	Install of tile and stone
Slab	Install of slab, stone, and quartz surfaces
Flooring	Install of finish flooring materials
Glass	Install of glass tub/shower enclosures, etc.
Painting	Painting and finishing of exterior/interior surfaces
Landscaping	Install of landscape materials

3.014 CONTRACTOR'S LICENSE

Whether a contractor is a GC or a sub, they must hold a license from the state where your project is located. They typically have a company wherein the contractor is the person who holds the license for the company. Researching a contractor's license is one way to legitimize a candidate, but it's not the last way. Your first step will be to examine if your candidates have a license, how long they've had it, and if it's assigned to the company they represent. You can quickly accomplish this by looking at your state Contractors' Board.

I emphasize this fundamental step because occasionally unscrupulous individuals may claim to have a license but actually don't or they may use other people's license numbers for their business. It's amazing how many homeowners hire unlicensed people to build their projects! This violation is illegal for the contractor, plus it makes homeowners wide open to liability. A contractor's license status can divulge some particularly important things to you:

- License numbers are usually issued sequentially, so the lower the number is, the longer the contractor has held the license. At a glance, a low license number instantly conveys experience, wisdom, and longevity. That said, it could also mean a person who's *not* up to current times, construction methods, and levels of project management sophistication.

- Higher license numbers would seem to imply that a person has less experience and a new business, but that's not always actually the case. If a tradesperson has been working under a GC for 20 years and then ventures off to start up their own business, they could be a person with a new license but a lot of experience. Likewise, a person working in the family business who succeeds the parent GC must get their own license or create partnerships with two or more experienced individuals. Either of these scenarios triggers a new license.

The bottom line is that you must understand each candidate's license status and the background behind it. Doing so will give you some tidbits of knowledge that you can then use to make intelligent choices.

3.020 ATTRIBUTES OF QUALITY GENERAL CONTRACTORS

The value that a general contractor can provide to a construction project can be summed up in three elements: expertise, project management, and team building.

A general contractor has the construction experience and knowledge to navigate the complete building process, including collaborating with your design team and interpreting complex plans and specifications. It's a daunting task! Next to knowledge, experience, and wisdom, having strong relationships combined with solid project management skills is how a good GC builds your project per the plans and specifications on time, within budget, and at a superior quality level.

3.021 CONSTRUCTION EXPERIENCE VS. EXPERTISE

The overriding attribute of a GC is the construction experience and knowledge they bring to a project. A qualified contractor has built many projects like yours and is always learning by taking steps to increase their knowledge no matter how seasoned they are. Transforming into an expert happens when people couple knowledge with real-life scenarios (a.k.a. experience) and learning from the results. You need an expert, and you need to be confident that you're talking to one by asking the right questions. The TAH Planning Workbook will help you tackle that.

A general contractor's expertise can be compared to what people in other management-level positions have—a qualified GC possesses specific skills and experiences, understands the big picture and overall goals, and assembles a team possessing the specific skill sets that are required to accomplish the goals of a given project. A general contractor doesn't necessarily know the intricacies of what a plumber or electrician does, but the GC *does* hold them accountable for installing their systems per the plans, the scope of work, and building codes. A GC needs to know a little about a lot; they need to assemble the right team and take full responsibility and liability for their work. Trusting that they can do all of this is one of the many leaps of faith you'll need to take with your GC.

3.022 PROJECT MANAGEMENT

A variety of proactive actions and resources all must come together at the right time to ensure that a project is constructed properly and on time. You'll soon be learning about your options for hiring contractors, but regardless of the option you select, certain fundamentals go into managing a residential construction project. All of these always tie back to the one person who's your conductor and guide: your GC.

THE FUNDAMENTALS OF WHAT A GENERAL CONTRACTOR (I.E., THE PROJECT MANAGER) DOES

- Disseminates plans and specifications into a multifaceted battle plan.

- Prepares detailed project schedules that allocate the proper resources (subcontractors, suppliers, employees) to each task.

- Disperses pertinent information to each member of the team (subcontractors, suppliers, employees).

- Utilizes the schedule to procure materials in a timely manner.

- Utilizes the schedule to deploy subcontractors and employees to the job site.

- Supervises construction methods, which materials are used, and the installation of equipment.

- Implements and monitors the quality level of construction.

- Maintains the schedule on a regular basis.

- Possesses superior communication skills and interfaces between all parties.

- Communicates with architects, owner's agents, and homeowners during construction.

- Requests and attends all Building department inspections.

- Provides budget tracking (if necessary) during construction.

- Initiates any extra or change-order work orders.

- Completes the project on time.

3.023 SCHEDULING

Managing a project involves tackling the one thing we don't have complete control over: *time*. No matter what we do, we can't stop time. The next best thing is to manage time efficiently and effectively! Successful project management starts with the almighty keystone of a construction schedule.

A construction schedule focuses on foresight, planning, material procurement, resource allocation, and persistent communication. Pretty easy, right? Unfortunately, many GCs fly by the seat of their pants when it comes to scheduling. This leads to unnecessary delays, cost overruns, and—you guessed it—*missed expectations*. Managing your project is what you're paying a contractor for. If there's no schedule, you aren't getting what you paid for.

"Critical path" is a term used to manage any project schedule. Whether you're designing software, a robot, or a high-rise building, some things must happen before another thing can occur. It's as simple as that. You can only put the countertops on if you have the cabinets in place. A sign of trouble is when your contractor comes to you and says, "What tile do you want for your master bath? We need it Monday!" and you haven't even picked out the tile, let alone ordered it. Something must give: either timing, cost, or quality. All three often apply to an unscheduled project. Now, that being said, it's not always the contractor's fault—the problem could be you getting in the middle of the process or wanting to save a buck or deferring choices during the design process or insisting that something special you personally ordered be installed.

Let us open the door to what must go into a project schedule to keep your project on track. A schedule created before groundbreaking can show when specific materials should be ordered and when construction should start. A schedule should be created before you sign a contract with your contractor. Why? Because having a schedule ensures that they fall into the "expert" category.

Having a tangible schedule in place *before* you commit to a contractor accomplishes several things. First, you know that the project has been thought out in detail. Second, you know when your contractor will expect progress payments. Third, a well-written schedule will identify when certain materials need to be ordered. And fourth, a schedule will expose the almighty completion date. Having a schedule builds accountability and sets expectations for everyone involved.

Most reputable contractors deploy software programs to build a project schedule. That way, right at the beginning, all of the special-order materials that the GC knows will be needed on-site at certain times will actually be there. GCs can only determine these dates if a schedule has been completed and lead times have been established.

Below is a snapshot of scheduling software from a project my team and I did. As you can see, the highlighted cell tells us to order the windows by a specific date. This is tied to a date later in the schedule to when we plan to install the windows. This task is also tied to how long it takes to get the windows and when we need to install them so that the construction process can continue. If we had no schedule to expose these various deadlines, then inevitably, the windows wouldn't arrive when we prefer them to arrive. This is just one example of many critical-path, special-order materials typically needed for a project.

SAMPLE JOB 1 / 73795 S DELLEKER RD
Job 100 Schedule

NAME	%	✓	📅	🕐	👤
Overall	☐		Mon, May 12	80	
Material Procurement	☐		Mon, May 12	13	
ORDER: Windows and Exterior Doors	☐		Mon, May 12	1	
ORDER: Plumbing Fixtures	☐		Tue, May 20	1	
ORDER: Interior Doors and Millwork	☐		Mon, May 26	1	
Start Date	☐		Mon, Jun 2	1	
Windows and Exterior Doors	☐		Mon, Aug 11	2	
Set windows - Entry and Stairwell	☐		Mon, Aug 11	2	

Visit theawakenedhomeowner.com to see samples.

Everyone depends on materials to do their job, but good project management goes deeper than that—assembling human resources such as employees and subcontractors can be just as challenging. A schedule will uncover the dates when each person is required to be on the project. A well-written and well-managed schedule can tell the plumber weeks and even months out when they're expected to be on the job site. Subs like plumbers and electricians (and frankly *everyone*) genuinely appreciate having this kind of detailed schedule because it allows them to properly manage their workload. Beyond scheduling the obvious tasks that need to happen for a construction project, crucial milestones should also be included in the list of tasks. Let's look at a few of those:

✓ City or county Building department inspections: During construction, the county requires inspections at certain times. For example, after the new foundation for your home is excavated and the concrete forms are in place but *before* any concrete is poured, the city must inspect the site and sign off on it. There are several other times when inspections must occur; you'll learn about those in the TAH Building Workbook.

✓ Special inspections by third-party agencies or consultants: The city may require outside agencies to inspect and document construction milestones. Examples of these are structural engineering observations of hardware placement and surveyor certifications of proper setbacks.

One way to maximize your protection is to observe what's happening. By that, I mean have the consultants involved in the project's design visit the job site and inspect the contractor's work. For example, after the home or addition has been framed up but before the walls are closed, the engineer of record can inspect and certify that the work has been built per the specifications. Although this is not necessarily mandated by anyone, it's a good idea, especially if you have concerns.

Progress payments is another method of protection. Indicating when each progress payment is due within the schedule is helpful for managing your finances and provides solid protection because the schedule is directly linked to the contract, or at least it should be. Seeing as it's not uncommon for payments to be linked to the items above, that's all the more reason to show them on the schedule.

Each contractor and business will have their own methods and tools for scheduling a project. What matters is whether the schedule exists, how seriously it's taken, and—most importantly!—how often it's updated. Having a project schedule can be equated to having a plan to hike a summit in the sense that no matter how much planning and scheduling you do, adversities will also play a role. Maybe you hit an unpassable part of the trail or there's a delay to your job site due to weather conditions. The point is that once you break ground, the schedule becomes a working tool that *must* be used, modified, and cared for.

3.030 CONSTRUCTION TEAM

Much of a GC's value lies in assembling a team of qualified employees, subcontractors, and suppliers with whom the GC has longstanding relationships. These are the resources the GC depends on and is liable for. Some GCs are armed with employees who perform some or all of the work; others subcontract everything. The latter are known as "paper contractors" or "suitcase contractors." Often, GCs have a blend of employees and subcontractors. This allows them to have a reasonable level of control while also having the ability to tap into trade subcontractors to perform specific tasks.

GENERAL CONTRACTOR

EMPLOYEES

SUPPLIERS

SUBCONTRACTORS

Suppliers play an equally important role in a construction project since nothing can get done without materials. The process of vetting reliable suppliers (and subs, for that matter) takes time and strong relationships. A seasoned contractor has established, solid relationships with suppliers, which is a testament to their credibility. From paying bills on time to ensuring fair exchanges, a supplier will jump whenever their best customer asks them to. This is where a GC provides value by circumventing a maze of challenges.

3.031 EMPLOYEES

In today's world of construction labor, the average worker is over 50 years old. Many of these veterans came up the ranks over the past 30 years and are now established as builders or GCs. Compounding the average-age reality is that many young people today are not entering the trades, therefore limiting growth and capacities for existing contractors. It's a nationwide issue that hopefully will be addressed by a wage surge, trade schools, and more women entering the workforce.

A contractor with a team of employees is best positioned to serve you. The value comes in the form of control—if a builder has their own employees perform core tasks such as foundations, framing, and carpentry, then schedules and quality are inevitably better maintained.

A GC operation with a crew of employees is often structured as a hierarchy. It begins with a job foreman and then goes to journeymen, carpenters, apprentices, and laborers. A foreman is the supervisor who's specific to a job site and is often the right-hand man of the old wise GC. Many of these foremen are just as knowledgeable as GCs since they see the actual application of the plans daily on the front lines. You want to bond with this person! Bring water to the crew and maybe even a few adult beverages at the end of a hard day. It's prudent to dig into how your contractor candidates are organized from a personnel perspective when you conduct your interviews. More on this when the time comes to plan your project.

3.032 SUBCONTRACTORS

Subcontractors play a vital role in constructing a project. A qualified GC brings an established, prequalified network of trusted subcontractors with whom they work regularly. Your GC will tap into their relationships to ensure quality work and timely project completion.

These companies are part of your contractor's team and imperative to a well-run project. Subs are considered single-trade contractors; therefore, they bounce between projects and are not on your site for the entire duration of the project. This matters to you because subs like to work for GCs who schedule them accurately, have the materials ready, and pay them on time. If a sub gets called to a job and it's not prepared for them, they walk and go to another project, leaving you in the dust. A good GC schedules a sub just like they schedule material purchasing: they create a task in the schedule, assign the sub to it, and notify the sub weeks or even months in advance. The GC communicates with the sub again as their arrival gets closer and then implements the plan.

A GC could have crews of three to six people, but if you're building a custom home, the odds that they can perform *all* of the necessary tasks are unlikely. Thus, it's quite common for a GC to subcontract out a large percentage of the work. The larger the project is, the more subcontracting will take place. The subs play an even more significant role in this kind of project! Their work might begin with excavation and foundation and move on to handling the plumbing, electrical, heating and air-conditioning, insulation, sheetrock, roofing, and so on. You could have ten to thirty different specialty subcontractors involved in your project. Once again, this is the value that a good GC brings to the table.

3.033 SUPPLIERS

Think of suppliers as being like mama bird returning food to the nest. The subs and crews are hungry for materials, and if they don't get it...well, you know the rest. Suppliers provide materials to the GC and subs. They do not physically work on the site and they do not require a license. The materials they supply encompass a vast range of items, starting with concrete for your foundation, lumber for your structure, etc.

Supplies represent a considerable percentage of the cost of a project and are the number-one critical-path item on a schedule. The crew could be on-site, but with no lumber to feed them, you got nothing. This is where your GC comes in. A qualified contractor has longstanding relationships with suppliers who smooth over the acquisition of materials. The responsibility of procuring materials should remain under your contractor's wing.

There's one way to undermine the value your builder brings, and that's inserting yourself into the supply chain. For a variety of reasons (but usually cost), homeowners want to be the mama bird and intercept the acquisition of materials. This causes numerous issues and hidden liabilities for a homeowner. Unless you're experienced in this area, I recommend resisting the temptation to enter the ring of ordering materials. Instead, you can obsess over what you want but leave the ordering to the pros so that the entry door you love actually fits.

HINT!

A prevalent contributor to a poor construction experience is the absence of material specifications when the time arrives to place orders and then install the materials. Way back in step two of the design process, I emphasized the importance of having detailed specifications. Your contractor can only act on ordering materials if you have made absolutely all of your decisions. Once you break ground, it can be too late. Focus on what you want and document it in the design process! Your contractor will then be empowered to meet your expectations.

3.040 HOW A GENERAL CONTRACTOR MAKES A LIVING

Contractors make their living by marking up the labor, materials, subcontractors, and equipment they use to build your project. Sometimes referred to as P and O (for "profit and overhead"), this profit margin covers all of the overhead associated with hiring employees: their wages, payroll taxes, benefits, and insurance policies. GCs also pay themselves, plus they make the profit they need to make (and should make) in order to build their business.

3.041 LABOR COSTS

In a GC business, labor plays a large factor in the cost of construction. The total cost of labor goes beyond an hourly wage, and a GC includes the company costs of employing personnel. The term that's used to come to a total hourly cost for an employee is called "burdened labor" and is often based on a percentage of the hourly wage. For example, if a carpenter is paid $30.00 per hour, a contractor will add an additional 35% to cover the employment costs, making the hourly cost $40.50 per hour before any profit is earned by the GC. Depending on the profit percentage the GC desires, this carpenter could be billed to the project anywhere from $60.00 to $100.00 per hour. You may care about how labor costs are calculated depending on the type of contract you and your contractor have. We'll drill down into the standard methods that contractors use to structure their agreements in the next section, which is about understanding contracts.

3.042 SUBS AND SUPPLIERS

The value of a GC team comes at a price. And it should! GCs go to great lengths to source, qualify, and interact with numerous trade contractors and suppliers. Once your builder has been provided with a set of plans and specifications, they'll distribute them to each subcontractor and supplier, obtain costs, and apply their percentage of profit and overhead. The overhead dollars are intended to compensate the GC for the following:

- ✓ Having a qualified set of resources as part of the team.
- ✓ Putting in the time needed to perform all project management responsibilities.
- ✓ Covering the cost of assuming liability for the teams' materials and installations.
- ✓ Covering operating costs.
- ✓ Delivering a completed project per the plans, specifications, and owner's expectations.

✓ Having the funds they need to support and grow their business.

A hint and a caution: There's one pervasive obstacle that homeowners are tempted to erect, and that's hiring some of their own subcontractors. Don't be that meddling homeowner! Interfering in a project managed by a GC can cause numerous problems. To avoid this disruption, refrain from interjecting yourself into the management of the project—let the GC do their job. If you can't resist hiring some of your own subs or performing some of the work yourself, you may be what's called an owner-builder. I will explain this method of building your project later.

SUMMARY OF WHAT GENERAL CONTRACTORS DO _____

✓ Contractors come in two varieties who work together: your general contractor who oversees the entire project and their team of specialized subcontractors.

✓ GCs have varying profiles and business models, all of which should be considered.

✓ The values that a GC brings to the project are construction expertise, project management, and managing the construction team.

✓ A GC makes their living by adding overhead and profit to all of the costs of a project. This is usually expressed as a percentage.

3.100 ESTIMATING YOUR PROJECT COST

The day when you obtain the final costs on your project is the day when all of the time, effort, and money that went into the design process pays off! This section aims to enlighten you with all of the project estimating aspects. A warning: these can be quite involved. My goal here is to introduce you to a methodology that includes important steps and materials you can use to arm yourself with knowledge. Once you're ready to begin planning your project, in the TAH Planning Workbook, I provide the ideal steps you can take at the ideal times to hunt for the right people. I also show you how to obtain estimates, how and when to monitor costs, and how organizing costs will help you make important decisions before it's too late.

WHAT WE'LL COVER

- ✓ What a project estimate is
- ✓ Who estimates the project cost
- ✓ How estimates are broken down
- ✓ When estimates are obtained
- ✓ How estimates are secured

Requesting estimates may be your first foray into working with a contractor. Your plans and specifications are the first thing you have to build credibility with said contractor—a solid set of plans and specifications motivates a contractor to spend the necessary time to cost out your project, and believe it or not, when reliable, dependable information is at the contractor's fingertips, you may even get a better price. In contrast, a mediocre set of plans with no specifications can drag out the process and influence a contractor's pricing. It may even impede you from finding a contractor at all! So now is the time to polish up those specifications.

Remember, the specifications and scope of work document supplement the plans with information that either didn't make it onto the plans or was inappropriate for the plan pages. This supplemental information includes a detailed list of materials that your contractor will depend on to provide an accurate estimate. You will and should expect the contractor to include these costs in their estimate.

3.101 WHAT A PROJECT ESTIMATE IS

Earlier, we took on the task of building a budget. The budget is the first layer of thinking about cost from different angles and how your dreams can affect costs, what kind of investment you make, and your comfort level. We built a budget based on some soul-searching and theoretical costing methods to get you beyond your delusions. Your budget was your sanity check; it has been a good benchmark up to this point.

But whereas a budget is high-level thinking about cost, a project estimate comes along deeper in the planning stages as a direct result of the design and planning steps I've been laying out throughout this book. Although it's a project "estimate," your contractors will actually establish a cost based on your final design plans and specifications. The theoretical aspects of the budgeting exercise are out the window—now we have hard costs. The more thorough your plans are and the more detailed your specifications are, the more accurate the costs will be and the fewer surprises you'll have down the construction road. And you don't want surprises.

3.102 WHO ESTIMATES THE PROJECT COST

Although you, your architect, or your agent will facilitate the process and you won't personally be calculating the project cost, it will be your job to facilitate the process and ensure that your contractor candidates have the information they need to provide you with accurate estimates. If you haven't already touched base with contractors, the estimating process can accomplish two things simultaneously: you can find your contractor and you can estimate your project.

You may recall that you had a few budget checkpoints during the design process. Those were in place to ensure that your project was still on track. Budget checkpoints could be as simple as having discussions with the design team and rechecking your budget calculations or as complex as engaging with engineers and contractors. Bringing in a contractor at the checkpoints is not a bad idea for several reasons. First, they'll add construction knowledge to the team. Second, they'll have a better pulse on current construction costs. Third, it's an early opportunity to begin the contractor selection process. And fourth, the contractor will have early insights into the project when the official estimating time arrives. Some contractors are amenable to engaging that early in the process and some are not. If your architect has a strong working relationship with a contractor, they may be able to bring in a construction expert who's interested in your project.

INSIGHTS AND HINTS! _____

- It takes a tremendous amount of time for a contractor to estimate a project—depending on the project size, it can range from 40 to 400 hours. This time suck is the first thing on the contractor's mind when they receive your invite. The second thing is do you have the money?

- Attempting to obtain estimates from more than three contractors can be overwhelming and complicate the process. Letting a builder know you're getting seven estimates will likely undermine their motivation. That's not for fear of competition, but more about the odds of inexperienced or sketchy characters surfacing and undermining the bidding process.

- A skilled and experienced builder will review your plans in detail and build the project in their mind. This has immense value.

- The more thorough the plans are, the more precise they are to a contractor. If a plan set is missing information, contains unrealistic details, has incomplete details, lacks specifications, is missing engineering, and so on, the less likely a contractor will be to want to bid on the project. This will directly affect their price.

- Conversely, suppose a set of plans is thorough and includes everything a contractor needs to see. In that case, they'll be motivated to provide a proposal because they know that a greater percentage of their costs will be protected.

- You might think, "I'm the customer, so if he doesn't like my plans, I'll just find someone else." But searching for a mediocre contractor to bid on your crappy plans is counterintuitive! Way too many homeowners provide inadequate plans and boast about the low fees they paid...and inevitably end up with an inferior contractor and a lousy project.

- Pay close attention to the builders who ask many questions about the plans and your scope of work. This interest saves you money and time and protects your expectations. The question-askers are the guys you want on your side! Oh, and don't take advantage of this tendency—the seasoned guys can sniff you out and will move on to the next project.

After learning about your options for hiring contractors in upcoming sections, you can form a plan to estimate your project as you move into planning your project.

3.103 WHEN TO OBTAIN ESTIMATES

There are at least two opportunities to obtain estimates. These will depend on a few factors:

- The size, scale, and complexity of your project.
- The design process and how complete your plans and specifications are.

BEWARE!

Suppose serious budget concerns arise during the design process. In that case, this may be the time to go beyond a budget checkpoint during the design process—you might want to have a contractor consult with you and your architect to provide you with a preliminary estimate. This estimate may not be as precise as the final one will be, but it will surpass what's available using the budget checkpoint method. Knowing when to approach estimating beyond just looking at a budget is certainly one of the more precarious decisions a homeowner must make. Ultimately, you'll have to make the call with input from your design team.

GETTING ESTIMATES DURING
STEP TWO OF THE DESIGN PROCESS

The first opportunity to obtain an estimate is at the end of the design development phase *provided that* you have all of the necessary information a contractor needs. (See Bid Package on page 298.) The best candidates for early estimates are projects that are relatively simple, such as:

- Remodeling projects where no space is being added to the home.
- Small addition projects where the design is straightforward.
- Kitchen and bathroom remodeling.

For larger or new home projects, an estimate can be obtained at the end of the design development stage...with the caveat that the estimate could vary depending on the final outcome of the construction documents step.

The advantage of attempting to gather some form of estimate at this stage empowers you to make informed decisions before the plans are finalized. For example, you may decide to defer a portion of the project or change material and/or equipment specs.

GETTING ESTIMATES DURING THE CONSTRUCTION DOCUMENTS PHASE (STEP THREE OF DESIGN PROCESS)

When you complete step three of the construction document phase, that's the official and best time to obtain accurate estimates of the project. Construction documents provide your GC with all the information they will need to provide an accurate and dependable estimate. The key components of construction documents are:

- Architectural plans and details.

- Construction material and systems specifications.

- Consultants' plans, details, and material and equipment specifications.

- Interior design plans, details, and material specifications.

- A scope of work detailing the work to be performed and materials to be provided by the GC.

Remember, though, the design process is finished at this point. If you require revisions to your design and specifications as an outcome of the estimating process, you could incur costs because the plans will need to be revised to fit your new scope of work. This conundrum is one of the largest obstacles you could face and why specific steps are in place during the design process to remedy this challenge.

HINT!

The overriding objective of the construction documents phase is to prepare a completed set of plans to submit to your city for permitting. If cost is a concern, it's wise to obtain estimates *before* the construction documents are 100% complete.

3.104 BREAKING DOWN ESTIMATES

Comparing estimates between contractors is at the top of the list of challenges for homeowners. This stems from not knowing how to control the process and instead accepting bids in varying formats, making it impossible to know who has the most accurate estimate. Fortunately, this widespread problem can be overcome with good plans and specs and a system to wrangle all of the costs. We call this having a work breakdown structure. Does that sound familiar? I first introduced the WBS during the design process to use as a tool for structuring specifications. Now we'll use the same framework to attach costs to each category.

To begin the estimating process, you or your architect will prepare a bid package (coming up next), which is essentially a compilation of all of the work that was done during the design process. A breakdown structure becomes part of your bid package and is how you'll analyze costs before contracting with a firm to build your project.

THE BENEFITS OF A WORK BREAKDOWN STRUCTURE

- Gives you a method to organize your project costs.

- Ensures that you have thought of *all* areas of construction.

- Provides you with a format to outline the specifications and scope of work.

- Allows you to compare contractor candidate costs.

When a contractor estimates a project behind the scenes, they'll have their own methods and tools to use for assembling costs. These are almost always organized by category and include the four elements of labor, materials, subcontractors, and equipment. The problem is that each contractor will have a different way of breaking down their estimates. When you receive estimates in various formats, it becomes impossible to compare costs and be confident that each contractor has included every single thing.

The solution is to turn the tables and issue a uniform work breakdown structure to each contractor candidate. This structure should outline how you would like the project to be broken out. The best part is that you already set this up during the design process—now you just need to tweak the sheet a little.

In this section, I'll show you a WBS format that contractors can identify with and that you can use to obtain costs. This isn't something *you* will fill out, though! Instead, use it as you request and compile estimates. Imagine handing this to three contractors and asking them to break out their costs by category. The results would be eye-opening.

A work breakdown structure is a list of construction categories that almost always go into a project. Breaking your project down into such categories can help you better understand the different elements that go into the project and their associated costs. My intention here is not to train you in how to run a construction company—I just want to enlighten you as to how contractors think about a project. Or, to go back to our favorite phrase, I want to tell you how to know what you don't know.

Before we look at a WBS more closely, however, it's helpful to understand a particular aspect of construction costs, namely that the four elements of construction apply to each WBS item. Knowing this industry standard is essential as you're analyzing costs from your candidates.

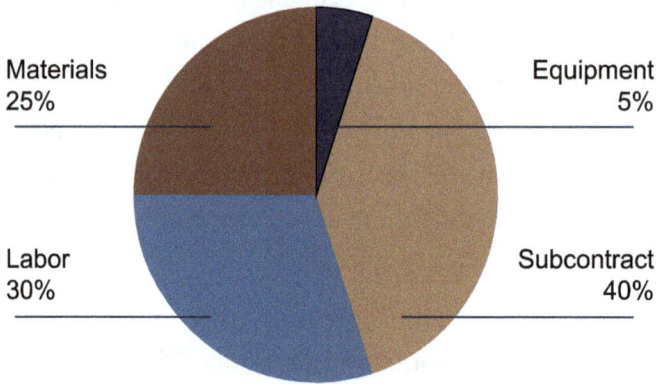

Labor: *This is labor provided by your contractor, typically by their employees.*

Materials: *These are materials provided by your contractor that are included in the contract. For example, under Category 25: Rough Carpentry (see below), your contractor would include all of the lumber, hardware, and supplies needed to build your home or addition.*

Subcontractors: *These are trade contractors whom your general contractor may hire to perform certain aspects of the project. Good examples would be an electrician, a plumber, a roofer, a tile-setter, etc.*

Equipment/Other: *This is primarily reserved for equipment needed on the project to perform specific tasks. A good example could be scaffolding to install stucco or siding material. "Other" costs could be permits.*

The pie chart above gives you some insight into how the four elements are often divided amongst a project. This is bound to vary depending on the project size and complexity and the capabilities of your contractor.

THE WORK BREAKDOWN STRUCTURE

DIVISION	CONSTRUCTION CATEGORY	
	MASTER PROJECT	
22	Site preparation excavation	$0
23	Demolition and disposal	$0
24	Concrete	$0
25	Rough carpentry	$0
26	Sheet metal and waterproofing	$0
27	Roofing	$0
28	Siding and exterior trim	$0
30	Skylights	$0
31	Windows	$0
32	Exterior doors	$0
33	Stucco and masonry	$0
34	Plumbing	$0
36	Electrical	$0
37	Low-voltage work	$0
38	Mechanical	$0
40	Fireplaces	$0
42	Insulation	$0
43	Sheetrock	$0
44	Interior doors and trim	$0
45	Stairs	$0
47	Cabinetry	$0
48	Hardware	$0
49	Tile	$0
50	Slab: stonework	$0
51	Solid surfaces	$0
52	Flooring	$0
57	Appliances	$0
60	Glass	$0
65	Painting	$0
68	Landscaping	$0
90	Specialty	$0
	Total	$0

The first column is a numbering system called "divisions" that organizes the data. The second column is the categories of construction. These categories are how a construction project progresses, from site preparation and demolition to the final steps of painting and landscaping. The third column is where your contractors enter a cost. These costs include all four construction elements. Based on a fixed price contract, each line item would consist of the contractor's profit and overhead and the total you'll pay. For example, Division 31: Windows would include all of the materials needed to provide and install the windows, the labor required to do so, the subcontractors who are needed, and necessary equipment such as scaffolding, lifts, and/or cranes. This organization method helps keep things in a logical order while maintaining simplicity when it comes to compiling and comparing costs.

✓ There are even more benefits to using a breakdown structure as you move down the path of planning and you hit the estimating and contracting stage.

✓ During the design process, we touched on specifications— which are the materials, equipment, and scope of work— and their importance. The WBS structure is how we organize the specifications. When the time comes to request estimates, the contractor can reference the corresponding division categories within the specifications and include them in the cost.

✓ When signing a contract with your contractor, using the breakdown helps you understand the payment schedule that the contractor presents to you. Having a breakdown to validate the payment schedule can come in handy.

✓ To organize the inevitable mounds of files, you can use the WBS system as a folder structure hierarchy to organize estimates and specifications. You can find out more about this in the online TAH bonus content.

This section will be precious to you later in the process as we navigate through the Planning Workbook! Understanding how estimates are organized and presented will help in numerous ways, such as categorizing costs, comparing costs between contractors, and making informed decisions about how to select your contractor.

3.110 THE ESTIMATING PROCESS

The person who's the most intimate with your plans and specifications is your architect or designer. It's not unheard of for an architect to assist in facilitating the estimating process. Although this service usually falls outside the scope of design and more into construction administration, the extra cost you'll incur by involving your design pros could pay off immensely. However, since the estimating process is also your time to engage with contractors, I wouldn't necessarily relinquish the responsibility entirely—instead, I recommend teaming up with your designers for the best outcome. An overriding benefit to having help with the estimating process is that architects possess far more industry- and project-specific knowledge than you do. This professional disposition can produce more thorough proposals from contractors thanks to your architect projecting credibility and simultaneously building in accountability and expectations for the estimate.

Let's dig into the bidding process and what I believe should be your baseline attempt to obtain costs. As we do, keep one overriding principle in mind: the bid package is your accountability mechanism for the design team, the contractor, and *you!*

3.111 BID PACKAGE

A bid package includes the following:

- ✓ A cover letter inviting a contractor to provide a proposal with detailed instructions and deadline dates.

- ✓ A scope of work document organized by category to articulate the materials and equipment that will be provided for and installed on the project.

- ✓ A work breakdown structure detailing how you want the costs organized and broken down.

Plans titled "Bid Set" and dated provided by your design team.

- ✓ Architectural pages (see Understanding Plans, Architectural Pages on page 213)

- ✓ MEP pages (see Understanding Plans, Architectural Pages on page 213)

- ✓ Fire suppression pages, if applicable (see Understanding Design Professionals, Fire Sprinklers on page 101)

- ✓ Civil plans, if applicable (see Understanding Plans, Civil Plans on page 230)

- ✓ Structural pages (see Understanding Plans, Structural Plans on page 231)

- ✓ Energy pages (see Understanding Plans, on page 236)

- ✓ Interior pages (see Understanding Plans on page 237)

Consultants Reports

- ✓ Geotechnical report, also known as soils report.

- ✓ Other consultant reports or plans as they apply.

1. **Bid set:** Have your design team prepare a completed plan set that includes all of the pages listed above. The set should be titled "bid set" and be dated and stamped Not for Construction or Preliminary. The titles and dates of plan sets are crucial to managing the process. The date the document is published is typically found in the lower right-hand corner of the architects' border. Title your soft copy file accordingly: "Jones_BidSet_xx-xx-xxxx.pdf" ("Last Name_BidSet_Month_Day_Year"). The Not for Construction stamp prevents plan pages that are no longer relevant from surfacing during construction.

2. **Revisions:** Do not change the bid set once it has been "published"! Issuing revisions during the bidding process can increase confusion, delays, and misunderstandings, leading to your wallet being emptied. Instead, as you discover any changes, keep a running list post-bid set so the changes can be included in follow-up estimating requests.

3. **Proposal request:** Issue the bid set, scope of work, and material/equipment specifications to the builders you've selected. Because you've invested time and money in a quality set of plans and specs, call attention to these documents so that the candidates can disseminate the information.

4. **Invitations:** Whichever way you decide to facilitate the proposal request process, encouraging the candidates to visit the project site and meet with your design team is a prudent way to build a relationship, obtain possible revisions to add to your list, and expose the builder to the existing structures and site. The underlying benefits of a site visit are to give the builder a fair look at the site-related scope, meet the design team, and see how engaged they

desire to be. Having your potential builder meet with your design team will provide you with another source of input when the time comes to make the final decision.

5. **Format:** Establish a format for the proposals. Rather than try to compare estimates in different formats and cost breakdowns, turn the tables here and request that the candidates organize their costs by your format. The WBS system I've created is an option that empowers you to compare estimates side by side as builders enter their costs into each category. This levels the playing field for all and addresses the objective of comparing apples to apples, so to speak.

6. **Options and Alternatives:** Pre-identifying portions of a project during the bidding process can save an immense amount of time for both you and the builder. **Options** are defined as areas or a particular scope of a project that you'd like to understand the cost of before committing to it. For example, a separate cost for a Bath #1 remodel or a separate cost for hardwood flooring throughout the entire home, not just the primary suite. **Alternatives** are related to scope and materials; you want to understand the cost of replacing certain materials with a different material. For example, say the scope of work specifies ¾" thick by 3" wide red oak flooring in the primary suite as your baseline cost, but you'd like to understand how much more it would cost for walnut wood.

7. **Phasing:** This identifies a portion of a project that you'd like to understand the cost of, enabling you to understand the value of a particular area and empowering you to make an informed decision about it. For example, say you've designed an addition to the front of the home for an office

and the rear of the house for a primary suite. If you elect *not* to do both simultaneously, you would like to have the two areas broken out as two separate projects. Informing a contractor that phasing the project is possible makes their estimating process more efficient.

One of the most significant project planning milestones is receiving bids from your contractors. You now have essential data to make the final scope of work decisions and a better idea of who your contractor may be. Based on the cost breakdowns provided, at this point, generally one more round of estimating is needed to complete the process.

The revisions step is your chance to close the loop on questions, make final material selections, and make decisions related to options, alternatives, and phasing. The revision step can also be your time to work towards your final contractor decision by engaging more with your contractor candidates. Being able to gauge their response time and accuracy to your revisions affords you an opportunity to check their level of interest and availability to begin construction.

3.112 REVISIONS

During the estimating process, revisions will inevitably occur on your project. A handful of situations can trigger revisions to a project:

- Input from builders during the bidding process. Questions that arise—usually clarifying a detail or material or spotting an error—can often require revising plans.
- Inaccurate or incomplete proposals from builders.
- Changing your mind on design, scope, and/or materials.
- Final decisions on options, alternatives, and phases.
- Results of the approvals and permits process.

At the end of the first bidding process, it's advisable to gather *all* input from your builder, design team, and Building department and then combine it with your final revision requests. Doing so will allow you to issue *all* necessary revisions, minimizing confusion during the bid process. Also, as a result of interfacing with all three builders, now may be the time to narrow down the candidates to two rather than three. It's best to thin the herd if you feel you cannot work with one of them.

The steps I've outlined below depend on the number and degree of revisions. Let's assume that you want to tighten up your project cost with one round of revisions. Taking these steps should get you there.

REVISION STEPS

If you already have the permit application feedback, become aware of the requested revisions through your architect or designer. These could impact the design and cost of the project.

1. Provide a list of your revision requests to your designer if they pertain to the plans. A universal way to differentiate revisions from the original design is to place a "cloud" border around them within each plan page or scope of work document. Because many Building departments require this, your builders will be used to this method of identifying changes and responses to Building departments.

2. Have your architect date the plans and mark them with Revised or Permit Submittal. There's an industry standard that many (unfortunately not all) architects and designers use to track submittals and revisions: in the upper right-hand corner of the plan pages, there should be a box to record revision dates, while the date in the lower right-hand corner of the plans remains the original date. I have seen

this handled in a variety of ways, so be sure to become aware of how your designer manages changes through their plans.

3. Prepare your list of revisions as they pertain to scope, material, and equipment specifications. Perhaps you'd like to increase the allowance for the kitchen backsplash, for example. Supplement your revised plans with your document.

4. Select the options and alternatives you had separated earlier in the bid process if you're ready to commit.

5. Date your plan file much the same way as before, but this time, include "...REV1_xx-xx-xxxx" ("...REV[Revision-Number]_Month_Day_Year") so that the file can be differentiated from the original.

6. Submit your plans to your builder candidates or meet directly with each candidate. This is an opportunity to call attention to the revisions and interface with your builder more. By letting your candidates know your final decisions on options and alternatives, that (perhaps) you've narrowed down the candidates, and that the permit is in the process sends the message that you're close to deciding. Giving them insight into the final inclusions of options, alternatives, and phases helps candidates understand the project as a whole, thus potentially influencing their final bid submission.

Finally, assemble your final proposals, sit back, and compare the costs with the following ranking criteria.

3.113 RANKING

Here, we'll rank each proposal using a list of questions. At this stage, we're not necessarily making a final decision but more using a tool to separate emotion from the selection process. You may like Ace, but Fred sure was thorough and asked many questions.

RANKING QUESTIONS

- ❑ How did I find this candidate? Internet, invite, referral, advertising, neighborhood?
- ❑ How long have they been in business?
- ❑ Have they completed projects for someone I know?
- ❑ Have they worked in my neighborhood?
- ❑ Have they demonstrated competency with similar projects?
- ❑ Have I seen their work?
- ❑ Have I spoken with at least three past customers?
- ❑ Have I spoken with a customer currently under construction?
- ❑ Have they worked with my designer before? If so, does it appear to be a strong working relationship or just an acquaintance? How well did they communicate with me and my designer?
- ❑ Does technology play a large part in their operation?
- ❑ What was their response time to a proposal request?
- ❑ Did they visit the job site?
- ❑ Did they request meetings with me, the architect, and/or the consultants?
- ❑ Did they ask for clarifications and further information?
- ❑ Did they respond well to my work breakdown structure request?
- ❑ What was their response time to a revision request?
- ❑ What is the projected duration of the project?

From requesting bids to ranking, by now you should have a good sense of who you'd like to build your project with. In the soon-to-be-released online Planning Workbook, you'll find a bid and ranking process ready for you to use.

SUMMARY OF HOW TO ESTIMATE YOUR PROJECT COST _____

- ✓ An estimate goes beyond a budget—it gives you hard costs based off your plans and specifications.
- ✓ Your contractor candidates will provide you with estimates.
- ✓ There are two primary times to obtain estimates: near the end of step two of the design process or at the end of step three.
- ✓ Using a universal way to break down estimates empowers you to intelligently understand and compare costs between contractors.
- ✓ There are prescribed steps to an estimating process. These can be accomplished on your own or with help from your architect or agent.
- ✓ The estimating process could be your first foray into working with and qualifying contractors.
- ✓ Revisions should be carefully managed so as not to confuse the process.
- ✓ Ranking your estimates is a good time to sit back, analyze the data, and ponder your candidates.

3.200 CONTRACTING METHODS

Finding the right general contractor is clearly one of the biggest challenges and milestones in the world of designing and building your new home—after all, your team will consist of your designers, consultants, and general contractor. There are two common paths to take as well as some alternative routes to approach the design and construction of your project. You'll learn more about those in Options for Hiring Your Team *on page 346*. In the meantime, this section aims to enlighten you about two completely different ways that a general contractor may operate their business from a financial perspective. These options will matter to you when the time comes to obtain estimates and enter a contract. With this information in your knowledge bank, you can better go from understanding contracts to completely understanding agreements with your builder.

WHAT WE'LL COVER _____

✓ The cost-plus method of contracting

✓ The fixed price method of contracting

_____

3.201 TWO METHODS OF CONTRACTING

How the contracting method is addressed in your contract boils down to your risk tolerance. How much does the risk tip in your favor or your contractor's favor? How high does price rank on your priority list? Maybe you're saying to yourself "I'm in a hurry and I want to get started! I'll figure out that material later" or you're thinking "Maybe I'll raise the ceiling or maybe not—let's wait and see." Either way, you expect to understand the project's price beforehand. Worse yet, you think you'll be 100% sure about the price.

Does that approach work for you? Many homeowners don't realize the risk they're taking and wind up heading down the wrong trail. They inevitably become entangled in a mess…and the bridge behind them just washed out. There's no turning back.

The project's total price can be expressed in two ways: a fixed-price contract or a cost-plus agreement. A fixed-price contract is the safest for both parties, but it does require a thorough set of plans and specifications and a contractor who can pin the costs down to the dollar. We'll start with the higher-risk method of cost-plus contracts and then compare it to the lower-risk option of fixed-price contracts. Here we go with the first of two forks in the trail!

3.202 COST-PLUS CONTRACTS

Remember Ace the Builder in the section about delusions early on in the book? The contractor who said "Three hundred bucks a foot? No problem!" for your new primary suite? Say you threw together some plans and leaped into a cost-plus contract with Ace. You can guess how the rest of the story goes: you're locked in the car and in the back seat as Ace takes you for a ride. But you can't put *all* of the blame on Ace—you didn't know or didn't want to see the truth and you took a leap of faith. What happened after that is mostly on you. If you have a thick skin and high tolerance for this approach, you may pull it off, but it likely won't be cheaper and won't be on time.

COMMON TRIGGERS FOR COST-PLUS CONTRACTS

✓ The homeowner is anxious to start construction.

✓ The plans are mediocre.

✓ The specifications and scope of work are incomplete.

✓ The homeowner is unaware and inexperienced.

✓ Price is not a high priority for the homeowner.

A cost-plus contract is also sometimes referred to as a time-and-materials contract. It essentially means the general contractor is reimbursed for all of the expenses (costs) incurred on your project PLUS an agreed-upon profit added to all of the costs. How this can work in your favor boils down to two considerations: you genuinely don't care how much the project will ultimately cost or your project is tiny and has a limited duration. You can then open your checkbook, sign all of the blank checks, and hand them over to your GC.

Why does this method even exist? Landing a cost-plus large project is a dream come true for a contractor because there's no financial risk for them. This contractor heaven is especially true if they had nothing to do with creating your plans—they can just go to work for you and send you bills for what seems like an eternity.

But it's not all on the general contractor! Many projects take this path because the plans and specifications are incomplete or inadequate. Estimating a project off crappy plans coupled with a homeowner who can't decide on things is a recipe for disaster. This situation can morph into a cost-plus contract, change-order hell, and inevitable disagreements down the path.

All that said, a cost-plus contract does have some benefits and can be beneficial if both sides manage it properly. This method can work exceptionally well for a homeowner with a lot of experience in remodeling and building homes, for example. Perhaps you have a great GC who provides a high level of quality work but may not be the best at administration. If you allocate enough time to manage the GC, you may end up with a project with the most value. But don't fool yourself! You need to know a lot and be able to spot "mistakes" in billing, because there will be plenty of them. First and foremost, you'll need full transparency—seeing the actual costs of what the contractor paid to their suppliers, subcontractors, and employees empowers you to understand the costs that drive decisions down the line.

If you want to rappel the cliff of a cost-plus contract, I have some suggestions for ensuring that the rope is secure at the top. A cost-plus/time-and-material agreement can be wide open and should be closely scrutinized. It's prudent to identify the hourly rates, profits, overhead percentages, and calculation methods when they're included in the contract for a cost-plus project. If a budget has been created in conjunction with a "not to exceed clause" in your cost-plus agreement, this should be referenced and attached as an exhibit to the contract. If any incentives are agreed to, they should be inserted as well.

In the Estimating Your Project Cost section on page 285, I introduced a work breakdown structure, which is a list of construction categories for organizing the scope of work and costs. This tool allows you to categorize expenses as they come in. Agreeing on how costs are delivered and identified along with how frequently you'll be billed for said costs is a start. Properly attaching profit and overhead is paramount to making this approach work!

WHAT NEEDS TO BE IN A COST-PLUS CONTRACT

Identify how frequently billing will occur, such as once a week, twice monthly, etc. This is often tied to the contractor's payroll periods.

1. Agree on the billed hourly rate for each employee. This does not include the contractor's profit and overhead but should consist of the overhead for employing each person. Translation: one guy's $30.00 per-hour cost may be $45.00 (40% to 50% higher) for you depending on the benefits provided. Watch this one, because some contractors double-dip here and tack P and O onto each hour and then add the P and O again at the bottom of their bills to create the total.

2. Agree that ALL employees on the job are on the payroll and are receiving all of the benefits you're being charged

for. This is another loophole contractors can latch onto by hiring day laborers, paying them in cash, and then billing the homeowner for the agreed-upon rate. This behavior is illegal and it's insurance fraud, but it happens way too often. So talk about it and support the agreement with the documentation requirements.

3. Agree on how the contractor's time will be handled and what their rate is. Contractors can spend a lot of time off-site dealing with your project: ordering materials, meeting with designers and architects, making calls and sending emails to the teams, even billing you to send you a bill. Have this discussion and consider agreeing that any time spent on-site working with the tools or having meetings with you or your representative will be billed hourly and properly categorized; otherwise, time spent will be covered in the overhead percentage at the bottom of their bill. Remember, if your contractor must call the plumber when they're on another job, they're going to add a percentage to that plumber's cost to cover their time and expenses.

4. Mistakes will occur and can be a source of contention. Agreeing on how mistakes will be handled on-site can circumvent conflicts. Arguments generally stem from whose mistake it was, why it happened, and who should pay to rectify it. In a cost-plus contract, it can be argued that you as the homeowner must pay for ALL time and materials used regardless of the reason. This is part of the risk. It can also be argued that the contractor should pay by using their P and O. Often, these mistakes occur because of poor plans, insufficient details, and a lack of information. Have this conversation ahead of time and agree on how mistakes will be handled.

5. Agree that all backup copies of receipts, bills, statements, and time cards submitted by the original vendor will clearly identify YOUR project. Do not agree to pay any bills that do not identify your project or are handwritten by the contractor. All suppliers, even Home Depot, have ways to tag purchases to projects, so this is a very reasonable request. Come up with a code for your job. It could be your street number, first name, or last name. Be consistent.

6. Each document provided by your contractor for reimbursement should identify the work breakdown structure to which it's attached. This allows you to track the budget and helps you during the review process.

7. Set a time to review the bill and backup copies. Seven to ten working days is reasonable. Consider spot-checking the bills by checking dates and calling a few suppliers to see what the material might be for or to confirm it's for your project.

8. Consider another third-party person to assist with this review. That could be your architect or what's known as an owner's agent. You can delegate this responsibility wholly and extend it to the supervision of construction on-site. The fees you pay to architects or agents to do this can quickly be recouped when they spot billing errors or construction defects.

If for whatever reason you decide to embark on a cost-plus contract, there are a few ways to mitigate the risk. These methods inch a cost-plus contract towards becoming a fixed-price contract.

✓ Establish an overall budget for the project by asking your contractor to prepare a high-level look at the cost broken down by a WBS. By pairing their experience with some plans and specs, they should be able to assemble a budget that can serve as a reference.

✓ Use this budget to establish a "not to exceed" clause in your contract. This clause will rein in the contract a bit and will at least establish some sort of comfort level for you.

✓ Consider including an incentive the contractor can earn by completing the project promptly.

Empowered with this last bit of information, you can then connect your expenses to the budget and track them, thus winding up with more insight into what's going on. You'll also be able to build a safety net for the overall cost and motivate the contractor to finish the project yet maintain an acceptable level of quality.

In my opinion, the cons of cost-plus contracts outweigh the pros, but if you're an experienced homeowner anxious to get the project started, maybe a cost-plus contract will work for you. Just be sure to first ask yourself:

✓ How concerned am I about the total cost of the project?

✓ How tolerant am I with *not* knowing the exact cost of the project before we get started?

✓ How concerned am I about the duration of the construction?

✓ Can I tolerate delays due to delayed materials or unexpected construction complexities?

✓ Am I interested in investing the time and money to thoroughly document my project?

✓ Is my contractor willing to create a budget and manage costs along the way?

✓ Do I have a good feeling about my contractor candidates or am I selecting the least expensive one?

✓ What incentive does my contractor have to finish my project efficiently? (I suggest answering this with "In a way that achieves maximum productivity with minimum wasted effort or expense." Note that generally, this answer does not align with a cost-plus contract.)

3.203 FIXED-PRICE CONTRACTS

A fixed-price arrangement with your contractor is a complete contrast to a cost-plus contract. As you now know, it takes a substantial amount of knowledge, time, and management to go into a project on a cost-plus basis, with the alleged benefits being that you can start more quickly and save some costs. However, the odds are that you *may* begin construction earlier but will finish later and spend more money than you expected. Still, regardless of whether your contract is cost-plus or fixed-price, it will take time to complete your project. The choice becomes how smart you'd like to be about how you use your time, how you rank the various decisions you'll need to make about your home, and who will help you package up the myriad snippets of information.

Another necessity regardless of contract type is that you need thorough and detailed information in order to build something. A well-designed and thoroughly documented project goes hand in hand with a fixed-price contract; such detailed information empowers you and protects you during bidding and construction. That said, it requires investments in time and money to achieve this summit, and frankly, gathering this level of information can be a grueling process. I emphasize *investment* because the extra time and money you spend with design professionals will help you align with the TAH overriding guiding principles and expectations.

But back to fixed-price contracts. From the homeowner's perspective, it's quite simple: when a contractor prices out a project within a fixed-price structure, they calculate all of the labor, materials, subcontractors, and equipment they've been asked to provide on the plans and then they submit a fixed price. The price only changes if changes are made to the plans or specifications outside the boundaries of what was initially agreed to.

FIXED-PRICE CONTRACT STRUCTURE AND METHODS

In a fixed-price contract, the contractor's profit and overhead are built into the project, so there's no need to micromanage this within the contract other than providing a clear statement saying that yes, the P and O are built in. The contractor will build the labor overhead into their cost and will apply a profit margin to the subcontractors and suppliers to arrive at a final contract price. Suppose the contractor missed something in the plans—say it took longer than expected to frame the house or the material was more expensive than originally determined. In that case, the contractor is liable for addressing the situation. You should never hear anything about the cost until a request comes in for a progress payment that is documented in the contract. Granted, a fixed-price contract might prompt the contractor to establish a higher profit level to cover any oversights, but I'd argue that this could happen with a cost-plus contract, too.

A fixed-price contract comes with peace of mind. It also comes with time, work, and investment. However, seeing as a fixed-price contract can set realistic expectations, any bumps in the trail will be minor. When you first interview your design professionals and contractors, open a conversation about cost methods and gain an understanding from their perspective that you can bank into your knowledge base. Their positions can be very revealing. From an architect's perspective, if a cost-plus basis is acceptable, then this factor may be represented in their plans, meaning that they'll only provide you with bare-bones information. While this mindset isn't always the case, if the architect senses that you're not prepared to pay them for the level of work required to generate comprehensive plans and specs, they may suggest you go the cost-plus approach, in effect transferring the liability back to you. Generally, they'll prefer to design the project thoroughly and protect you, but again, remember: *you* are the driver, and if you handcuff your design pros, you might end up in a bad spot.

Contractors, on the other hand, can approach contract types from different angles. Experienced and smart contractors know that a cost-plus contract can be a very slippery trail and that it will only work with the right client. Going into a cost-plus contract as a standard operating procedure is a recipe for disputes, delays, and dissatisfied clients. But if your plans are mediocre, contractors will be discouraged from entering a project on a fixed-price basis for obvious liability reasons.

Opening a conversation about contract types will help you make informed decisions about whom you genuinely want to deal with. Remember, your plans become part of your contract with your contractor. This can work *in* your favor or *against* you if the information is missing or inaccurate. Consider telling your architect on Day One that you prefer to contract the project on a fixed-price basis and thus a high level of information will be needed.

To benefit from a fixed-price contract, you must enable the contractor to provide a solid cost. Whether or not they can will be a reflection of how thoroughly your plans and specifications were developed during the design process.

A FIXED PRICE CONTRACT DEPENDS ON THESE CRITICAL COMPONENTS

- ✓ A set of plans tailored and detailed to your desires.
- ✓ Thorough specifications and a detailed scope of work document.
- ✓ A homeowner and design team who are willing to invest the time and money to deliver thorough information.

✓ A builder who's comfortable enough with the information provided to agree to a fixed-price contract.

Remember, specifications and a SOW document supplement the plans with information that either did not make it onto the plans or was not appropriate for the plan pages. The specs and SOW should include a detailed list of materials that you expect the contractor to provide at their stated price and those that you prefer they *not* include. In my opinion, the pros of fixed-price contracts outweigh the cons. Still, ask yourself:

✓ Do I have the bandwidth to invest a sizable percentage of my time during the design process?

✓ Am I interested in mitigating risk by investing enough money with the design team to allow them to document my project thoroughly?

✓ Am I okay with prioritizing my financial security over the construction start date?

✓ Is my contractor willing to enter into a fixed-price contract based off of my plans and specifications?

✓ Do I have a good feeling about my contractor candidates or am I just selecting the least expensive one?

3.210 UNDERSTANDING CONTRACTS

There's more than one way to conduct business with a general contractor, and it's best that you know the ins and outs of the two prevalent contracting methods a GC may propose for your project. Regardless of your arrangement with your contractor, some core components should be addressed within the contract. I'm going to bring these to your attention next.

✓ Whom you contract with

✓ Contract basics

✓ Change and extra work orders

3.211 WHOM YOU CONTRACT WITH

Before we get into contract details, let's review whom you'll contract with. In this section and throughout the book, I've used the terms general contractor, GC, contractor, and builder. These are all terms used in the industry and they're all one and the same: the primary person responsible for building your project. Your GC hires subcontractors and therefore is not part of the agreements you would enter into with your contractor. That said, when it comes to hiring a company to build your project, there can be some exceptions tied to the options you select. I'll cover those options within Part Four, Building Your Team, but for now, here are a few key points:

✓ Hiring a general contractor is the most common method. This is when you only contract with one entity.

✓ If you have the necessary experience, you can act as your own GC and contract directly with each subcontractor. Be careful here!

✓ You can hire a company to handle all aspects of design and construction under one umbrella. This kind of company is called a design-build business. (See Options for Hiring Your Team on page 346.)

3.212 CONTRACT BASICS
(NOT LEGAL ADVICE, BUT WHAT MATTERS)

Full disclosure: I am not a lawyer, so I will touch on the contract basics purely in terms of what I believe will matter most to you. Depending on your risk tolerance and project size, it's always a good idea to have an experienced construction law attorney review the contract presented to you.

First, *have* a contract. That sounds dumb to say out loud, but it's unbelievable how many contractors break the law and how many homeowners enter projects without a contract. This omission surely undermines the project from the start. Hundreds of conversations and emails mount up during the design and bidding, and how these are remembered (or conveniently *mis*remembered) is where the problems begin. Homeowners are as guilty as contractors and designers for not recalling conversations about inclusions in the design and specifications. *This is why documentation exists.* A contract goes beyond boilerplate legal text—it should reference your particular plans and specifications. Hopefully you also have a supplemental scope of work document that aggregates all of the back-and-forth communications in one central location.

As you narrow down your contractor candidates, consider requesting a copy of their standard contract for your review. Their response time and the quality of the contract can help you know who you may be dealing with. Asking for their standard contract gives you a couple of benefits. First, it allows you time to review the contract comfortably, and second, it provides you with a copy of the contract that can be compared to the one ultimately provided to you for your signature. If there are any differences, ask why.

There will surely be a section in the contract dedicated to payments. Look at this section to see how payments to the contractor are handled. Is there a schedule of progress payments and milestones, or does the contractor want all of their money upfront? (If they do, YIKES!) Being armed with a sample contract and knowing how payments are handled will position you well when *your* particular contract comes around.

3.213 COMPANIES AND LICENSE NUMBERS

Confirm that the construction company and license number that are listed for the contractor match the entities you've been dealing with. On occasion, individuals will "partner" with another person who has a license because their own license may not exist or may be in jeopardy. Remember, this is a mutual contract between you and the contractor. Not only are you on the hook, so are they. Look for signature areas for the contractor and be sure that the person is qualified to sign the contract.

3.214 CHANGE ORDERS VS. EXTRA WORK ORDERS

Since change orders are such a controversial topic in construction, this one deserves a deeper dive. The term "change order" implies that some scope of work item or product specification initially included in the project has changed. This could mean that the kitchen backsplash tile material make and model changed, for example, or that you want the ceilings six inches higher in the primary bedroom. These types of "changes" can range from insignificant to major. Another possibility that could lead to a change order being issued would be if the scope or specifications were never included in the plans or contract originally, as in you later decide that you want to install a security system or remodel the hall bath. In my business, I differentiate between these two instances: the former is a change order and the latter is an extra work order. This helps define the origin of the revision.

Not surprisingly, change orders and extra work orders can be stressful on a project. They stem from a few sources, with a lack of information on the original plans and specifications undoubtedly being the number-one culprit. Certain points might have never been addressed or discussed during the design phase or might have never been documented. Still, the homeowner may have thought, "But I assumed that was included!" Beyond that, conflict can occur when the information *is* on the plans and specs and the contractor misses it. In theory, you should never hear about this as a customer—instead, the work and materials should be performed and the contractor must absorb the oversight. This is yet another reason to get the proper information on the plans.

Think back to when you obtained project costs from a few contractors. Presumably, some of those other builders read the plans and thus included the same omission in their proposal. It's only fair to hold your contractor accountable for the scope as specified. On the flip side—and this occurs often—maybe your designer never put the information on the plans and therefore the contractor never knew that you wanted a heated tile floor in the master bath. What's fair is fair! Remember, it's a two-way street.

Handling change orders can get more complicated depending on the arrangement and cost type you've agreed to. This becomes a less formal process for a cost-plus contract unless a budget and a subsequent "not to exceed" clause have been specified. If that's the case, then a formal change order or extra work order should be generated by the contractor and approved by you. A documented change order allows the value to be separated from the original budget and the "not to exceed" clause since these costs were in fact not considered during the estimating and contract stage. A fixed-price contract requires a documented work order that both parties must approve before the work commences.

Change orders and extra work orders can be time-sensitive. A sense of urgency must be instilled! Orders should always be approved before the work is started, and this liability falls on the contractor. This is where conflicts often surface. The nature of a contractor is to keep moving on with the immediate tasks at hand, frequently neglecting the administrative parts of the business in the midst of the action. This leads to work being performed without the proper approvals…and then the contractor comes knocking for payments. The worst-case scenario is when a contractor performs extra work, never tells you about said work, and then asks for payment. This stems from contractors being uncomfortable with confrontation and instead trying to recover costs the hard way, thereby unfairly compromising the relationship. I liken this to your guide on the trail changing the itinerary and not telling you about it and then requiring you to scale a cliff when you have zero experience in cliff-scaling. You can't get upset because you're depending on your guide for survival, but you're steaming inside. Setting out firm rules before you embark on your trip sets expectations and holds others accountable.

A clause in the contract on how change orders or extra work orders will be handled is vital to a project. Some states require this clause in addition to a sample of the form that the contractor will use for approvals.

3.215 SCHEDULE

Identifying a start and end date within a contract is ideal; in some states, it's the law. For a contractor to intelligently determine realistic dates, a construction schedule must be developed. Numerous software programs and web-based platforms are specifically designed for this task and should be used, especially for larger projects. It can't hurt to attach this schedule to the contract as an exhibit even if it's identified as being a preliminary schedule. If a schedule doesn't yet exist, be aware! Perhaps include a statement that a schedule is forthcoming.

3.216 INSURANCE

An insurance declaration identifying the insurance carriers and policy numbers should always be included in the contract. Again, many states require this. Insurance should include both liability and workers' compensation. It's always prudent to include statements stipulating that insurance certificates must be provided by the carriers that identify you and the property as being additionally insured entities. See the Managing Risk section on page 329 for more information.

3.217 PLANS AND SPECS

The plan set should be identified as part of the contract since it's the primary document governing the work to be performed. Hopefully you've invested time and money into creating a detailed plan set. (Remember, your primary objectives are to achieve your desired project and to hold all involved parties accountable for building it.) Ideally, this is the set of plans stamped by your city when the permit was issued. If it's not, a plan set should be identified as being the build set for the contract and be appropriately dated. Be careful here! All sorts of plan revisions have been flying around in emails and hard copies, and zeroing in on the FINAL plans and specs is hugely important.

You or your agent may have created a SOW document that supplements the plans. If that's the case, then include this document in your contract. Of course, in all fairness, the contractor will only be responsible for what's within these documents, so take the time to be meticulous about what the scope of work is. Then the project experience can be smooth sailing!

3.218 PAYMENTS

A payment schedule should be included in the contract, especially if the project is a fixed-price contract. In some states, this is the law. If the project is a cost-plus contract, then agreements regarding billing periods, methods, and profit margins can be included in this area. Regardless of your cost and contract type, periodic progress billing should be part of your contractor's standard operating procedure.

In a fixed-price contract, certain milestones are identified after the completion of work and are reflected within a construction schedule so that the homeowner can anticipate when payments will be requested. For example, Payment #1 may be related to the completion of demolition, Payment #2 to the completion of the foundation, Payment #3 to the completion of the floor framing, and so on. The key here is that you're paying for work that has been completed rather than for future work to be done.

Utilizing a work breakdown structure at the beginning of the bidding and costing steps empowers you to monitor the project as it moves into the contract stage. This method is essential for both fixed-price contracts and cost-plus contracts. At my company, I break down costs for the client by WBS, which follows the project's progression. For example, the first WBS category is called Site Preparation, followed by Demolition. These go hand in hand, and I will submit a payment request when this work is completed. A certain percentage of each milestone payment is taken out and moved to the last payments of the project for the customer to reserve until they're sure that they're satisfied with the work. See the example below:

Payment	Description	Amount	Date
	Deposit upon signing of contract	$ 1,000	1/1/XXXX
1	Completion of demolition	$ 15,000	2/24/XXXX
2	Completion of concrete underfloor	$ 14,000	3/15/XXXX
3	Completion of wall/ceiling framing	$ 15,000	4/1/XXXX
4	Completion of plumbing/ electrical rough-in	$ 29,000	4/24/XXXX
5	Completion of mechanical/ fireplace rough-in and inspection	$ 12,000	5/10/XXXX
6	Completion of sheetrock and hardwood floor rough install	$ 9,000	5/24/XXXX
7	Completion of cabinetry install	$ 18,000	6/10/XXXX
8	Completion of slab counters and tile set	$ 9,000	6/22/XXXX
9	Approval by city; final inspection	$ 8,886	7/1/XXXX
10	Completion	$ 6,000	7/15/XXXX
		$ 136,886	

Here you see what a typical kitchen remodel schedule of payments can look like. It's not a perfect science and some WBS categories are combined and crossed over in some areas, but it's darn close and it equalizes payments relative to the progress. The last column identifying the forecasted payment dates is a nice-to-have that we created in response to numerous customer requests. But a caveat: the only way to provide this information is to have a completed construction schedule! Reality will play a factor as construction progresses and the dates may move, but having some kind of schedule is better than having none.

DEPOSITS

It's not uncommon for a contractor to request money up front; sometimes it's a necessity because many contractors are small business-people who have limited cash flow. These deposits are usually related to the ordering of materials. Materials can be classified in two ways. The first is consumable materials such as lumber, hardware, and any material that could be used on any job and returned if not used. The second category is special-order materials specific to your project, such as custom cabinetry, tile, stone, and anything that cannot be returned or used on other projects. Each type of material should be handled differently when it comes to forking out money before the project has started. As far as the consumable materials are concerned, a deposit should not be required by the contractor since these materials can either be billed to you after they've been delivered to the site (in the case of a cost-plus contract) or included in a progress payment (in the case of a fixed-price contract). If a contractor asks you for a deposit for consumable materials, you may want to stew on that request for a while before writing a check.

Special-order materials are a bit more complicated since many of them can be high-ticket items with long lead times. Materials such as cabinetry, windows, entry doors, tile, stone, etc. are just a few examples of special-order materials. Sometimes they need to be ordered before the project even starts construction. To ask a contractor to fork out tens of thousands of dollars of their own money before the project even starts is an unfair situation, but believe it or not, some states have outlawed a contractor from taking money for exactly this purpose. It gets complicated and how the law is interpreted comes into play. For now, I'll focus on how I think this issue can reasonably be handled for both parties.

Let's break down materials by cost type and assume that you've signed a contract with your contractor.

- **Cost-plus contract:** This is one of the areas where a cost-plus contract is a bit helpful, but remember, this type of contract is inherently riskier. If the contractor's supplier requires a deposit to order the windows, then your contractor submits their supplier's bill to you for payment, including the profit and overhead. You can then make a payment to the contractor and they in turn can pay the supplier. For optimal protection, you can pay the supplier directly. The benefits of direct payment are that you know who the supplier is and that yes, they have in fact been paid. Regardless, always obtain a receipt or acknowledgment that you've made the payment. The balance of the material cost should not be paid until the materials have been delivered correctly and in good condition.

- **Fixed-price contract:** A fixed-price contract is not as transparent as cost-plus in that you don't necessarily know what your contractor's profit and overhead is, nor should you care assuming you're comfortable with the overall cost. This leads to the contractor not sharing their costs with you. Therefore, you don't need to know what they're paying for the windows, but you *should* know that the suppliers are getting paid. Again, not as transparent as a cost-plus contract, but it's safer for you financially.

Deposits for special-order materials can be handled a bit differently. Your contractor will likely submit a request for a payment tied to one of your progress payments. In our example, the payment could be tied to the category of Install

Windows. In order for this to occur, your contractor needs the windows and it could take eight weeks to get them. A draw against this progress payment could be submitted by your contractor. Must-knows are: how much of the draw is relative to the total payment, who is the supplier, and how do you know they're getting paid? Before submitting your payment to the contractor, request to know who the supplier is and that you would like an acknowledgment from the supplier that they have indeed received the deposit payment. This can alleviate potential unknown concerns and hold your contractor accountable.

THE CASH TRAP

It seemed exciting when Tad the Builder said, "If you pay cash, then I can discount your project by 10%." Ten percent of a $130,000 kitchen remodel is $13,000! "Wow—that could pay for all of my appliances!" you say. Why would a contractor offer this? Let's dig in here, because this is a huge red flag regarding the integrity of the person you're dealing with. Unbeknownst to you, they're gambling with your liability and safety.

For contractors, the benefits of accepting cash payments are twofold. Assuming the cash is not run through the company's accounting system (which is the only way to hide income), the contractor is avoiding taxes related to income and payroll. But if a contractor isn't running the money through their payroll system, then they're not paying for workers' compensation insurance, and that insurance protects the employee *and* you! Isn't that nice?

Now let's look at the benefits for you if you paid in cash. You saved $13,000. That's it. Here's what you're risking:

1. For a contractor to qualify as a dirtbag—which they do if they accept cash payments—there must be no written contracts to document the transaction. That said, many still do these document-free transactions at significant risk. The IRS doesn't leave too many stones unturned.

2. Cash payments don't usually come with evidence of payment. If your contractor were to write you a receipt, that'd be pretty dumb since then they'd have a record of receiving payments, and that record could bite them given their scheme to pay under the table.

3. Having zero records of payments that both parties have agreed on means the door is kicked wide open for conflicts. Misremembering when payments were made and for how much and for what comes to mind, to name a few potential problems. It will all become a tangled mess.

4. With no record of payments, you are unable to officially account for the project. Being able to legally account for the project could benefit you when Tax Day rolls around and it comes time to minimize capital gains or maximize rebate programs.

5. The reason you were offered a 10% discount is because Tad the Dirtbag is not paying the proper insurance or taxes. Therefore, you've been placed at risk if an employee should get hurt. Oh, and by the way, Tad the Dirtbag is saving more like *30%* of his costs by operating under the table.

This is a sensitive subject for those of us who operate a business in a legitimate manner. When a contractor who lives outside the rules enters the arena, this makes for an unlevel playing field. And be aware, many "contractors" who bring up the cash idea are not legitimately licensed. It's a shame, but this kind of cash-only payment scenario goes undetected way too often. So before you run to the bank and get a big pile of cash to become your contractor's best friend, THINK TWICE!

✓ The most common approach is to contract with your general contractor.

✓ There are two types of contracts: cost-plus contracts and fixed-price contracts. Which one you choose depends on your tolerance for risk and the time and money that might be required to mitigate the risk.

✓ Certain important items specific to your project should be included in the contract.

3.300 MANAGING RISK

Reducing your risk with perhaps the most significant investment of your life seems prudent...right? Risk *exposure* begins with simply not knowing how to mitigate risk. Even worse, many homeowners do the polar opposite and risk it all by hiring unlicensed and uninsured people. This puts out the welcome mat for risk. Remember, *you* will assume all responsibility for any human being who steps onto your property if your contractor does not have the proper forms of insurance. And it gets better! This applies to *any* subcontractor, supplier, or any other human being who is somehow associated with the project. Another reason to make sure your contractor is insured is that many states legally require a contractor to have insurance. So why not be absolutely *sure* that they do?

✓ Liability insurance

✓ Workers' compensation insurance

✓ Builder's risk insurance

✓ Liens

3.310 LIABILITY INSURANCE

Many states (but not all) require that a general contractor carry a liability insurance policy. If an event occurs that an uninsured contractor caused, the GC can become personally liable for the fallout. Thus the gamble gets even riskier if your contractor doesn't have the assets to remedy the damage caused by the event. Reputable contractors carry liability insurance and smart homeowners require it. It's just about standard today regardless of whether or not it's required by a state. Liability insurance policies commonly start at one million dollars and cover contractual liability, liability for accidents and injury, liability for events caused by an employee or subcontractor, and the products produced by the contractor.

3.311 WORKERS' COMPENSATION INSURANCE

While liability insurance is related to damage caused by the contractor, workers' compensation insurance protects employees of the contractor in the event that an injury occurs that prevents them from working and making an income. Unlike liability insurance, most states require contractors to carry workers' comp insurance.

As a property owner, if you hire a contractor who does not have workers' comp insurance, you are taking a HUGE risk, because if an employee of your contractor gets hurt while working on your property and your contractor isn't covered, that employee has every right to recover their lost wages directly from YOU.

There are ways to confirm that a policy exists by checking with your state licensing board and the certificate mechanism, but be aware: illegal contractors play some dirty games here. First, on the state board, you can quickly check the status of their workers' comp. It will state that either a policy is in place (and the expiration date of said policy) or that the contractor has claimed they have no employees. If a contractor claims they have no employees, that is indeed a possible scenario—they may subcontract all the work out to other subcontractors. However, that's often *not* the case. More likely, they're a sleazy contractor who claims no employees and then pays workers cash under the table to avoid the costs associated with carrying a workers' comp policy. Not only is that contractor almost certainly breaking the law, they have you dangling from a cliff and risking your entire investment. This unscrupulous way of conducting business happens way too often! Don't be that horror story. An excellent way to qualify your contractor and achieve instant transparency is to do a bit of interrogation.

QUESTIONS TO ASK YOUR CONTRACTOR

- ❏ "Do you subcontract all of the construction work?" Wait for their answer and then say, "I see that you claim no employees on the state site."

- ❏ "Do you carry workers' compensation insurance?" Give it another pause… "On ALL of your employees?"

- ❏ "Can you please include your policy on an insurance certificate if I select you?"

And it gets even better! As I mentioned earlier, a big responsibility of a GC is to assemble a team of subcontractors to build your project. Guess what? *They all need the same insurance policies.* It's the GC's job and liability to confirm that each sub has the proper insurance policies, so they obtain certificates from their subcontractors listing the GC as an additionally insured party to protect themself and ultimately you.

Many insurance companies audit GCs every year to manage their risk. This risk multiplies with many human bodies looking to get hurt on your property. In the meantime, you don't even know they're on-site. *You must manage your risk!* To continue with your peace-of-mind mission, ask your contractor the following questions:

❑ Look them in the eye and ask, "Are all of your subcontractors properly insured?" When the GC says, "Yes, of course!", then follow up with…

❑ "When the time is right, can I get a list of all of the subcontractors and copies of all of their insurance certificates?"

So how do you know your contractor has you covered? Insurance certificates are a mechanism that exists to give you peace of mind. A certificate is a document provided to you directly by your contractor's insurance agent. It must list the insured party, the policy carrier, and the coverage amounts. It can take 24 to 48 hours at most for an insurance company to produce a certificate. If it takes longer, then bank that, because it's possible that your contractor candidates made a mad dash to get insurance after you requested proof of it.

Two critical inclusions must be on an insurance certificate in order for you to achieve peace of mind. First, require that you are named as an **additionally insured** party with your property address. Second, verify that the policy exists by contacting the carrier directly. Policy terms are usually in place for one year, which could mean that the policy could lapse in the middle of your project. Listing you as an additionally insured party builds in a mechanism to automatically notify you if a lapse occurs. But don't depend on this as the be-all and end-all of making sure that your contractor has insurance throughout the duration of your project! Flag the policy's expiration date in your calendar and *follow up*.

3.312 BUILDER'S RISK INSURANCE

This insurance (also known as course of construction insurance) is a specialized type of insurance that helps protect buildings while they're under construction. The primary items it covers include weather-related events, fire, lightning, hail, explosions, theft, and vandalism. Consulting with your insurance agent is a prudent step, and you may want to seriously consider requiring your contractor to have builder's risk insurance. Or you can obtain this coverage on your own.

3.313 HOMEOWNER'S INSURANCE

As the owner of the property, you also have a responsibility to obtain insurance. This could be in the form of a typical homeowner's insurance policy that's required by the mortgage holder, but even if you have this policy already, don't assume you'll be covered throughout your project. Also note that many typical construction contracts include a clause that you as the property owner *must* obtain insurance. Why are you on the hook? Because many events can occur that would place the burden of liability on your shoulders as opposed to your contractor's shoulders. First, if a destructive event occurs on the property that is *not* the fault of the contractor or any subcontractor or supplier under their contract umbrella, then replacement costs will revert to being your responsibility. For example, perhaps a project is halfway complete and you decide to have the roof replaced by your own subcontractor. Now that you've brought your own subcontractor onto the site, you're assuming all liability for the work they perform. If the roofer causes damage to the home and to work that has already been completed by your contractor, *your* insurance company will cover the damage, not theirs. Your insurance company will then seek to recover their payout from your roofing contractor. Things can quickly spiral out of control if you didn't verify that the roofer had insurance, so be sure to obtain evidence of insurance before you bring anyone onto your property!

And finally, once your project is completed, contact your insurance company to see if any discounts are now applicable because of the work you've completed.

3.314 LIENS

Just the word "lien" can make a property owner nervous. Again, I am not a lawyer, so if you want to dig into this topic, I suggest contacting a real estate attorney. My job here is to inform you of the existence of liens, break them down in understandable language, and describe how lien processes can protect you but also hurt you. A caveat: my experiences are based on California laws. If you're in another state, I recommend doing some research to learn about your state's specific process regarding liens.

A lien is defined as the legal claim of one person upon another person's property to secure the payment of a debt or the satisfaction of an obligation. Companies and individuals that provide materials and services to real property—a.k.a. your home—have recourse to collect the money owed to them once the materials are delivered or the services are performed. A preliminary 20-day notice is a required mechanism within the lien process that subcontractors and suppliers use to notify property owners that they have performed work and now expect payment. If subcontractors and suppliers follow the process to the letter and are still not paid, they can execute a mechanic's lien and ultimately force the sale of the property to get their money. While it's rare for things to escalate to this point, it's important to be aware of the possibility. Additionally, if a lien is not remedied, it can prevent you from refinancing the property, adding further complications.

The lien process also protects homeowners. If you hire a general contractor (GC) to build your project, it's impractical to know who all of their subs and suppliers are. The first step for a provider is to file a preliminary 20-day notice. This notice notifies property owners who have an interest in a property. For providers to protect themselves, they must file this notice within 20 days of starting services or delivering material and deliver it by certified mail or personally to the property owner, general contractor, and lender (if there is one). If the provider did not file a 20-day notice, they have relinquished their ability to collect unpaid money through the lien process. On the positive side, this notice also gives homeowners visibility into who is working on their project. You can then use this information to ensure providers are paid through your general contractor.

For example, imagine your project starts, and lumber from your contractor's supplier shows up on your site. A few days later, a 20-day notice arrives in the mail declaring who the supplier is and how much they have filed the notice for. Retain the notice, and when your contractor comes knocking for a progress payment, request a lien release before you issue any payment. A lien release can only be provided by the person who filed the 20-day notice, and they will not release their rights until they've been paid. The contractor must return to their supplier, pay the bill, and then provide the lien release document to you. Depending on your comfort level, you can verify with the supplier that they have been paid or proceed with issuing payment based on the lien release.

Unconditional waivers and releases are preferred, indicating payment has been made. Conditional waivers, on the other hand, go into effect once payment has been reconciled. In such cases, issuing a two-party check can ensure the money streams to the provider. This process protects both parties and provides peace of mind for the property owner.

With larger projects, reviewing payments and any 20-day notices as the project nears completion to address unpaid amounts is essential. Some subcontractors and suppliers don't file 20-day notices, often due to strong relationships with the GC or lack of organization. If a notice is filed late, the provider can only collect money for services delivered 20 days after the filing date. For instance, if a lumber company delivered materials three months ago but forgot to file a notice, and then the notice appears, they cannot claim money for the initial delivery. As your contractor wraps up the project, it's prudent to request lien releases from all subcontractors and suppliers, whether or not notices were filed. This release ensures any residual payments owed by your contractor are settled.

A notice of completion (NOC) or certificate of occupancy (COO) officially declares the project complete and is recorded at the county or city level. These documents are key milestones in the construction process, as they end lien rights. Afterward, there's a 60-day window for anyone who filed a 20-day notice to file a mechanic's lien. General contractors (GCs) don't need to file 20-day notices since you've contracted directly with them, though they can file a mechanic's lien if unpaid. However, if a construction lender is involved, a 20-day notice from your GC is required.

The lien system is designed to protect all parties involved in a project and does not need to be adversarial unless payments are delayed. During the contract stage, it's a good idea to let your contractor know you're informed about liens by asking, "Tell me more about pre-liens and releases and how your company handles them." Being proactive ensures that all parties are aware of their responsibilities and helps avoid misunderstandings or disputes down the line. By staying informed and organized, you can protect your property and keep your project running smoothly.

- ✓ There are ways to protect yourself and your property with insurance.

- ✓ Understanding the different types of insurance and having you and your property listed as being an additionally insured party is vital.

- ✓ The lien process is normal and is *not* a direct reflection of your contractor's integrity.

- ✓ There is a pre-lien process that protects you by adding transparency—then you know who could potentially file a claim.

- ✓ A lien only happens if a subcontractor or supplier doesn't get paid by your contractor.

PART THREE CONCLUSION

Hopefully learning about the world of construction has enlightened you with the essential knowledge you need to transform your design, plans, and specifications into a reality. You now know that your primary point of contact during the building process will be your general contractor, and you're familiar with various types of contractors, their qualifications and attributes, and the value they bring to the project.

As you begin working with your GC, you'll need to obtain a cost estimate, which is why we waded deep into *the estimating process. At* a minimum, you'll oversee that process; you might even facilitate it. I pulled back the veil of how *general contractors make their living* to help you understand costs and how GCs structure their business by using one of two contracting *methods.* We also delved into how to *understand contracts*, and I emphasized critical components of a contract agreement with a contractor. Lastly, now that you're familiar with how to *manage risk* during construction, you can ensure that you're protected as your home is being built.

"We had a great experience working with Bill and his team. Bill is a really good, honest, family guy and these qualities are reflected in his staff as well. Bill and his staff are respectful and trustworthy and take pride in their work. We were lucky to have found them for our project."

Mei C.

PROJECT BY BILL REID OF REMODELWEST

"We may have all come on different ships, but we're in the same boat now."

Martin Luther King, Jr.

BUILDING YOUR TEAM

4.

BUILDING YOUR TEAM 4.

4.0 INTRODUCTION

Your team comprises three components: design, construction, and you. As you now know, subsets of design and construction (such as consultants and subcontractors) are made up of several players who form the team. While you may indeed have to engage with all of the players, that's not common—in most cases, you won't hire every single one of them. Instead, you'll evaluate each architect and general contractor candidate who brings the rest of the team to the project.

The knowledge you acquired of the fields of design and construction in Parts Two and Three laid the groundwork for hiring the right resources to achieve your goals. We'll now begin narrowing down the players by categorizing your project within a matrix. I'll present options for building your team, with different degrees of your own involvement tailored to your experience and availability. Lastly, I'll offer strategies to help you search for the right team.

WHAT WE'LL COVER _____

- ✓ The Design Pro Matrix: This tool identifies which team players you may need. These options are tailored to your expectations and experience
- ✓ A guided design-build experience: If you want a one-stop shop, you may want to pursue this option.
- ✓ A self-guided option: This is the conventional path.

✓ The owner-builder option: If you choose this path, you'll be on your own.

✓ The owner's agent path: This lets you extend yourself.

✓ Search strategies: Ways to find your team players.

THE DESIGN PRO MATRIX

The type of designer and contractor you hire is often project-specific. An interior designer may suit an interior project such as a kitchen and bath remodel, while an architect may be the best route for an extensive renovation, addition, or new home. Bottom line: you'll need a designer to capture your ideas into plans and specifications and a contractor who can demonstrate they're capable of executing your project type.

Using the matrix below to classify your project is the first step in your hiring process. This tool is designed to filter out design professionals based on your project track, helping you identify the most suitable candidates. Armed with this information, you can then decide whether to manage the hiring of all design professionals yourself or hire a company to handle the entire design and construction process (more on that in the next section).

PROJECT TRACKS

A. Interior renovations with no expansion or structural changes. Projects include kitchens, baths, replacements of windows, installations of skylights, etc.

B. Renovations and remodels with expansions and structural modifications

C. New homes.

Required or recommended	**R**
*Optional or possibly required**	**O**
N/A	**N/A**

* Optional generally means deciding if you would like to hire this professional. In some cases, your city or county may require this design professional to be involved with your project.

DESIGN PROFESSIONAL	A	B	C
Architect	N/A	O	R
Residential designer	R	R	N/A
Interior designer	R	R	R
Kitchen and bath specialist	R	O	O

CONSULTANTS	A	B	C
Surveyor	N/A	O	R
Civil engineer	N/A	O	R
Geotechnical engineer	N/A	O	R
Structural engineer	N/A	R	R
MEP engineers	N/A	O	O
Low-voltage specialist	N/A	O	O
Fire suppression specialist	N/A	O	R
Energy specialist	N/A	O	R
Solar power specialist	N/A	O	O
Arborist	N/A	N/A	O
Landscaper	N/A	N/A	O

4.000 OPTIONS FOR HIRING YOUR TEAM

Before you set out on your path to hiring your design and construction pros, let's investigate a few options that align with your experience and preferences. You have two primary paths to manage all of the players and processes you've learned about: the self-guided path, which is the most common, and the guided path, which integrates design and construction into a streamlined, one-stop-shop approach. Ultimately, both options will involve the same players—it's about finding the path that suits you best. Beyond the self-guided and guided paths, we'll explore a couple of other specialized options, too: going solo as an owner-builder or bolstering the two primary paths with an owner's agent.

4.010 GUIDED: DESIGN-BUILD A ONE-STOP SHOP

A guided remodeling or building experience is much like going on a European vacation where you show up at the airport with the next two weeks planned by a travel guide. Or you hire a fishing guide to navigate a famous stream and simply arrive at the banks with your cooler in hand. In any guided trip, you spend the time to find a guide who fits you well and then you sit back and enjoy the experience, knowing that you have someone with knowledge and experience by your side.

The guided path to designing and building your project wraps up all of the numerous design and construction pros, companies, processes, and resources into one package, with one entity looking out for the project from the very beginning to the very end. This full-service business model is often referred to as a design-build company.

THIS PATH MAY BE RIGHT FOR YOU IF...

- Your project is a significant remodel with extensive details.

- You have limited time to devote to planning and overseeing the project.

- You have limited to no experience in hiring design and construction pros.

- You prioritize the quality of the experience and construction over cost.

- You have a strong design-build company referral and an elevated level of trust.

- You prefer interacting with just one person.

THE THREE ATTRIBUTES OF THE GUIDED-PATH APPROACH

The design-build method has some perceived benefits, but they also come with some serious considerations.

1. You'll relinquish some control and visibility.

2. The process will be seamless from design to construction.

3. There's built-in accountability for the design-build company.

The design-build business model couples the design process with the construction implementation within one company. A company offering a guided service has gotten its start in a variety of ways, but often such a company consists of a general contractor who offers in-house design services done by their employees. On the flip side, architects or designers can sometimes offer construction services. In either case, though, *one* entity is taking full responsibility for the project. A professional knows what challenges may arise and how they can be avoided. Since they're along for the entire journey of design through construction, I'm confident in saying that the survival mindset of the design-build company triggers built-in accountability that benefits both you and them. Let's look deeper into this accountability and its benefits.

4.011 THE MERGE OF DESIGN AND CONSTRUCTION

Selecting a company that offers both design and construction services can extract you from being in the middle of the transition and handoff all the way from design to construction. This guided solution allows you to focus on the creative aspects of the project while the full-service company takes charge of the planning, design, and construction, making sure it all flows seamlessly. Although one person oversees the project as a whole, feasibility studies of the proposed design ideas are initiated to protect everyone. Progressing through all of the design steps with the same person alongside you can provide comfort and protect you from being blindsided by challenges that could otherwise turn into cost escalations and delays.

4.012 BUDGET, COST, AND VALUE BENEFITS

You may remember that in Part One, I brought up the budget and how to get your arms around what a project may cost. That's about as far as we can go until design begins. Keeping a finger on the pulse as the design develops and relates to cost can and should be a priority regardless of how much money you have. This is where a company experienced in overseeing design and construction comes in.

The person operating the design-build business model has been alongside you from the beginning. They understand your budget priorities and have the best sense of what your ideas may ultimately cost. Perhaps you were dreaming about a new basement. After budget discussions, it's determined that your limit is 700K for a new home. Guess what? No need to design a basement, because your contractor says no way will you ever accomplish that given your budget. Therefore, the directive to the design team is "No basement." Or maybe you have the money but want to understand the cost of a basement. Concepts can be developed early on, discussions can take place with a concrete contractor, and enough information can be obtained to allow you to make an informed decision. Sounds logical, right? Well, many people hire an architect and do *not* discuss a budget, yet they design and even engineer a basement and price it out…and then never build it. Meanwhile, thousands of dollars are spent on plans and engineering. Conflict ensues. The design-build model can facilitate a more pragmatic approach, which will in turn lead to a more efficient design process.

Digging deeper, value engineering can play a huge role as a design develops, and if one knows to prod the design team as ideas are being presented and discussed, then it's possible to remain in the driver's seat. Whether or not to include a design element boils down to the cost of a feature relative to its function and aesthetics. I have examples galore of this, but here's a good one. My team was once deep into the design development stage of a rebuild for a new home. The client whipped out a picture of a forty-foot-long glass door wall along the back of their house, saying it would be amazing to have the ability to open up the back of the home to the yard for entertaining. As we progressed with the design, however, and engaged with a structural engineer, it became apparent that this wide-open span would require steel beams, posts, and huge concrete footings to support the roof of the home *and* the glass door system.

The project was not supported by an unlimited budget, so I posed the question of how much was the steel going to cost? What was the value of such an open wall relative to its cost? Well, it was north of $50,000 just for the steel contractor, plus then there would have been engineering and other costs. This brought on more dialogue with the client, the engineer, and my crew. To cut to the chase, we simply included one 6" wide by 6" tall post within the span. That added additional support within the mid-span, thus eliminating the steel. We saved over 40K, the value of the glass wall became much higher, and best of all, our client ended up liking having the option to open the wall in a couple of areas. It's examples like this that can make or break a project. Check it out: https://tinyurl.com/5ew5szht

Ensuring your own satisfaction begins with knowing that there's more than one way to achieve your goals and also with knowing to ask questions of and challenge your design team. This is where having one entity take full charge of the experience pays off.

4.013 DESIGN-BUILD FRAMEWORK

A design-build company structured with a design agreement independent of the construction contract is ideal for a variety of reasons, one of which is that having a separate contract for design services empowers you to understand the value of the design services relative to the construction cost and potentially other providers. This knowledge makes it much easier to compare your options. Here are yet more benefits:

1. A separate design agreement (meaning that it's not rolled into a construction contract) protects you from committing to a project with one company so early in the process.

2. If the cost for design feels like it's higher than you expected, a quick calculation can tell you what the rough percentage of construction hypothetically is. This can be

compared to samples of the company's work product and those of competitive providers to understand the value.

3. If the cost for design feels low, don't immediately see that as a benefit. Remember, you get what you pay for! Companies that devalue design commonly just recoup the time that would have been spent in design within the construction contract. Worse yet, they provide minimal design, which leads to other problems.

Design can be a very personal experience, and you may not gel with your designer or they may not perform to your expectations. Establishing a cost for each step of the design process places a value on what you've purchased and by default identifies the deliverable.

WHAT TO ASK BEFORE ENTERING INTO AN AGREEMENT WITH A DESIGN-BUILD COMPANY

- ✓ Are your design services separate from your construction services?
- ✓ What are the qualifications of your design team?
- ✓ Do you have a licensed architect on staff?
- ✓ Are there stages to your design services? And can we stop at any point?
- ✓ How do you come up with the value of design and then break it down?
- ✓ How are design fees billed? Hourly? As a lump sum?
- ✓ Do I own the plans? If I decide to stop, will the plans be released to me?

The "build" portion of "design-build" is a separate construction contract to build the project off the plans and specifications that the same company provided. This is probably the largest benefit of using the same company to design and build your project, because this naturally removes any problems that may arise when the design arm of the company hands everything off to construction. For example, if your new kitchen remodel calls for a wall removal and the design work and subsequent plans did not consider the structural ramifications of an open kitchen, then escalated costs could be incurred…but not by you. It's very tough for a design-build company to approach a client for extra work when *they* have dual responsibility for plans and construction. I call this built-in accountability. This is why good companies perform extra due diligence during design—then they won't be forced to absorb surprise costs.

Compare this design-build scenario to the self-guided model wherein you hired a separate designer and contractor and the designer missed structural details on the plans and consequently the contractor did not include them in their cost. Guess who pays for the extra cost? YOU. Unless, that is, you can sweet-talk your designer into paying for it… Good luck.

SUMMARY OF THE DESIGN-BUILD OPTION _____

- ✓ A design-build company offers you the chance to deal with *one* entity from the beginning of design to the completion of construction.
- ✓ Built-in accountability reduces stress and unforeseen cost escalations.
- ✓ There's seamless communication between design and construction.
- ✓ This approach frees up your time so that you can enjoy the creative parts of the experience.
- ✓ Ideal for busy and/or inexperienced homeowners.
- ✓ Potentially carries a premium cost…on the surface.

✓ Maybe you won't be faster to break ground, but you'll still win the race.

4.020 SELF-GUIDED, A.K.A. THE CONVENTIONAL PATH

Taking the self-guided conventional path can be compared to preparing your own travel plans: researching transportation methods, what sights to see, and which accommodations to reserve. It takes a lot of time and preparation. It also means that you have more control…but you simultaneously take on the risk of visiting uninspiring places or worse. Those who tackle such extensive travel planning often begin informing themselves by reading guides, browsing the web, and consulting with others. This guide and TheAwakenedHomeowner.com developing resources will act as your travel guide.

"Self-guided" is my term for the most common method of planning and building a project, but it doesn't literally mean that you're alone. Instead, you're in the thick of things! You're armed with some experience, you know what the needed resources are, and you have specifics in mind to plan your project. As the homeowner, you're the point person, orchestrating the planning strategy, assembling the design and construction team, participating in depth within the design and construction processes, ensuring quality outcomes, and facilitating all of the processes that are introduced so that your expectations are met.

THIS PATH MAY BE RIGHT FOR YOU IF…

- You have some experience with projects in your current or past homes.

- You have connections to qualified design and construction pros.

- You have ample time to devote to the planning stages.

- You enjoy or are excited to learn about the remodeling/building process.

- You have a disposition well suited to handle daily challenges with equanimity.

- You are a control freak.

THE SELF-GUIDED PATH BENEFITS FROM THREE POWERFUL FORCES

This most common method of approaching a project has perceived benefits, but again, those come with some serious considerations.

1. You have maximum control of the process.

2. You have optimal visibility of how the design and construction phases are progressing.

3. You have increased accountability.

4.021 DESIGN TO CONSTRUCTION COORDINATION

The transfer and translation of design work and specifications from a designer/architect to the builder or GC is probably the biggest contributor to misunderstandings, cost escalations, and schedule delays. The conventional path places you in the middle of the two by requiring you to facilitate the handoff and transition from design to construction.

Within the self-guided or conventional method, the design process inevitably progresses independently from construction studies and cost analyses. Even though design professionals and homeowners should take early steps to engage with an independent general contractor for feasibility and costs, that doesn't happen often enough, and even when it does, the outcome doesn't impact the accountability for each party. Meaning, if something was left off the plans or didn't work and the builder requests a change order, guess who gets to pay? Yep! YOU. The *homeowner* assumes the responsibility for streaming details to those who are selected to provide materials and build the project. This comes with responsibility, accountability, and a certain amount of risk. All of which can be tough for a homeowner since... yep! You don't know what you don't know.

SUMMARY OF THE SELF-GUIDED OPTION _____

- ✓ You hire a designer and a general contractor independent of one another.
- ✓ You are in the middle of the process and thus assume more liability and accountability.
- ✓ There's a higher risk of inferior or missing information leading to cost overruns and delays.
- ✓ Requires doing some retrospection to determine if you're ready.
- ✓ Requires a substantial time commitment.
- ✓ Ideal for experienced homeowners.
- ✓ Potential cost savings...on the surface.
- ✓ Your architect can help you and act as your advocate.

HINT!

Hiring an architect and general contractor and mediating between the two adds a layer of responsibility between you and the project, whereas the alternative paths I'm about to lay out add or subtract layers of responsibility.

BONUS HINT!

One of the biggest challenges for homeowners and contractors is obtaining complete and accurate costs that are *comparable between candidates*. Taking charge of the project cost estimating process is one of the most important aspects of a project. Taking the self-guided path positions you to take charge *provided that* you are empowered with all of the information that was completed in the design steps.

Before you embark on this journey, it's prudent to take some time to determine if you truly do have the time, knowledge, real-life experience, fortitude, and stamina to deal with all aspects of the project.

4.030 SPECIALIZED OPTIONS

You have two other options for designing and building your project. Being an owner-builder goes even further past the self-guided option, placing you squarely in the trenches. At the other end of the spectrum, an owner's agent fortifies all of the planning and building steps, thereby freeing you of the day-to-day requirements. I'll briefly introduce these concepts, and if you think either or both of these paths are an option, you can visit the TAH site for a more detailed description of the pros and cons of each one.

4.031 OWNER/BUILDER:
YOU ARE THE GC…YOU THINK

Perhaps you want the most freedom possible and decide to backpack through Europe indefinitely, yet you don't fully grasp the cost or what sites you'll see. You're still planning your trip, but now you are the only one who's responsible for finding food and water, and it's very possible you'll be sleeping in hostels cuddled up under a blue tarp with a character named Trail Dog to save a buck and take in the "experience." Traveling this way can be rewarding, sure, but you had better have experience, fortitude, stamina, and deodorant.

Perhaps you've likewise thought about being your own contractor. Instead of depending on a general contractor to lead the journey, you could tackle it on your own! As an owner-builder, you are no longer just the owner of the team; you are in the trenches as the general manager, recruiting and coaching all of the players, managing the egos, acting as the bat boy/girl, and being the person who cleans the stands (maybe even the bathrooms) after the game. It can be done if you have the time, brainpower, and experience.

THIS PATH MAY BE RIGHT FOR YOU IF …

- You're in the construction trades.
- You have plenty of experience with past projects.
- You plan to construct much of the project yourself.
- The project completion date is not a top priority.

Imagine yourself as the General Contractor, right in the thick of things—managing subcontractors, sourcing materials, navigating building codes, and ensuring every project detail aligns with your vision. For some, this hands-on, owner-builder approach seems ideal for saving money and maintaining control. But is it the right path for you?

SOME OF WHAT OWNER-BUILDERS COMMONLY DO

- Design and create plans themselves...or hire an architect or designer to design and create the plans.

- Select all of the materials and equipment.

- Develop the specifications and scope of work documents and details.

- Handle the approval process themselves.

- Source and hire all of the consultants needed.

- Perform most of the work with their own hands...or source and hire subcontractors to perform some or all of the work.

- Work closely with subs and suppliers to ensure that work is completed accurately and to code.

- Coordinate all city inspections.

An owner-builder role is typically best suited for seasoned homeowners with direct experience in the construction field. While many jurisdictions allow property owners to act as contractors without a license or formal training, doing so comes with responsibilities and risks. Filing a declaration with your building department and signing waivers related to subcontractor insurance are just the first steps. From there, the burden of compliance, coordination, and liability rests squarely on your shoulders.

At first glance, the potential cost savings of skipping a General Contractor's overhead and profit margin may seem like a smart move. However, this perceived advantage can quickly unravel if mistakes occur, schedules slip, or relationships with subcontractors and suppliers aren't solid. Acting as your own GC might save money in theory, but the reality is often far more complex—and costly—than it appears.

A LESSON IN ACCOUNTABILITY:
THE OWNER-BUILDER JOURNEY

When you decide to act as an owner-builder, you're taking on more than just a project—you're stepping into a role that requires responsibility, knowledge, and accountability. Let's explore a real-world example of how seemingly straightforward decisions can spiral into costly complications.

You've decided to replace all the windows in your home. Sounds simple, right? They'll all fit into the existing openings, so you confidently take charge. You assume the role of Owner-Builder, dive into research, and call the city building department to ask questions and gather information. Feeling prepared, you write a detailed scope of work and are proud of the effort you've put into the process.

Contractors begin showing up to provide bids. They're impressed by your research and thoroughness, and you feel validated. The bids come in: one is sky-high, another is shockingly low, and one sits right in the middle. After reviewing qualifications and experience, you choose the middle bid. Feeling wise, you place the window order (because lead times are long) and apply for permits to "do things the right way."

And that's when the lessons in accountability begin.

It turns out the clerk at the city building department—despite sounding knowledgeable—left out some critical information. **Mistake #1: Egress requirements**. Modern building codes require windows in bedrooms to meet specific size and placement criteria for emergency access. Your 1960s-era window sizes are no longer compliant. Four bedroom windows you ordered are the wrong size and must be reordered. **Mistake #2: Tempered glass requirements**. Windows near tubs, showers, or swinging doors must be tempered for safety. You didn't know this, and now two bathroom windows are incorrect and must also be reordered.

You can only look in the mirror. Mistakes like these aren't rare—they're inevitable when navigating uncharted waters. These are just two of the many missteps that could occur in a seemingly simple window replacement project. Each mistake costs time, money, and energy.

Now, imagine scaling this up to a more significant remodel or even building a house. The stakes only get higher.

THE ALTERNATIVE PATH

Let's revisit this scenario, but with a different approach. Instead of taking on the role of Owner-Builder, you contact a contractor specializing in window replacements. You invite them to your home, point to the windows, and say, "I'd like to replace all these windows up to current code. What's your plan?"

Now, they are responsible for measuring correctly, ordering the right products, ensuring code compliance, and handling the installation. They take care of permits, coordinate the work, and assume accountability for the results.

By relinquishing control, you focus on managing the big picture—evaluating contractors, reviewing qualifications, understanding costs, and making informed decisions—while letting experts handle the technical details.

THE BIGGER LESSON

The window replacement story is a microcosm of what happens during large-scale remodels or new home construction. As an owner-builder, you're taking on the burden of ensuring compliance with codes, sourcing materials, coordinating labor, and troubleshooting problems. It's not impossible, but it requires meticulous planning, a willingness to learn, and the ability to adapt when things go wrong.

Being an owner-builder can be a viable option for seasoned home-owners with experience in construction and ample time to manage the project. On the surface, acting as your own general contractor seems like a cost-saving solution. By dealing directly with subcontractors and suppliers, you eliminate the middleman and retain control of the budget. However, the reality is that these savings are only achievable if you have strong relationships with subcontractors and suppliers and the knowledge to avoid costly mistakes. The most significant savings often come from hands-on homeowners who perform some tasks themselves.

It's important to note that many jurisdictions allow property owners to act as contractors even without a license or formal experience. Remember, taking this path involves filing a declaration with the building department and signing waivers related to insurance for each subcontractor you hire. The liability you assume as an owner-builder is comparable to that of a licensed general contractor. For this reason, following the steps outlined in the earlier Managing Risk section (see page 329) is essential to ensure your protection.

If you choose the Owner-Builder path, understand that big and small mistakes are part of the process. They're the cost of independence. However, consider relying on professionals if your goal is to manage risk and ensure a successful project. Trust their expertise, hold them accountable, and focus on the broader vision.

The choice is yours, but make it with eyes wide open. Know what you're signing up for, and weigh the rewards of control against the risks of costly errors. After all, being accountable isn't just about getting the job done—it's about doing it right.

4.032 OWNER'S AGENT:
YOUR GUARDIAN ANGEL, A TRUE ADVOCATE

With this approach, you're at the private concierge level. Not only is your vacation planned by your concierge, but they also travel alongside you every step of the way and turn down your sheets at the end of the day.

An owner's agent does not replace your contractor or architect—instead, an agent adds a wrapper around of all the aspects of planning and building a project. It's still your home, and the more you participate in decisions, the better, but your agent will tackle the project on your behalf, thus allowing you to focus on the fun aspects of building or remodeling while still enjoying your daily life.

THIS PATH MAY BE RIGHT FOR YOU IF...

- Your project is a significant distance from your current location.
- Your project is large and complex.
- Your personal schedule does not allow you to dedicate enough time to the project.
- You have no experience.

Known as a CMA (construction manager as agent), think of an agent as being an extension of you. An agent is a guardian angel, a person who's the most experienced and objective about the project and who has your priorities, happiness, and safety as their top priorities. In certain situations and conditions, a CMA is appropriate, such as if you're building a second home in an area far away from your primary home, if you have a large project, if you're a busy person who cannot allocate ample time to focus on the project, and/or if you lack experience with the increasingly complicated world of design and construction. Your agent would facilitate all of the functions outlined in this guide, such as sourcing and vetting contractors, architects, and suppliers, orchestrating the land purchase and design process, receiving approvals and permits, and overseeing the construction right up until the day when you find the keys to your new home under your pillow.

As you can see, there's more than one path to achieving your destination. It's wonderful to know that each path can fit individuals in different ways and that there's no wrong way as long as you make 100% sure that you have the core knowledge you need for whichever option you choose. If you're interested in learning more about these specialized options, I'm in the midst of building a plethora of knowledge on the TAH site that will allow you to learn more.

4.040 SEARCH STRATEGIES

Now that you understand the different paths you can take to begin planning your project, let's delve into a few methods you can use to begin your search for resources that fit your preferences.

Two leading players in designing and building your project are your architect and general contractor. The search usually begins with assembling a list of candidates for both roles. We'll start with suggested strategies for finding architects and contractors beyond the obvious Google searches.

OPTION 1: CONTRACTOR AND THEN DESIGNER

Engaging with a contractor before you search for your designer can benefit you in a couple of ways. First, you already have a potential contractor candidate on board, and second, you may have a channel to a recommended architect whom they work with. Having a contractor waiting on the sidelines can be greatly beneficial, but eventually you'll need a set of plans and specifications before you can obtain estimates and actually hire said contractor. Therefore, you'll end up starting your project with a designer and then loop the GC in at prescribed times during the planning process.

For example, during the design process phase, I stressed the importance of doing budget and design checkpoints. That's a perfect time to engage early with a GC, allowing the two of you plenty of time to get acquainted while also giving the GC a chance to provide you with valuable input.

OPTION 2: DESIGNER AND THEN CONTRACTOR

Conversely, your first contact may be an architect who came via word of mouth or whom you hunted down yourself. This approach also works, and frankly, it can be even more beneficial. Architects and designers often work with multiple contractors on projects, and those contractors can be resources for you to consider when the time is right. A strong architect-contractor working relationship has many benefits.

Regardless of how you find the two main players on your design and construction team, the better the relationship between your architect and general contractor is, the better positioned your project will be. Make it your goal to find team members who are already familiar with each other or at least do your best to play matchmaker to ensure a harmonious relationship. And don't forget about the guided option as you're searching! That can smooth out design and construction relationships.

SOME BENEFITS OF RESILIENT DESIGN AND CONSTRUCTION TEAM RELATIONSHIPS

- Better communication: A strong relationship between the architect and contractor promotes familiar and open communication channels. An established relationship also carves off the honeymoon stage and gets directly to the issue at hand. This ensures that the homeowner's vision, needs, and preferences are clearly understood and effectively communicated between both parties.

- Efficient problem-solving: Collaboration between the architect and contractor allows for more efficient problem-solving during the planning and building stages. They can work together to address any challenges that arise, offering creative solutions while keeping the homeowner informed and involved in the decision-making process.

- Streamlined planning process: When the architect and contractor work closely together from the beginning, it streamlines the planning process. They can coordinate schedules, timelines, and resources more effectively, reducing delays and potential conflicts that may arise during construction.

- Cost management: A strong relationship between the architect and contractor can also lead to better cost management. They can collaborate to identify potential cost-saving opportunities without compromising the quality or integrity of the project, ensuring that the homeowner's budget is respected.

- Quality assurance: By working closely together, the architect and contractor can ensure that the homeowner's expectations for quality are met or exceeded. They can monitor the construction progress, address any issues promptly, and ensure that the project is built to the highest standards.

- Enhanced design integration: Collaboration between the architect and the contractor allows for better integration of design and construction elements. This ensures that the end result will align with the homeowner's vision while also being feasible in terms of construction techniques and materials.

- Peace of mind: Ultimately, a strong architect-contractor relationship provides the homeowner with peace of mind throughout the entire planning and building process. The homeowner can trust that their project is in capable hands, with both parties working together towards a successful outcome that meets the homeowner's needs and expectations.

When you're ready to begin building a list of names of both architect and contractor candidates, you can approach your search from both directions—contractor and then designer and designer and then contractor—to see what materializes. As you search, though, keep in mind the benefits of the two design pros having a strong relationship.

4.041 SEARCH METHODS AND RESOURCES

REFERRALS

Recommendations from your neighbors or friends are the best direct line to a design professional and contractor—this classic approach can greatly expedite the selection process. But first be aware of a few things! Don't have referrals from friends and colleagues be your only qualifier. While speaking with your friends, pry a little to understand their project scope and how it is or isn't similar to your project. A designer or contractor may have done an excellent job on their kitchen remodel project, but you may be planning a much larger project that would be out of the designer's or contractor's comfort zone. Still, neither design pro might be inclined to share their lack of comfort because they want the project, so dig in deeper with your friend or colleague to learn more about their experience.

WHAT TO ASK A FRIEND OR COLLEAGUE

❏ Tell me about your project.

❏ How did you find your contractor?

❏ How did you find your architect?

❏ Did they work well together? Have they worked together before?

You'll find a more comprehensive checklist in the TAH Planning Workbook.

DOING A NEIGHBORHOOD WATCH

The moment you start thinking about a project is not too early to begin your search! Keep an eye out for active projects in your neighborhood or surrounding areas—spotting those can uncover resources and multiple benefits. Start by looking for job site signs that identify the contractor, architect, and subcontractors. Compile a list and then monitor the projects.

BENEFITS OF FINDING PROFESSIONALS VIA OBSERVATION

✓ Architects and contractors doing projects in your area would be familiar with working with your city or county.

✓ You already have a sense of the kind of style the architect may specialize in and if it's a good fit for you.

✓ You glean a look into the future to see how projects progress and are maintained.

✓ You can have a built-in reference by speaking with the property owner about their experiences.

SUPPLY HOUSES AND SUBCONTRACTORS

A stealthy way of cutting through the fluff is asking the people who supply contractors for their materials and services who those contractors are. These folks are often free to offer information and frequently love to talk about it. There are a few ways to tackle this:

✓ Visit the local lumber yard that supplies your area. Look for a business card wherever builders may drop off their cards and ask the sales staff who seems to be the most organized and liked contractor.

✓ Visit local suppliers of windows, doors, tile, flooring, fixtures, etc., and accomplish two things simultaneously: start your materials research and ask for referrals for their best contractors.

✓ Don't be afraid to stop and speak with the contractor who's on the site during your neighborhood travels. You can start by asking the first person you see if they're the contractor. If they aren't, it's likely they're a subcontractor and will point to where the GC is. If the contractor isn't on-site, this is an opportunity to ask the sub about the contractor. Either way, you can talk directly with the contractor or get info from the subcontractor and start adding to your lists.

LOCAL CITY AND COUNTY RESOURCES

Taking a close look within your community is an excellent way to begin your search.

✓ Visit your Chamber of Commerce and search by category for members.

✓ Visit your local Building and Planning departments in person. This allows you to accomplish two things. First, you can obtain information like finding out how the city's approval process works (there are usually info packets on this kind of thing), and second, you can see if the person at the counter is willing to recommend a few architects and contractors. This idea may take some shmoozing on your part as there may be a policy that they cannot refer people.

✓ You can perform a permit search in your city and learn what kinds of projects are going on and who the contractors are. Each city is different as to how they present this publicly available information, but it's worth a shot. You can then search for the contractors' and architects' names on the web and see if they're worthy enough to make your short list.

✓ You may research specific candidates via your state Contractors Licensing Board. The type and status of their license and insurance requirements is a big takeaway!

✓ Here's a sample from California's site: https://www.cslb.ca.gov/OnlineServices/CheckLicenseII/checklicense.aspx

INDUSTRY RESOURCES

The design and construction world has industry associations with which your candidates can be affiliated. Searching these directories can uncover companies and individuals who demonstrate their commitment to their craft by participating in the industry. Let's look at a few specific associations.

DESIGN PROFESSIONALS

American Institute of Architects. Here's a link to locate your closest chapter: https://www.aia.org/community/chapters

American Society of Interior Designers. Here's a link to locate your closest chapter: https://www.asid.org/find-a-pro. For some projects, an ASID designer can be your leading designer or can collaborate with your architect as the interior designer.

The National Kitchen and Bath Association is a national organization dedicated to kitchens and baths. You can find your local chapter and potential designers who can design your remodel project or collaborate with your architect: https://nkba.org/resources/directory/

CONTRACTORS

The National Association of Home Builders has different designations, from national home builders to remodeling contractors. Here's a link to the directories where you can learn about and search for a pro in your area: https://www.nahb.org/nahb-community/nahb-directories

The National Association of the Remodeling Industry is a national association dedicated to remodeling. The NARI site has a section specifically for homeowners: https://remodelingdoneright.nari.org/

SOCIAL MEDIA AND APPLICATIONS

Houzz.com is an online resource for researching styles, products, and professionals. The unique aspect of Houzz is that you can create your own idea books, search for both design and construction pros, and share your idea books with them: https://www.houzz.com/professionals/

SUMMARY OF SEARCH STRATEGIES_____

- ✓ You can approach your search from two angles: either begin with a contractor or begin with a design pro. Work both angles.
- ✓ The stronger the relationship is between the architect and designer, the better the outcome will be for everybody. Keep that in the back of your mind as you're on the hunt.
- ✓ Don't overlook the search methods and resources that go beyond the abyss of a Google search.

✓ Have the estimate bid package completed, including all of the outlined variables.

✓ Research candidates' licenses and insurance policies.

✓ Review qualifications based on portfolios, references, and project management tools.

✓ Review scheduling systems.

✓ Get a preview of the construction contract and type (i.e., fixed-price or cost-plus).

✓ Obtain a sample schedule of progress payments and cost breakdowns.

✓ Find out the professionals' availability to start your project.

✓ Rank your candidates based on the combined price factors, their established expertise, and your gut feelings.

"We immediately felt in "good hands" with Bill and his team as they are genuinely great people who care about the quality of their work and that we were happy with the process and the results."

- Layne H.

PROJECT BY BILL REID OF REMODELWEST

PART FOUR CONCLUSION

In Part Four, I've aimed to enlighten and empower your first planning step: hiring your team of design and construction pros. We began with a summary of all the design pros (wrapped up in a matrix) who may be involved in translating your *discovery* exercise into your most powerful tools: real-life designs, plans, and specifications. As you stand at the trailhead, you can now see different paths you can take to assemble your design and construction team. Each path is a viable option, and with your newfound knowledge, you can choose the path that's best suited to you. Now that you've chosen a path, searching for the right pros will be the precursor to actually stepping onto the trail. You can utilize various methods to find the right fit; in the section on *search strategies*, you found out how to go about a search beyond the obvious web searches. The destination beckons!

"A house is made with
walls and beams;
a home is built with
love and dreams."

Ralph Waldo Emerson

LET'S MAKE IT HAPPEN.

AFTERWORD

As I've continued to orchestrate projects for over half of my 60 years, I have developed an itch to spread my knowledge beyond the services I provide to my loyal clients. For a minute, I dreamed about building a construction empire to take over the world, but I quickly discounted that as a bit of an overreach. I pondered creating programs and systems that fellow design and construction businesspeople could use, but that arena seemed fragmented and flooded. The path wasn't coming into focus until I peered back at my most valuable asset: my customers. It's the people who desire to improve their lives who need knowledge, power, and guidance. It's YOU!

The big picture came into focus: I would construct a bridge of knowledge to *enlighten, empower, and protect* homeowners. I began with the idea of writing a book and putting it out there and that would be that. The path and destination seemed clear. As I began to organize and write the content, however, a force was lurking about, but I couldn't pin it down. The destination went out of focus. I pressed on anyway. It wasn't until I was deep into the manuscript with my editor as my guide that I realized this book wasn't a book. It's the beginning of something much larger: a mission.

As a new author, I became enamored with the whole writing process. I consumed a plethora of information about writing and publishing, but it took one small but significant statement from my editor to move the mountain. That happened when Jennifer said, "What do I do with this information?" My pause seemed like an eternity. As Jennifer continued assessing the manuscript, themes began to develop. The content needed to reach far beyond informing homeowners, I realized. They needed direction and an action plan to put it all to work. And *boom!* The Awakened Homeowner was born.

I began to dismantle and reconstruct the manuscript with many of Jennifer's incredible suggestions hovering over me. I became overwhelmed…and I finally really understood how my clients feel in the midst of designing and building a project. I took a long pause of probably a year to reevaluate the mission. (Have I mentioned that this entire process took four years?)

The manuscript's reorganization resulted in a clarity that's hard to describe. The book has been transformed into a resource to address what I know causes you as a homeowner anguish when you're considering a project. Still, I've striven to offer insights and methods that will allow you to gather your thoughts and ideas and then embolden your own pursuit with your own newfound knowledge. I quickly realized, however, that it would be impossible to achieve my entire mission within the covers of one book. That's why the ever-evolving TAH community is under construction.

Between homeowners' personal circumstances and the continually shifting world of construction, it was inevitable that I would need to build a home to care for the TAH community. My website is constantly developing and is my home base where I can elaborate on what I've learned over the years, build a fellowship, and provide resources, templates, forms, lists, and applications that I have created and continue to develop.

The Awakened Homeowner will be your destination for resources designed to support you every step of the way. Among these offerings will be an exciting, thoughtfully structured application currently in development that follows the chronological steps of planning and building. This app, aptly titled BuildQuest, takes the guesswork out of applying your new knowledge by providing clear guidance and actionable steps to empower you in successfully designing and executing your project. Through these evolving tools, I aim to make the process more accessible and rewarding.

The adventure of remodeling or building a home is very personal and unique to your desires and property. Inevitably, you may need more information specific to your needs and your project. I'm here to help you with that, too! I'm excited to engage with you one-on-one via my private consulting and coaching services to help you achieve your dream. These personal services include:

Coaching: Coaching means providing you with guidance, instructions, and even classes on how to tackle your project—in other words, tailoring your newfound knowledge to your particular circumstances. You'll have a shoulder to lean on and bounce ideas off of.

Consulting: We delve deeper into property and project specifics, assess your discovery exercise, and tailor the overall knowledge and the content within the guide to your specific needs.

VISIT US, PERUSE THE SITE, AND JOIN OUR FELLOWSHIP OF EMPOWERED HOMEOWNERS WHO ARE ON A HOME BUILDING AND REMODELING PATH!

WWW.THEAWAKENEDHOMEOWNER.COM

I sincerely appreciate you taking the time to read *The Awakened Homeowner,* and I look forward to seeing your project materialize.

William W. Reid
wwreid@TheAwakenedHomeowner.com

EPILOGUE

Remember Ben and Jane and their horror story? Remember the Mc-Millans and their storybook project coming to life? I couldn't help myself—I wanted to know what had caused such a contrasting experience. So I dug into what had happened…and what I learned was so very revealing.

It turned out that the McMillans had been living several hundred miles away from the new lot and had only tackled a kitchen remodel in their previous home. They'd had some bad experiences, so when they decided to build a new home, they decided to hire an owner's agent who could help with the construction. They also hired an architect at the same time. Guess who those two guys were huddled at the corner of the lot as Ben and Jane drove off? Yep: the owner's agent and the architect. That potential lot had multiple rock outcroppings that would have had to have been blasted away to accommodate the home, and who knows what else was lurking below the surface? Their team called all of this to their attention, causing the McMillans to purchase a different lot. In other words, they abided by all three Guiding Principles. CHECK!

Meanwhile, Ben and Jane fell prey to the excited salesperson who worked for the developer who built the lots. They purchased the lot the same day without first getting any professional input. The consequences were multifold but mainly related to the costs of the foundation, utilities, delays, and the overall design.

Building on a steep hillside with a miraculous view can add anywhere from 30% to 50% to the cost of the foundation, not to mention the complexity of the remaining structure. Utilities are always a concern—that long driveway forced a hundred-yard-long excavation, adding tens of thousands of dollars to the cost. To top it off, Ben and Jane had never done any remodeling before. But since they were already all-in on the project, there was no turning back even though the price substantially exceeded their budget. Before this discovery, Ben and Jane had skipped some critical steps and had begun searching for an architect. At the same time, the McMillans took a more systematic approach by working on their investment goals, budgets, and dreams.

The McMillans already had their architect. Ben and Jane found theirs online. His name was Bob the Gatekeeper. Does that ring a bell? His cost was "very reasonable," but getting him to the site to begin the design was hard. Instead of showing up in person, he gruffly proclaimed, "Just send me some pictures of the lot, and I'll get started," so that's what Ben and Jane did. Bob didn't visit the site until the plans were completed...or at least completed in his eyes. With a big roll of plans tucked under Ben's arms, Bob exclaimed, "Let's get a permit and get this project started." At that, Jane yelled, "Whoopee!!" and cheered everyone on. Never did Bob ask about their budget or if they had a contractor.

By now, the McMillans had completed their wish lists, built their idea books, and had an excellent idea of the look, feel, and layout of their proposed home. They had their first design meeting with their architect, Stu the Outfitter, at the site, where they all stood on the bare ground, waving their hands around and visualizing their ideas. Stu was armed with a site survey previously authorized by the McMillans that helped them site the house and minimize the utility work. After their on-site meeting, Stu excused himself and retreated to his studio to conceptualize their new home.

Back at Horror Central, it was getting worse, but Ben and Jane didn't know it. The permit was issued, so Bob the Gatekeeper told them, "We're ready to break ground!" A celebration exploded. But one small detail had gone unaddressed: *who's* going to break ground? Calls to contractors went unreturned, and the ones who did arrive to review their project disappeared off the face of the earth. (I suspect the plans scared them off.)

Bob finally lets the cat out of the bag and says that he knows "a guy." We'll call him Jack. Jack is a contractor but has never built an entire home. He has his name on the side of his truck and has been in business for a long time. Plus, Bob knows him…or does he? The handoff occurs. Jack yanks the plans out of Ben's hand and says, "I'll get back to you with a price." He never asks for material specifications or what to include or not include. Weeks go by with no sign of Jack.

While crickets are chirping on Ben and Jane's empty lot, the McMillans are progressing with their design—on their lot, Stu shows up equipped with a laptop and accompanied by an assistant who's also an interior designer. Stu then proceeds to blow the McMillans away with 3D renderings of their home as it would sit on the site. "After reviewing your wish lists and idea books, let me tell you how I've achieved almost everything you desired," Stu humbly says. He nailed it! Decisions are made on the spot.

High above, looking down, Ben and Jane notice the group of people walking around while passing a laptop with the 3D drawings on it back and forth. With a grin, Jane says, "Wow, they're still designing! We're way ahead of them—*we* have our permit!" Ben agrees, pumping his fist in the air. Little did they know a day of reckoning would come.

Back to the pleasantries of the McMillans' life. Stu decides to reward the McMillians by announcing, "Since I feel like you've done your homework, I thought I would introduce you to Mary, our local interior designer." Mary continues to zoom in on the 3D plans she and Stu had collaborated on behind the scenes to further confirm that the team has nailed it. As a result, they quickly move into the second step of design development, hire the necessary consultants, and pin down a multitude of decisions, decisions that Ben and Jane didn't even know they needed to make.

It's been a month. Finally, Jack resurfaces, apologizes that he went fishing in Idaho, and proceeds to share his personal problems with whomever will listen. Leaning against his 1980s-era truck, Jack pulls out a handful of papers with numbers on them and hands one to Ben—it has a big number on it—while exclaiming, "Boy, this one is for the record books!" Ben and Jane gulp. It's almost double what they wanted to spend! And Bob the Gatekeeper is nowhere to be found. How can that be? Well, did anyone ask him to show up? Did anyone tell him about the meeting? I doubt it.

To rein the project back in, the home must be redesigned and scaled back. Bob magically reappears. Unfortunately, there's only one place to site the house, so the foundation and utilities are what they are. With the engineering completed and their permits in hand, Ben and Jane have no choice but to pay again.

The small bell jingles as the McMillans enter Mary's quaint interior design studio in the rustic small town nearby. As the door slowly closes, a vehicle races by outside. Inside it, Ben and Jane are screaming at each other. The McMillans turn their attention back to Mary, who's prepared with multiple potential ensembles of materials for the entire home. Within hours, all materials are specified and written up in a specification sheet Mary has developed. Mary divulges, "Once we're wrapped up, Stu wants to meet with you and your agent Bill to discuss the project." The McMillans nod happily. They meet up, discuss options, and proceed with doing a cost study. Stu announces, "Design development is wrapping up, and as soon as we know the final scope, I can begin the construction documents and get ready for permits." The McMillans are elated and wait for Bill to crunch the numbers.

Selecting all of the materials and Stu completing the design development step takes three or four months. This gives Ben and Jane time to catch up. Bob spews out a revised plan, proclaiming, "It's closer to your budget." How he knew what their budget actually was, Ben and Jane have no idea. Regardless, they take his word and send the plan back to the HOA, Planning department, and Building department for a new permit. Thank goodness Bob knows them all and gets the approval ramrodded through! Jack the Contractor returns and somehow has a revised price in a week. (That's scary.) Ben and Jane accept his bid, don't read his contract, and sign off. The job starts on Monday.

Dirt begins to pile up as the foundation gets started. Down below, the McMillans are walking their lot, looking up and wondering how the other couple have gotten started so fast. The day of reckoning is still lurking.

The big cost analysis meeting is held with the entire group around a table. Stu and Mary are prepared with the plans. Bill whips out his laptop and papers and is flanked by a new person on the team: a general contractor whom Bill has worked with many times and is one of the candidates he has filtered out for the McMillans. A detailed spreadsheet presents various options for the McMillans to choose from. The budget is close to their expectations because Stu prioritized said budget and collaborated with Bill behind the scenes to ensure that he was on track. Long story short, everyone agrees on what to remove from the scope and they negotiate the price.

Over the next two months, Stu completes the construction documents while Bill works with the McMillans and the GC to finalize the cost, contract, and administrative items. Soon enough, the plans are ready to submit for the permit. The McMillans can now relax, sit back, and watch their home take shape. (Well, it's not quite that easy, but I'm sure you get the gist.)

Months have passed while the McMillans were completing their plans. During a site visit with the contractor, they all three glance up at Horror Hill, only to still see the same mounds of dirt still piled high. They look at each other, shrug their shoulders, and continue their pre-construction meeting.

The salmon season was on, and Jack had to head out for "a few weeks." But really, that didn't matter, because he had hit boulders that needed to be blasted apart. Come to find out, Bob the Gatekeeper never did a soil report! Somehow, that got through the permitting process. Ben and Jane get their first change order before anything has even been built. The law of attraction is a real thing! They eventually narrow the gap between their original bid and the revised bid.

I could go on and on with this story—it has hundreds of positive and negative consequences for each path each couple took. This story is close to real-life examples of what people go through. Even though Ben and Jane started their project before the McMillans did, they finished it over six months later. They were over budget by 40% and compromised on just about every finish decision. Their kids had to pay their own way through school. In contrast, the McMillans' home was completed within two weeks of the original schedule. Their budget increased by 10%, but only because they added back one of the options they had taken out earlier. Believe it or not, the McMillans spent *less* on design than Ben and Jane did! It doesn't take somebody with an MBA to figure out that designing a home once and not twice costs less.

I'LL LET YOU DECIDE WHO THE AWAKENED HOMEOWNER IS.

ABOUT THE AUTHOR

WILLIAM REID

William Reid developed a passion for construction at an early age. At age 22, he became a minority shareholder in a startup construction company with his mentor, learning the ins and outs of managing a business. In 1992, he launched his own company, RemodelWest, located in the San Francisco Bay Area, where Bill was born and raised. Over the past 30 years, as RemodelWest proliferated into a full-service design and construction company, Bill developed processes and systems to meet the high demands of Silicon Valley's discerning homeowners who were desiring to build and remodel their homes. Now the time has come to continue the mission by sharing his wealth of knowledge through his latest venture: The Awakened Homeowner. In doing so, Bill hopes to empower homeowners to achieve their dream home successfully and pleasantly.

These days, Bill resides in the northern Sierra Nevada mountain range in California with his family. Along with spending time reading and writing, he likes to enjoy the outdoors by going hiking and fly fishing whenever he gets the chance.

HELP SPREAD THE MISSION.

If you enjoyed this book,
please share by posting a review at:

Amazon.com

Goodreads.com

or your favorite online bookstore.